John D. Mackintosh.
14 Spylaw Road.

THE SPAN OF TIME

THE AUTOBIOGRAPHY OF A DOCTOR

THE AUTHOR IN HIGHLAND DRESS WHEN
HE WAS IN SCOTLAND

THE SPAN OF TIME

THE AUTOBIOGRAPHY OF A DOCTOR

by

J. T. Bell Nicoll

London

HODDER AND STOUGHTON

FIRST PRINTED . . . SEPTEMBER 1952

*Made and Printed in Great Britain for Hodder & Stoughton, Limited, London,
by Wyman & Sons Limited, London, Reading and Fakenham*

To LUCY

FOR BETTER FOR WORSE,
FOR RICHER FOR POORER,
IN SICKNESS OR IN HEALTH

. . . .

TILL DEATH US DO PART

CONTENTS

CHAPTER | PAGE

FOREWORD - - - - - - - - - - 9

I. HOME - - - - - - - - - - 11

II. PREP. SCHOOL - - - - - - - - 25

III. GEORGE WATSON'S COLLEGE - - - - - - - 30

IV. THE CHURCH - - - - - - - - 50

V. THE UNIVERSITY - - - - - - - - 70

VI. HOUSE SURGEON - - - - - - - - 91

VII. INDIA - - - - - - - - - - 112

VIII. AFRICA - - - - - - - - - - 118

IX. MY FIRST PRACTICE - - - - - - - 141

X. MY SECOND PRACTICE - - - - - - - 160

XI. MY THIRD PRACTICE - - - - - - - 175

XII. SCOTLAND - - - - - - - - - 193

XIII. A VILLAGE IN SURREY - - - - - - - 210

XIV. KING FOR AN HOUR - - - - - - - 228

XV. NOT THE END BUT THE BEGINNING - - - - 234

XVI. THE BEST YEARS OF MY LIFE - - - - - 251

FOREWORD

BY

H. C. EDWARDS. C.B.E., M.S., F.R.C.S.

Surgeon to King's College Hospital, London.

" GARDENING ? " I straightened up, and met the gaze of the kindest eyes I had ever seen. They were smiling, quizzical and humorous all in one, and set in a handsome face lit with good humour and glowing with health. This was 23 years ago, and was my first meeting with Dr. J. T. Bell Nicoll. I had just moved into a newly built house, and was trying to start a garden. Later that day the doctor returned with boxes full of cuttings and roots from his own garden. I have often thought that generous action to a complete stranger the perfect commentary on the man. It goes far to explain his patients' devotion to him. Dr. Nicoll seemed to exude goodwill like some tangible quality, and both in sickness and in health we felt the better for having seen him. He was always ready with some practical solutions to the manifold problems with which his patients ceaselessly confronted him. He never spared himself in their service, whatever their station in life. Although in his younger days he enjoyed radiant health, the strain of work during the early years of the war, when he was, owing to shortage of doctors, doing more than could be expected of any man, proved too great, and a serious operation became necessary. His convalescence was shortened by his insistence on returning to his work. Again he toiled, and again his health began to suffer and, just over four years ago, when in the plenitude of his professional power and when reaping the reward of a quarter of a lifetime of service, it became necessary for him to retire. These past four years have, far from being embittered and disillusioned, been the happiest of his life. That this is no attitude of mere bravado, all those who are close to him will testify. There is indeed a solid enough reason for this paradox. Through the agency of the written word, and the B.B.C., he has been able to teach a way of life and reach out a helping hand to those many thousands of fellow sufferers for whom, through ill health, almost all would appear lost. This he does not do in the doubtfully scientific way of the psychiatrist, who himself, perhaps, has never plumbed the depths, but from his own personal experience of the valley of the shadows.

And now comes this book, written patiently, and with much toil. Books are usually the word of technical experts whose views are narrowed to a single field ; or of those with literary gifts, but with little to say. It is indeed rare for a general medical practitioner to find the leisure to become an author, though no profession can better fit a man for the purpose. In this one respect Dr. Nicoll's enforced rest has enabled fruit to be born. His many friends and acquaintances, and all those who have listened to his compositions spoken from Broadcasting House, will rejoice at this opportunity to learn of his life story in such detail as this biography makes possible. But it is more than a biography, for it contains a message of hope which will bring comfort to all who have to bear the burden of enduring sickness.

CHAPTER I

HOME

EVERY child must have heard its mother repeat stories of her childhood over and over again. Two of these stories in particular remain in my memory. One was of a wild stormy night when she stood at the front window of her parents' house at Newport on the South bank of the Tay idly watching the lights of a train as it made its way over the Tay Bridge. Suddenly there came a terrific gust of wind and when it had subsided the lights of the train had gone out. The bridge had blown down carrying the train with it.

The other story was of my grandfather " the Baillie "—who was deputed as one of a party of three to go to Balmoral with a humble petition from the Town Council of Dundee that Her Majesty would graciously open the new bridge across the Firth of Tay on her way south. Alas, the Queen was absorbed in her grief. At any rate she would not see them and they were just returning crestfallen through the grounds when they were accosted by a rough-looking man who asked them their business. The upshot of the conversation was that the deputation returned to the Castle and was received by Her Majesty—successfully, I believe. The rough-looking man was John Brown.

As my grandfather died before I was born, my recollection of him is nil. Not so with my grandmother. She overflowed into my childhood. Alas, she overflowed in other directions as well, for she was a stout woman. She exuded that supreme virtue of Victorianism—solid respectability.

One of my earliest recollections is of her paying her annual visit to us in a cab. The old lady descended from the back seat of the vehicle and stuck in the doorway. I am afraid that my sense of humour must have been abnormally developed—even in these early days—for I have a vivid recollection of standing at the window enjoying the spectacle to the full. For some obscure reason the cabby proceeded to remove the roof, but the old lady was ultimately released—like a champagne cork—by the combined efforts of the jarvie pushing behind and the family pulling in front. Her arrival on the pavement was abrupt if not dignified and like her prototype Queen Victoria—she was not amused.

My father's family came of good farming stock. Cattle dealers and rearers they had been from time immemorial. Probably they were not above a bit of cattle lifting in the days before history was recorded. My paternal grandfather died before I was born, but cattle dealing seems to have been a pretty remunerative occupation, for I have vivid memories of a rookery in my grandmother's garden and of a large house where she lived. I have heard my sister, who had a romantic disposition, tell her husband that the house was surrounded by a moat. As a matter of fact it had a sunk basement.

There's a lot I could write about my forebears, but I will refrain. Sufficient to say that my paternal grandfather resembled my mother's mother in one respect. When he died and the coffin came to be carried downstairs prior to his funeral, it was found necessary to remove the bedroom window *in toto* and lower the coffin to the ground by means of ropes.

As my father was alive even after I had graduated as a doctor, he was the dominant personality for the first part of my life, but my mother died within a few days of my seventh birthday and my recollection of her is dim and shadowy. She was a very sweet and gracious lady whom everybody loved. Of course, I recall isolated incidents in connection with her, but what made a deep impression on my mind was her funeral. I remember the black horses with their nodding plumes. I remember the black suit which I wore, complete with black cap, and I remember my father referring to us in the evening as his " motherless bairns ".

But I was too young to feel grief acutely. A succession of house-keepers stayed for a time and then left, all for the same reason. They couldn't manage the children. Looking back on that grim succession of foster-mothers, I don't blame them for not staying. The fact is that we were a handful. I had three elder sisters, and like a litter of healthy puppies we scrapped frequently among ourselves, but the spirit of family loyalty was very strong in us and it was a case of " who touches one touches all ". I remember one housekeeper who misguidedly thought that some chastisement would do me good, as doubtless it would have done. As soon as it was suggested, and opportunity presented itself, my sisters wrecked her room. She was particularly proud of a hat which was known as a " Paris model ". By the time my sisters had finished with it, it was more like a relic of the Battle of Waterloo. She gave in her notice the same day.

Another lady had been housekeeper to a Minister who, like my father, had one son. She insisted on telling me of his (the son's) virtues in such detail that a deep and bitter hatred of this paragon grew in my breast. Many years afterwards when I had grown up to man's estate, I was introduced in the drawing-room of a friend to a clergyman. His name sounded vaguely familiar. I sat down beside him and startled him considerably with my opening remark, " I have hated you with a deep and bitter hatred since childhood ". He seemed a very decent fellow.

To say that we were deeply devoted to our father would be an understatement. He was father and mother to us. When my father came home for his tea there was generally a little knot of us youngsters waiting for him at the end of the road. He was, however, a strong believer in discipline and loyally stood by the housekeepers when they had trouble with us.

Shortly after my mother died the whole family went down with diphtheria. For some reason or other we had periodic bouts of infectious illness and whether it was due to the situation of the house, or just bad luck, it was impossible to say, but it was a common condition for us children to be laid up simultaneously. On this particular occasion, so soon after my mother's death, our father naturally did not wish to send us away and he therefore took the somewhat unusual step of renting the house next door, which happened to be empty, and installing us there.

There are several different Edinburghs. There is the Edinburgh of the tourist who " does " the Castle and Holyrood and all the sights of the old town and the statues of the new. There is that other Edinburgh with its long lines of depressing looking tenement houses which line the tram routes in any direction out of the city. Then there is the squalid slum which the builder of the last generation put up so cheaply that it has already sunk to the level of a human rabbit warren. These are decently hidden away. We lived in a fourth Edinburgh which stretches chiefly to the south between arteries of tram lines. Districts of stone grey houses with inhabitants as grimly respectable as the houses they inhabit.

Changes on the actual roads of the city are so imperceptible that one has mentally to erect milestones over long periods of years to realise the change. There were lots of things to be seen on the roads in the days of my childhood which have since disappeared.

Dancing bears and German bands, leeries or lamplighters hurrying along in the dusk from lamp to lamp, and jingling away into memory's recesses is the tinkle-tinkle of a hurdy-gurdy. Punch and Judy shows and green watering carts, horse-drawn buses and Breton onion men with long sticks of onions over their shoulders. When first we came to live in Craighouse Road the sound of the corncrake was heard all day from the long grass in the fields at the back of the house. As time drew on towards the beginning of the first world war these birds disappeared from the countryside altogether and they went never to return.

We were very hard-up. As I have got older I realise that " hard upness " is a relative term. Till our grandparents died we had real penury to endure. In those early days I don't suppose my father's salary ever exceeded £250 per annum, out of which he paid rent and rates, school fees, doctor's bills and the hundred and one items which are forgotten in the most careful household budgeting. The Church didn't have a Manse. We lived, like St. Paul, in our own hired house. Curiously, these early habits of thrift have never left me and though I don't think I am in any sense mean, I hate waste in any form. Were I a millionaire I would instinctively turn an electric fire off when it was not really required. I think " hard upness " is a state which children should not be too frightened of, provided it is not carried as far as to warp the character. I am quite certain that none of our characters were warped, but that the early state of having to be " unco carefu " has taught us habits which years of admonition could not have done. Unfortunately, my mother never saw the more spacious days which the money from my grandparents' deaths brought.

I only remember one occasion on which my tendency towards thrift was misplaced. It happened long ago when I was a boy. It so chanced on the day I speak of that a young man called to see one of my sisters. I suppose he thought half a crown was cheap at the price to get rid of an adhesive young brother. Anyway, he gave me two and sixpence to go and buy some chocolates from a shop about a mile away. Alas ! I had never spent more than sixpence on sweets in my life and certainly could not imagine anyone spending half a crown. I hurried like a homing pigeon to the shop and bought sixpence worth of chocolates and brought back two shillings change. When I returned in record time, there was a marked lack of warmth in my sister's greeting and the young man insisted that I return forthwith and spend the remaining two shillings. The chill in the atmosphere was so marked that even I noticed it. I walked to the shop and spent the two shillings, and when I ultimately arrived home it was to find my sister and the young man considerably more amiable towards me.

Our family doctor was what is known as "a character". Not that he ever set out to be one. He was far above that and did not require any artifical stimulus to greatness. For he *was* a great man and one whose stature has not grown less with the years. At Edinburgh University he had been the Ettles scholar, which means the best student of his year. He brought all our family into the world and had attended us in all our various illnesses. We children respected and stood in considerable awe of him. His accounts, at least to us, were mere token payments, and yet he left over twenty-eight thousand pounds. It was characteristic of him that a consider-able portion of that sum was left to the church of his native village in Perthshire.

Among other things, he disliked motor cars. I don't think I ever saw him in one. Instead he rode a bicycle, which he mounted incidentally from the back step. The bicycle was never known to go more than six miles an hour and one of the surest signs that spring was coming was the arrival of a straw hat on his head. The straw hat had once been white, but advancing age had turned it yellow. Its arrival coincided with the snowdrops. The rest of his clothes are easily described. They consisted of a dark jacket (grey alpaca in summer) and trousers, a black band to keep the straw hat in position and—a dickie. He invariably used a wooden stetho-scope to which he bent down and applied his ear with much grunting and wheezing—for he was a heavily built man. When he bent down like this, the dickie usually escaped from the confines of the alpaca jacket and that is how I am in a position to be so dogmatic about his garments. Times without number I have been horizontal under the business end of that stethoscope at the critical moment when the dickie left the jacket and a vast expanse of hairy chest met my fascinated gaze.

I remember when one of my sisters had pneumonia, how he insisted on being given the key of the front door and how in the silent hours of the night we would hear his footsteps in the hall as he tiptoed to and from the patient's room.

One other memory comes to my mind. It is a summer's evening and the hour any time past ten thirty. The doctor is obviously on his way to a night call—probably a confinement from the bag in his hand. An ankle-length coat—or is it a dressing-gown—covers his garments, but below the dressing-gown, and almost sweeping the pavement, are the flowing draperies of a voluminous nightshirt. The straw hat is still upon his head and yet somehow or other this slow moving figure is not without dignity, rather like a clergyman in his surplice and cassock ponderously crossing the chancel on his way to read the lesson. He never married.

Looking back on one's childhood is like looking back on some dream state which once was familiar but now has become blurred and hazy with the mists of time.

My first romance was one of those peaks which stand out from these mists. I must have been about ten years old. She, I regret to say, was over thirty. She did not know it but I worshipped her from afar, she was kind to the little motherless boy and I think she understood children—at least she found her way to my heart. Curiously enough I have always been impressed by voices and she had a deep, rich voice, full of feeling. I lost touch with her shortly afterwards as she moved to a different part of the country. Half a lifetime later—when I was in my forty-fourth year to be exact—I found myself in an hotel in Edinburgh. I wondered if she was still alive. I found out that she was and 'phoned her. The same voice spoke to me over the 'phone as I remembered all those years ago—a deep, rich voice, full of feeling. We had lunch together the next day. She is now a white-haired old lady. We have become great friends and correspond frequently. The ring of romance has travelled full circle.

We seldom change our likes and dislikes from the days of our childhood. My distaste of dancing is an example of this. Least of all did I enjoy childrens' parties where I had to don a Little Lord Fauntleroy collar and dance with a succession of girls. An aunt of mine gave a party. I won't say that she went out to the byeways and hedges, for she did nothing of the sort, but she certainly gave a party and asked us among many others.

She was a woman of great wealth and of great charm and one whom young people clustered around and whose parties were always social events. I didn't want to go but there was no escape. I was hustled into my Lord Fauntleroy collar which had been specially ironed for the occasion, and was, incidentally, much too small for me.

A horse cab was hired for the event and the clop, clop of the horse's hooves fitted in with my own depression. The revels started with games, after which there was a first-rate supper with an unlimited number of meringues which were my special favourites. I had no fault to find with the supper. On the contrary I ate everything—every possible thing. The meal came to an end and then the children hurried upstairs to dance the old fashioned waltz. I have already stated that I did not like dancing. I therefore slunk back to the supper room and created havoc among the meringues. I don't know how many I disposed of, certainly more than a child's stomach could hold.

I have no recollections of going upstairs, but I have a distinct and vivid recollection of standing in the doorway watching the dancing couples. The waves of nausea come back to me after nearly a lifetime. Suddenly I felt ill. I was sick, actively and irrevocably sick in the doorway of the drawing room and on the parquet flooring. Of the shame of my sisters and their finding out that I had surreptitiously visited the supper table for the second time ; of what the maids thought who tidied up ; of what the other children thought who watched from afar ; and of what my aunt, who maintained her dignity and her kindness, thought of the whole thing, I know not. I was taken home in a cab, my sisters accompanying me. There was silence all the way home. My sisters liked dancing.

Among things which stand out clearly in the mists of memory are our annual holidays. It was a law of the Medes and the Persians that we had a month's holiday every summer. The preparations were begun many weeks beforehand and culminated in a porter's arrival from the neighbouring station with an iron trolley to remove the luggage. No one, unless they have seen it, can possibly imagine the vast pile of luggage which accompanied us on our holidays. They ranged from heavy tin trunks to a brown hat box, from the wraps containing all our overcoats and walking sticks to the tent which was to repose drunkenly on the beach. On top of this assorted mountain was placed the basket containing the cat. Its successor, the dog, was never induced to travel with the luggage, instead he led the family to the station, straining at the leash and only stopping when something particularly malodorous took his fancy.

In our younger days we generally went to Carnoustie. My mother was the second of seven children—five daughters and two sons— and Carnoustie was the spot where they all foregathered with their respective broods. My mother's sisters were what is known as well-built women.

One instance comes back to me as I write. One of the aunts felt that the offspring of the other aunts had injured her dignity. Our penance was as follows. The tent was opened at both ends. The assembled nephews and nieces went in at one end, apologised to their aunt, and took their departure through the opening at the other end. The five sisters were seated inside the tent like a bevy of Roman matrons. When it came to the turn of my youngest sister she did not repeat the normal formula of " I'm sorry Aunt so and so," instead she stood dumbly before her aunt and then screwing up her nose put out her tongue as far as it would go. My aunt arose with the light of wrathful dignity in her eye. She was too late. My sister went through the opening in the tent at speed and cleared a sandpit in her path with the celerity of a racehorse at Aintree. My aunt tried to do the same, but alas, like many of her predecessors at Beecher's Brook she failed to clear the obstacle and landed on all fours in the sandpit. The ranks of Tuscany— in other words the assembled cousins— could scarce forebear to cheer, for which we were all duly punished.

I must say a word or two about the cat in passing. The cat usually reposed on the ledge in front of the oven, but one day the inevitable happened. Its large and bushy tail caught fire and one of my earliest memories of childhood is of seeing the cat depart at high speed through the kitchen door and climb a tree in the garden in record time with a tail behind him blazing like a human torch in Nero's garden.

I must have been a peculiarly sadistic child, for I distinctly remember taking the cat up to the second storey and dropping him out of the window to see if he fell on his paws. He did, but I have a distinct feeling that the cat took a dim view of the proceedings.

Our house was on the flat ground below the Asylum and it was a common sight to see a section of the aristocracy of Britain taking the air in their carriages in front of the house.

Generally, things were quiet and humdrum. Life, however, had its more thrilling moments. It happened that I was seated one summer's evening at our sitting-room window when I heard a shouting up the road. A man ran down the opposite pavement pursued by a string of others, who in turn were urged on by a stout man in the rear. The stout man shouted to someone coming in the opposite direction. There followed one of the neatest tackles I have ever seen. The runaway lunatic went down with a crash.

It was unfortunate that the man coming up the road happened to be full-back of the Watsonian Rugby Club, then in the heyday of its fame.

One other thing connected with the Asylum comes to my mind. I was in the garden one Saturday morning when I heard a noise in the distance. The gable end of the cottage in the Asylum grounds abutted on to a main road. A patient had taken up a strong defensive position on the chimney and was engaged in taking out its stones one by one and throwing them with laudible accuracy at his pursuers. It was only when he had used up the chimney and started on the cottage that it seemed to occur to the authorities that sterner measures would have to be taken. The fire hydrant in the road was opened and a strong jet of water directed on the unfortunate man. The sympathies of the crowd, strangely enough, were with the lunatic and when a policeman essayed to walk along the ridge of the roof between the two gables and got the contents of the hose on his chest by mistake, the enthusiasm of the crowd knew no bounds. Ultimately the escapee was dislodged from his perch by the jet of water and captured by his keepers as he fell. I always think that the best of being a lunatic is that one can do absolutely anything one pleases and people will merely smile and say " Poor fellow, he can't help it ".

Family prayers—which were known as "worship"—were conducted by my father every day. Maids, visitors and family were expected to attend. My father seemed to have a genius for remembering " worship " at the wrong moment. How often have I been doubled up with laughter when the familiar words fell upon my ears.

" Jim, fetch the Book."

Worship consisted of father reading a passage of Scripture, after which we all knelt down and he prayed. If we laughed, as we not infrequently did, there would be a pause in a prayer and my father would say.

" So and so, leave the room."

It says something for the moral force of my parent when I recall that my sister was asked to leave the room long after she was married and her husband was among the worshippers.

One favourite cause of mirth was the behaviour of the dog. The dog behaved in a perfectly rational manner until we knelt down for the prayer. That posture seemed to rouse all his primitive instincts. Without any warning the dog would leap upon the back of the person nearest to him and then proceed round the room in a series of leaps on the backs of the kneeling worshippers. Of course, this aroused the worst instincts in us and not infrequently the dog was actually invited on to somebody else's back.

When someone came to the front door the nearest person rose from their knees and attended to the visitor. I remember an occasion during the 1914-1918 war when my father's brother and his daughter were staying with us. A telegraph boy came to the front door. My eldest sister was kneeling nearest the door of the room. She left the room and on receiving the telegram, read it to see if there was any answer. The telegram was from my youngest sister announcing her engagement. The occasion was too great to wait to the end of a prayer. My sister broke into the prayer to summon her father and tell him the news. He left us all in silence on our knees. One after another we left the room consumed by curiosity and did not return. Eventually my uncle and cousin were left kneeling together alone and after a few minutes of silence got to their feet. I regret to say that the family had forgotten all about them in the excitement.

In the course of time that sister married and was the first to leave the home. She and her husband came up to spend the holidays with us at the little village of Aberfeldy some twenty miles north of Perth. My brother-in-law has a marked English accent which was very evident among us Scots. It was necessary for him to go home to London somewhat sooner than his wife. On a warm summer's afternoon he and I walked along to the booking office of the station where a sleepy red-haired boy was the only occupant. My brother-in-law said to him in tones which were unmistakably from England and from Oxford."

" Boy, I want a sleeper up to Town."

The youth scratched his head for some time and then slowly replied.

" Wha' do you want a sleeper to go to Perth for ? "

We were practically unique in one respect. We had wedding cake instead of ordinary cake on Sundays. The reason was this. It was the custom in Scotland to give a large wedge of wedding cake to the minister who performed the ceremony. As my father frequently married half a dozen couples in the course of a week, it will be understood that a considerable amount of wedding cake had to be eaten. It was the custom to keep the first tier of the cake for the christening of the first baby. Sometimes the first child was long in coming and in any case the christening cake was not quite so fresh as the wedding cake. We became experts on the age, make and consistency of wedding cake.

The subject of wedding cakes immediately suggests the subject of weddings. In Scotland these were not necessarily celebrated in Church, but either at the home of the bride or at the minister's house. Friday evening was the great time for weddings as it gave the week-end for the honeymoon. It needed no Sherlock Holmes to trace the trail of confetti to our house on Saturday morning. The maid must have had bitter thoughts as she came to sweep it up.

A circular stone stairway descended from the upper landing to a stone-tiled hall underneath. Under the curve of the stairs was my father's study, where the weddings were celebrated. Unfortunately, we children discovered a new game which consisted of tobogganing down the stairs on a tin tray and landing at the foot on the tiled hall. Our activities were rudely interrupted by the arrival of my irate parent, who was conducting a series of weddings in the room beneath. He was normally a mild-tempered man, but I have rarely seen him so roused as on this occasion, when he explained to us that the noise up above prevented him carrying out the marriage service.

It was the custom of my father to ring the bell when the ceremony was approaching its close. The maid would then conduct the wedding party to the front door. Usually the best man tipped the maid substantially. In the course of years I noticed a definite tendency among my sisters to suggest that the maid take her night off on a Friday, for they were not above answering the bell themselves and showing the wedding party out after the ceremony.

Next door to us lived an old lady, and thereby hangs a tale. When I was about twelve years old I was sitting in the front room doing my lessons. It was a summer's evening. I saw a rough, uncouth navvy—like a man whom I knew as Tansy—come to the front of the house next door. He first of all rang the front bell and, getting no answer, proceeded to try the fastenings of the windows downstairs. I thought his actions were very strange, and watched him go baffled down the road. As I watched him he went round a bend at the end of the road and I felt almost sure that he intended to try the windows at the back of the house. I went to the back of the house to see if he would re-appear, and, sure enough, I saw him climb the wall, and finding the back door unlocked, go in. I went for help as quickly as possible, and at no great distance from the house was lucky enough to find a policeman, to whom

I told my story. He accompanied me back and we entered the house next door by the back entrance. The policeman led the way and I followed. As we stood in the hall debating where to go next, Tansy walked down the stairs carrying a bag of loot which he had gathered. I can remember yet the look of amazement, tinged with disgust, when he saw us. He offered no resistance and was led away handcuffed. Next day, accompanied by my father, I was taken to the cells at the police court in Parliament Square. I was taken along interminable passages and through many doors, which were locked after me. Ultimately the warder threw back a grilled iron door before opening it. I had never been in a cell before and will never forget the look of malevolent hatred which he gave to me. I did not have to attend the police proceedings where Tansy was sentenced to a long spell of imprisonment. I don't think I ever saw him again.

Once a year we were taken to see the procession of the Lord High Commissioner as he went in state to open the General Assembly. He is the direct representative of the King on these occasions, and the red coats, the busbies and the prancing horses of the escort were thrilling sights to a small boy on the pavement.

When I was a child the figure of Theodore Napier made a strong impression on my mind. One would generally see him in the course of the afternoon taking his constitutional on the Colinton Road. He was a fine figure of a man, striding along—the very epitome of the proud Gael. He always wore full Highland dress —complete with plaid and ruffles. I remember well his Balmoral bonnet with a feather up the front and his buckled shoes of goat-skin hide. I implicitly believed that the walking-stick which he carried was really a sword-stick in disguise. Rightly or wrongly, he was looked upon as a Jacobite and carried with him that air of mystery and romance which adherents of the House of Stuart have carried with them down the centuries.

I was brought up in a typically Scottish middle-class home. According to the standards accepted as normal down south, we were very hard up. No telephone, no car, of course no wireless, and everything new looked at in the light of what it would cost. On the other hand, we always had a maid (her wages, incidentally, were eighteen pounds per annum). We had plenty of coal (fifteen shillings a ton), and plenty to eat (fresh eggs fifteen for a shilling and butter one and twopence per pound). Life was generally speaking more leisured than to-day. People didn't travel as far then. I personally had my first visit to England when I joined the army in 1918, and I was typical of my generation. I remember seeing my first aeroplane in the " Round Britain " race in 1910. About that time, too, I saw my first taxi.

A maid's bedroom opened off the kitchen and was little bigger than the bed which it contained. She had one half-day free a week. Her bedroom and the kitchen both had a stone floor, but I never heard of anyone complaining. Probably even that was an improvement on the attic or basement to which maids were usually assigned. The hallmark of a maid was an apron and a cap with streamers on it. All the cooking was done on a cooking range which was an enormous affair and consumed a proportionate amount of coal.

My mother, like all her friends and acquaintances, had her " at-home " days. In small type at the foot of each visiting card was printed, " At home second Friday of each month," or whatever it was. I think these " at home " days stay in my mind largely because I helped to get rid of the food after it had been carried down from the drawing-room by the maid.

Actually, I never remember our drawing-room being used except for special occasions such as these. No one dreamt of sitting there. It was a chilly, uncomfortable place, and was so full of small tables covered with knick-knacks that one felt that if one was compelled to take a deep breath at least one table would crash to the ground. The " Soul's Awakening " was above the mantelpiece, but we were spared the imitation fruit and the stereoscope laid with studied abandon on a side table.

We were brought up frugally, but we didn't know it, not having any previous standard with which to compare it. My parents were strict teetotallers and looked on all theatres and music-hall entertainments as worldly and to be avoided. Drama and much of the cultural side of life was disregarded altogether. In fact, anything to do with the theatre was regarded as of the devil. It may have been narrow, but it was just the outlook of many of their generation, an outlook which was shared by the circle we moved amongst.

Sometimes that attitude resulted in catastrophe, as it nearly did for a boy with whom I was great friends and who had been brought up in a similar home to my own. In due course he found himself in France in the first World War, aged eighteen, and a second lieutenant in the artillery. Eventually he was detailed to go along with a sergeant to man a forward observation post at the head of a sap running out from the front line. His way led him through the front line trenches and the officers there hospitably invited him to have a drink before proceeding to his perilous position. They apologised for the fact that they had nothing to offer him except a bottle of creme-de-menthe liqueur. My friend thought that his position called for some stimulation, so he accepted their invitation. To the astonishment of everyone present, he proceeded to pour himself out a tumbler full. The other officers looked at him in wondering admiration.

" Surely you are never going to drink all that ? "

He saw he had blundered and only a bold front would carry it off.

" Oh, that's nothing," he replied, and he drank off the glass.

He then hastened as quickly as possible to his destination and had just got out of sight when he felt his legs give way and unconsciousness overtake him. Luckily the sergeant did all that was necesssary, and he told me afterwards that he had no recollection whatever of his time in the observation post.

Looking back on our home from a distance, I see it as a background for all the various doings of our later life. We were an essentially happy family. We could be natural at home. We felt secure. But only at this distance of time do I realise what security means to a child. Father provided us with not merely four walls and a roof—a house in which we could live—but he gave us a home. It wasn't a rich home, but it was just home, and however much we may have laughed at the wrong time, however silent we may have been about the deeper things of life, everyone of us knew instinctively that God was acknowledged to be the centre of our home and that father was a man of God.

CHAPTER II

PREP. SCHOOL

UNCONSCIOUSLY the character of a schoolmaster exudes through the pores of his skin and his pupils know him for what he really is only one degree less well than his Maker. I want to give therefore a very brief sketch of the man who was at once headmaster, proprietor and general overlord of the prep. school which I attended, as he appeared to a small boy during these early years. Externally he was stout, bald and had a large wen sticking up from the surrounding baldness of his head like an island in a placid sea. His baldness was covered with a mortar-board from which a tassel hung in the manner of certain Indians who release the spirit of the departed from it. Inside the school he wore a heavy black gown which hung about him in folds like an elderly matron who was shortly expecting to become a mother. Possibly a more fitting simile to his dignity would be to say that he wore his gown in the manner of a Roman wearing his toga. For this stout man was not without his dignity. In fact, I don't recall ever having seen him without that indispensable adjunct to a headmaster. I have omitted to say that he wore a pair of enormous whiskers which are associated with the name of the late Lord Dundreary.

I have said that he had a certain dignity in his bearing. He also had a very strong streak of kindness in him which was tempered by two things—fear of his wife and a wholesome respect for the God of mammon. Yes, I regret to say that even at that tender age when a child recognises character but is unable to articulate its meaning, I knew him for a snob who had the parents of the boys under his charge carefully graded according to their wealth, their profession and the size of the house in which they lived. He was no sadist, and he was, generally speaking, kind to his pupils, but I well remember getting my first thrashing from him, and that before the whole school.

On my way home from school I was caught fighting. Now, I wasn't punished for fighting. Fighting was looked upon as an honourable sport. No, I was thrashed for fighting the butcher's boy. He had laughed at my gaudy school blazer, and I got in one good blow in the region of his blue apron. Alas! it was the last blow I was destined to give him, as my opponent, who was at least twice my age, proceeded to make mincemeat of me. Thus I was doubly thrashed, and all for defending my own honour and the honour of the school. The injustice of it bit deep into my soul.

The headmaster was married. His wife taught in the school. All that I have said about her husband's character applied to her with even more force. She was the dominant character of the two, and it was of her we were frightened, not him. I don't think it was because she was not one of Nature's loveliest. A woman can be so plain as to be unfortunate in her appearance, and yet out of her eyes a child will recognise the gleam of love. It was not so in her case. I have never seen her raise her hand to a boy. I have never seen her behave unjustly or treat a boy with venom or deliberate unkindness. She had her favourites. What woman hasn't? She was a strict disciplinarian, but it was not that which made us afraid. Looking back over a lifetime to find the cause, the only one I can grasp is the one I have already stated, that the flower of love did not shine through her nature—and we knew it.

There were only three classrooms in the school, but there were many classes. It was the custom therefore for a class to depart to some quiet haven where both teachers and taught could achieve a modicum of quietness. These sanctuaries were very limited in number. There were two chief meccas, the cloakroom and the "business room". In both of these we stood round in a semi-circle, in the first surrounded by a halo of coats and mufflers, in the second by the desk and other office equipment necessary for the running of the school. The "business room" had a carpet on its floor and was much preferred as a place of instruction.

The boys had presumably grown in numbers, for one of the rooms underwent a metamorphosis into a gymnasium once a week. As gym was a "special" and my parents' budget for my fees did not run to "specials", I never saw the gymnasium in operation. Fencing must have been a "special", for I have vivid memories, even after nearly fifty years, of trying on a fencing mask in the absence of the master and of the joy of hitting my opponent over the head with all my force and hitting him with impunity. The change back to a classroom was as dramatic in its suddenness as the change into a gymnasium had been. When we returned from our conducted tour of the cloakroom or the "business room", we found the floor space covered with benches and the horse and the ladder and the other paraphernalia of a gymnasium placed in as inconspicuous a manner as possible around the walls.

Then there was the playground. It was about a third of the size of a full-length rugger pitch. The playground was frequently covered with a sea of mud and was innocent of grass except around the edges, like a bald-headed man with a fringe of hair around the circumference of his scalp. The playground was decorated with one pair of goal-posts, which had the highest cross-bar I have ever seen. The effect was like some new fashion where the waist is worn around the chest. Sometimes we played rugger transversely behind the goal posts if the ground threatened to bring proceedings to a sticky termination.

I may say that the rugger we played was not played with any degree of grit and abandon—but rather it was the custom for all players on the field to follow the ball at a gentle amble, rather like a flock of startled sheep. It was the custom to play in football boots, partly to save the appearance of our normal foot gear and partly to save the floor of the school. Sometimes if the referee did not blow his whistle immediately after the bell was rung we had not time to change into our ordinary shoes and had to sit throughout the following lesson in our football boots. This practice nearly led inadvertently to my being dismissed from the school. Had it not been for the financial loss which my fees would have meant to the headmaster I have no doubt whatever that my career as a pupil at that school would have come to an abrupt conclusion. It happened like this.

One day we were left without time to change out of our football boots and the ground was particularly muddy. As a result the studs of our boots were caked with sticky mud which was soon transformed into mud balls with which we proceeded to bombard each other as opportunity presented itself. The class was being taken, along with one on the opposite side of the room, by the headmaster. He wore a gown, as was his custom, but was also without his mortar-board, so that the shininess of his bald head remained uncovered. Soon the battle among ourselves began to pall and the boy next me suggested a " dare ".

I have been constitutionally unable to resist " dares " all my life, and lightheartedly took it on. The " dare " consisted of making a mud pellet about the size of a butter pat and at the moment the headmaster was addressing the opposite class, and was therefore presenting his back to us, for each of us to flick a mud pellet at the vast expanse of his back. There was no real risk of his feeling them, as the folds of his gown would prevent the sensation of anything touching him. The boy next me flicked first. His pellet struck harmlessly in the middle of the head-master's back and fell to the ground unnoticed. I flicked next, and the pellet sped for the headmaster like a homing pigeon. Unfortunately, I had concentrated on velocity rather than on direction with the result that the ball of mud went like a bullet for the wen on his head. The headmaster's dignity was outraged. I don't suppose I could have repeated the shot in a thousand years. I will draw a veil over the subsequent proceedings, which were both prolonged and painful.

I shall always look back, however, with gratitude and affection on the ladies who assisted the headmaster. They looked quite elderly to us then, but probably they were only young women. They certainly had a deep understanding of the heart of a child which served to soften the asperities of their superiors.

The preparatory school was unique in one respect. At it I gained my one and only prize for class work. Later on I was to win two prizes at Watson's, one for an essay on birds—about which I really knew a lot—the other for writing an essay on one of Sir Walter Scott's novels. Incidentally, as I had never even read the book, the second feat must be in a class by itself. It came about in this way. Those who were writing the essay were excused school for the rest of the day. Luckily, I had read a synopsis of the plot in the " Children's Encyclopædia " a few days before. With the bribe of a half holiday to urge me on, I entered for it, and, to my great surprise, I won it. To return to the preparatory school I was at, I was awarded a prize in my first year at school. As there were four in the class and we were all awarded prizes, the result is not surprising. Somebody certainly had to be first and apparently the choice fell upon me. I doubt if it was decided on merit. I am told I was a beautiful child—rather like a thinner edition of Botticelli's cupids. Maybe that was the reason why I was awarded the prize.

Looking back on my prep. school with the eyes of adult experi-ence, I can see that I was not happy there. I did not realise it at the time. Not that I was definitely unhappy. I did not nurse any secret grief or go to bed with a lump in my throat or any such thing, rather was I less full of *joie de vivre* than a little boy should have been. Possibly the fault was in myself—not in the school. Certainly the other boys seemed quite happy ; nevertheless, when the time came for me to leave I was glad to go. I was growing up. I went to my father and told him I wanted to go to Watson's. He thought the idea a good one.

CHAPTER III

GEORGE WATSON'S COLLEGE

WHEN I was eleven years old my father decided to send me to George Watson's College. Watson's is known beyond the bounds of Scotland for three things—the rugby football played by its old boys—the Watsonians ; the number of its old boys' clubs scattered over the world—in fifteen different countries, I believe ; and the high standard of its classical education. It provided a first rate education for the sum of five guineas per term, so far as I remember. Probably it was the latter which weighed with my father mostly, but certainly it was the rugby which attracted me. Our house faced on to Myreside—the school playing field—and the roar of the vast crowds watching the Watsonians on Saturday afternoons was enough to inspire any small boy.

The school was attended by about fifteen hundred boys, arranged in classes of about thirty boys each.

I passed the preliminary examination, and all that I remember about it is that it was conducted by "Goggles". To this day, I regret that I do not know his right name, but certainly " Goggles " was more appropriate than any surname could possibly have been. Sparsely built, with a slight stoop, a cut-away " swallow-tail " coat which had once been black but now was green, a long and straggling red beard turning grey, and thick spectacles with lenses like the bottom of lemonade bottles—such was "Goggles". He was in charge of the highest class in the Junior School and as I passed straight into the Senior School it never fell to my lot to know " Goggles " any better.

My first class master was " Butcher Munro," a typical dominie of the old school. Iron grey beard, an umbrella and an elder of the Free Kirk. I feared " Butcher " greatly but admired him secretly. He taught us mathematics and scripture. I always excelled at scripture but not at mathematics. The latter was the only subject in the classroom by which one gained promotion— or the reverse, and so I remained more or less stationary near the door, whereby I learned what has been more valuable to me than mathematics—the art of opening the door with dignity, in fact a smattering of butlering, an asset which has proved invaluable ever since.

"Butcher" sat on a platform, while we worked at sums in virgin white notebooks, with covers like gorgonzola cheese and a smell like cod liver oil.

The boys were a mixture. Probably a majority were sons of the manse like myself, others were sons of tradespeople. Some were distinctly hard up while others had more money to burn than I had. I was allotted a place next a youth arrayed in a red kilt and a red jersey. The jersey was rolled up to the waist and covered a large lump which looked like an umbilical hernia, but which I found before the morning was far gone, contained his lunch. There was no other way of carrying it when clothed in a kilt and a jersey. The lunch hour was from 12.10 to 12.45, but at 10.30 the jersey was unrolled and a surreptitious meal partaken throughout the course of the morning. I never remember that boy having any lunch to eat when the proper time arrived.

A very large number of the boys, including myself, wore kilts, and I can thoroughly recommend that garment to economical parents for their offspring. I had only one kilt which lasted me for many years and was lengthened by the simple expedient of inserting more material between the bodice and the kilt. A kilt never wears out and seldom gets torn.

I must say I thought my new classmates were a trifle boisterous. "Scragging" was the recognised method of fighting then. It consisted of trying to get your opponent's neck into the curve of your right arm, after which you proceeded to "bake" him, in other words you screwed his neck harder and harder. I am afraid my natural instincts soon found their natural outlet, and I "scragged" and was "scragged", "baked" and was "baked" before many days were out.

From "Butcher" we proceeded to "Tiger" to study French. "Tiger" was really a most placid man whose fierce moustache belied his natural gentleness. When any of us required corporal punishment we were sent next door to the gymnasium with a note for the gym instructor asking him to take action. The instructor was never backward in granting such a request, and most original in carrying it out. A long-handled brush with sharp bristles was his favourite weapon, and several jabs on the palm of the hand were things to be remembered. Another method was to give you a slight start, and then chase you the length of the gymnasium to the door, the while he urged you on your way with chastisement from behind.

It is a sad reflection on methods of teaching that I had French for six years—including some years at the private school—and could not translate a simple French composition at the end of it. Granting the fact that I was a slacker at French, that fact surely does not explain everything. It is a tribute to "Tiger" that even now I can sing " There is a Friend for Little Children " in undoubted French, but what the words individually mean I know not—nor ever did.

In later years at Watson's I dropped French, or to put it more exactly I was dropped from French, the immediate cause being a hornpipe exhibition given by me on the French master's desk during his temporary absence. It was rudely interrupted by the entrance of the little Frenchman (not "Tiger") who poured forth such a torrent of abuse in his natural tongue, that even I knew what he meant. I descended to explain matters, but was rudely taken by the back of the neck and literally thrown out of the room. My shame was even worse than my punishment, because I could have dropped him out of his window with one hand. On going home I decided on strategy and got my father —who knew nothing of the incident—to write the headmaster forthwith and suggest I took up Greek as I did not seem to be progressing at French.

I really liked Greek, and that was because I thoroughly learned the groundings of it. But the immediate cause of my learning Greek was like the conversion of St. Paul—a matter of a moment. On joining the Greek class I was under Mr. Allen—lest any Watsonian reader does not know who that was—let me give him his full title of Jimmy Allen, and then he will know his identity.

Now Jimmy Allen, like the other masters, sat on a platform on which was a desk, and on the desk were piles of lexicons and portly volumes. They were arranged to form three sides of a square so that it was possible for one or two boys to sit on the bench immediately beneath the desk and remain more or less unseen. Moreover, though an excellent teacher and a very shrewd man, Jimmy had one weakness, and we knew it. He always started at the same place in the class, and as a result, one row of unfortunates got the translation day after day. By right of conquest or diplomacy, I know not which, I occupied the coveted seat underneath the desk and remained unnoticed for several days. In order to improve my general education, I had sewn into the covers of my Greek book a volume entitled " The Memoirs of Sherlock Holmes ". One drowsy afternoon I got the biggest fright I ever got in my life. Jimmy leant over the top of the parapet and, indicating me, asked me to continue the translation. Hurriedly grabbing the next boy's book I arose without even the faintest notion where the passage for translation was. Jimmy descended from Olympus—in other words the platform—and I was caught red-handed.

Jimmy Allen never believed in corporal punishment. It was quite unnecessary. My punishment was to stay in after school hours for a fortnight and write out so many lines of translation, and thereafter bring my written translation to school every morning. And that was how I learned Greek.

But this simple story is not yet complete. There was a club at school called the field club. Their activities ranged from bugs to birds, and as I had always been enthusiastically interested in birds, I was a leading member of the field club.

Alas ! On the day of my encounter with Jimmy Allen I was billed to give a lantern lecture—my first—on " Scottish Birds ". I had better add here that in the course of preparation for the lecture I soon found that my knowledge could all be told in five minutes, so I decided to write it out. I did this in a note-book and copied it more or less *verbatim* from Hudson's " British Birds ", my father—like a sportsman—helping me. It is not difficult to imagine the quandary I was in about this lecture, to which, incidentally, a number of the masters came, and about which my father would certainly ask on my return home. I decided to tell Jimmy about it, and to my undying gratitude he let me off that first day.

One more word about how the lecture succeeded. I had my lecture written out, but foolishly omitted to tick off the birds for which I had lantern slides. The result was that only about one bird in six had a slide ; the others were prefixed by the monotonous repetition of the words " I am sorry we have no slides for this bird "—the full significance of which did not dawn on me till after the lecture.

The class turned out in force, and beyond a snigger every time I gave my sorrowful prefix, they never made a murmur. To this day I can't imagine why, because it was fertile with opportunities.

Later on in school I obtained one of the two prizes I ever got in Watson's for writing an essay on Scottish birds. My memory of Hudson served me well, but the prize had to be a volume on natural history. Alas! It was not long in my possession. Long before I left school I sold it to a second-hand bookseller in George IVth Bridge, and it supplied the capital for several jaunts to the pictures.

I thoroughly enjoyed school. What knowledge I had when I left consisted chiefly of a fair grounding in Latin and Greek, a real liking for English literature, a very deep and widely scattered knowledge of history, and a curious flair for geography. Of mathematics, modern languages and science I knew less than the veriest infant. I have never been able to spell correctly, but on the other hand, I find that I can work out sums in mental arithmetic much more quickly than most men.

My liking for English is entirely due to the teaching of that remarkable teacher, H. J. Findlay. "Henry John", as we affectionately called him, was one who courted no popularity, and got it because he was so transparently honest. Are masters aware of their eccentricities?

I am sure the spirit of the late "H.J." won't mind if I sketch the picture of him that comes to my eye most readily.

Always a fraction of a minute late after the bell had rung, he comes striding into the room twitching the business end of his nose the while, mounts the platform and announces "the verse for the day". Is he aware that I—and others—have read our lines, with gusto and fervour, from a page of Palgrave's "Golden Treasury" pinned on the coat collar of the boy seated in front?

Did he ever know that a certain myopic youth with bowed shoulders and peering eyes, who suffered from the delusion that he could recite, declaimed Wordsworth's "Ode to a Nightingale" with his shirt tails hanging out? It was a hot summer's day. We had our coats off, and a certain boy—lately a well-known legislator in India—edged gently but steadily the shirt tail from its usual resting place. I think that was one of the funniest sights I have ever seen in my life. I remember laughing till I was almost sick with trying to suppress it.

"Henry John" was a wise man and a gifted teacher, but he had one weakness, certain great and moving passages of English literature touched the fire that burned within him, and his voice would break with emotion when reading them.

A particular favourite of his was the scene in which Dickens describes the death of Little Nell ; when it came to the part where she died, the voice of "H.J." invariably faltered. I know that to be a fact, because I have heard him repeat the passage on three occasions. It was a moment that every one of the young barbarians in the class knew was coming, and yet in tribute to the boys' finer sense of honour and decency be it said, they never scoffed, and possibly not a few had a lump in their throats as well.

One could always tell how popular "H.J." was because of the number of old boys who came to see him when visiting the school. This, of course, was a godsend to us as these greetings were invariably conducted outside the classroom door. I think a large part of his success as a teacher was that he never tried to herd us into one groove in English literature. His own tastes were catholic and he respected catholicity even in boys. I remember him asking each boy in the class to name his favourite story. When the turn came to a certain youth we waited in expectation, because he was nothing if not original. His answer was "The Man with the Cream Tarts". Yells of derision from the rest of the class, who put an entirely different interpretation upon the title, were quelled by "H.J.'s" answer. "Yes, so and so, one of R. L. Stevenson's best short stories." Full marks to "H.J." as well as to so and so, a crest-fallen shamefacedness to the rest of the class. No liberties that I ever heard of were taken in his class, and he was certainly not severe with the boys, but rather allowed them considerable latitude.

While I was at school the art room was re-decorated, and plaster casts of various Grecian models were arranged on pedestals around the wall. This led to an unfortunate incident, when a normally quiet-mannered boy could stand the smell from the "still life" collection of fruit he was drawing no longer, and in a moment of freedom and despair shied a rotten orange right through Venus. How his father must have cursed him when it came to payment for the damage ! !

The Art Master was elderly and absent-minded, and probably was unaware to the end of his days that we had prised up a considerable portion of the floor, and could retire to the grubbiness of the foundations at our leisure, re-emerging when a suitable opportunity presented itself.

There was one boy in the class who was a real genius at art, and in later life took it up as a profession. It was he who sat next me in class, and he was many things besides an artist. Incidentally, he led me into one of the biggest thrills of my boyhood.

At the mouth of the Firth of Forth between Gullane and North Berwick are wide stretches of lonely sand hills—the site of that eerie story of R. L. Stevenson's " The Pavilion on the Links ". One summer holiday he, with one or two other boys, spent several weeks encamped on these hummocky sand dunes, having chosen their pitch as far from prying eyes as possible and near to a spring of water. They spent their time digging. They dug and dug till a vast and deep excavation was made, some nine feet deep and about sixteen feet long by nine feet broad. Into the floor of this pit they drove deep stakes at every corner and at suitable intervals between.

Time and time again the sand tumbled in on them, but they persevered, and ultimately built a complete house under the sand. The roof was raised in the centre and sloped from a central beam to the sides. The walls were lined with wood, chiefly driftwood, and the entire inside tarred and made proof against sand drifting in through the walls or roof. The floor consisted of pure white sand, and the entrance was a ladder, the top of which was covered by a trap door. The whole structure was covered with two or three feet of sand, so that absolutely nothing was to be seen by anyone walking over the roof. A chimney led out from an ancient stove by means of a funnel through the sand. When the stove was not in use, or when the house was left vacant, the top of the chimney was covered by a board, which in turn was covered by sand. Moreover, in order to avoid smoke being seen rising from the ground, a cowl was placed over the chimney so that the smoke ran along the surface.

The spot was so isolated that not even the builders could walk to it unguided. Inside were two beds with bed clothes, a table, chair and various cooking utensils.

The existence and location of this house under the sand was a secret known to only a select few. No one was allowed to divulge this without the permission of the others. As it was only two hundred yards from the sea where the bathing was ideal, we got a tremendous amount of pleasure from our occasional week-ends. The cost was nil, as we cycled the twenty-odd miles from our homes, and took our food with us.

I don't know what ultimately happened to the hut, but I was told that it was discovered by the military during the war years, and in view of its position at the very mouth of the Forth was thought to be the location of a German spy—a not unnatural supposition. I refer, of course, to the first world war.

Some years ago when on holiday in that part of Scotland, I took my wife and the children to look for it, but I was unable with any certainty to locate the particular cup of sand where it lay hidden. Maybe it is destroyed—maybe lost. Why not go and look?

To return to Watson's and the life there. It was essentially a happy life. If one did one's work and avoided trouble, no happier school life could be desired. Unfortunately, I went through school with the minimum of work, in sharp distinction to my University years, where I worked really hard. I have a vivid recollection of going to school unduly early, in order that I might glean the brains and homework of a particular bright lad in the class—now a well-known Q.C. He was always extremely generous with his brains at school. I trust that he may never have to use them on my behalf in later life. All the same I do not now regret not having worked at school, for my brain was fallow when I went to the University. Moreover, I was thoroughly interested in medicine, and that, combined with a naturally good memory, may account for any success which I may have found there.

Of bullying I remember none. Possibly because I would always fight, provided my blood was up, and certainly would try to give as good as I got.

The moral tone at Watson's was very good. There were, and are, at every school, a certain few who are unhealthy little vermin. They were usually sat on by the others very strongly.

I remember an incident when travelling to play some other school at Rugger—Glenalmond, I think. A certain boy produced a piece of paper and passed it round for the others to read. It had on it an extremely foul word. David MacRither, now lying in Flanders, was one of the first to read it. He tore it into several strips and threw it out of the carriage window. Not a word was spoken, but I shall remember that action all my life.

Swearing was taboo. I remember getting a ticking off for swearing in the scrum when playing for the school. I did not remember doing so, and anyway it could not have been very bad. But there it is. It taught me a lesson. After all swearing is merely a sympton of lack of self-control. Not that we were little prigs. Whatever we were, we were not that. I only

37

remember one rather half-baked group who formed a club called the " I.C.S.S.", which stood for the Institute for Chaps of Social Standing. I don't even know whether they were serious or not, as I was not a member.

Of roughness and horseplay there was a good deal. It was the custom for certain classes to assemble outside their respective classroom doors. Several of these had rather narrow passage-ways leading to them. Prior to the arrival of the master, the class would line the walls of the passage, and every late-comer would be pushed from one side to the other with considerable force, until ultimately he arrived at the other end of the passage a very different youth from the one who entered it. It was known as " running the gauntlet ". That custom was stopped, I believe, some time after I left.

Another amusement of ours which overstepped the limits of decorum was the game we played in the playground during the lunch interval. A ball was used, or maybe somebody's cap rolled up, and as many as liked could take part in it. Rough and ready sides being formed, the game was to touch with the ball a wall of the lavatories on either side of the playground. All on one side tackled the one with the ball who struggled on as far as he could and then passed it on to someone else, and so the game went on. As the playground was made of hard pebbles and asphalt in parts, and the tackling was fierce, clothes and bodies suffered as a result.

When the bell was rung for school a dash was made for the doorway, and the fight grew even fiercer as the moments slipped away. It was a grand game, though the score mattered nothing, and I never heard of anyone being actively sick, though we played it immediately after lunch. The weak-kneed could generally avoid these rowdyisms, but to those who took part in them it was the survival of the fittest and the battle of the strong.

It is natural that in looking back on one's school days, the things which stand out are the unusual incidents. The hours of honest toil are forgotten. For example, when I try to remember what we did in the science rooms, the incident which rushes to my mind is that of a certain youth being blown up. Curiously enough, it didn't happen in the science laboratory either ; it was in the Latin classroom. This particular youth cared not for the mysteries of O_2 and CO_2, but he was really interested in ex-plosives. Why or how, I don't know, but this I know that in the middle of our Latin lesson there was a deafening roar and a sheet of flame surrounding him. It all happened in a moment. One minute he was reading *Ovid*, the next moment he blew up. What happened was this.

Following a science lesson in which we were told that certain chemicals added together and heated would explode, he had managed to obtain a small quantity of the necessary ingredients from the laboratory, and put them in his waistcoat pocket, intending to pursue his studies further in the matter at home. Unfortunately, he forgot all about them, and the heat of his body did the rest.

The first thing that reminded him was when he came to himself in the ambulance on his way to hospital. His clothes had literally been blown off him, and to this day I treasure a trouser button of his picked up on the opposite side of the room. By great good fortune the explosion took place outwardly, and his injuries were not serious. It was a miracle that he was not blown to bits.

The only other incident that I can recall in connection with the science laboratories is the incident of the burst pipe. The same Latin room in which the boy blew up was situated immediately under the lab. A pipe was leaking up above, and about every second a large drip would descend on a desk of the Latin room. A zinc pail was put to collect the drips pending repairs upstairs ; meanwhile the class went on with its lessons.

Ping ! A large drop of water dropped on to the bottom of the pail. Another second passed, then ping again, and so on. It was a golden opportunity not to be missed. Ping ! in went a trouser button. Before five minutes had passed the collection of assorted goods in the pail was truly marvellous.

By one of those freaks of nature, the deception was only spotted by the master when one over-bold youth threw half an apple into the pail, when the result was not a ping, but a noise like a gas gong going off. I think we all got thrashed for that.

Thrashing was generally administered by a strap on the palm of the hand—occasionally by a cane on the other time-honoured seat of punishment. I preferred the cane to the strap any day. For the benefit of those of tender years who may still be called upon to suffer, let me point out three things to do, and one thing not to do.

First, if there is time, apply resin to the palm before the strap is administered. Secondly, let the hand give with the strap, don't hold it too rigidly. Thirdly, don't get the strap on your wrist if you can possibly help it—it hurts like the Inquisition. Now, as to what not to do : don't pull away your hand altogether so that the master gets it on his own knee ! ! You only get double strength next biff.

One of the most curious methods of thrashing was administered by one of the English masters. He beat you with a cane on alternate shoulders. It was necessary to stand or sit absolutely rigid, otherwise you would be severely struck on the head. He faced you while operating, and years of practice had made him expert, so that the cane flew with lightning rapidity from side to side. We feared that master greatly, and I can well remember an incident in his classroom when a certain lad ought to have got the schoolboys' " V.C." This master took us for scripture—it was in later years than the Gospel according to " Butcher "—and the Bibles were kept in a small cupboard on the wall behind the master's desk. There was always keen rivalry to distribute the Bibles, and on this day, by fair means or foul, the journeys to and from the cupboard were performed by a Highland lad, a descendant of one of the Highland chiefs.

After piling up the Bibles at the end of a desk, he re-entered the cupboard and sliding the door, apparently decided to stay there. We all saw this, but of course the master was unaware of it.

The second act in the drama took place when a boy was called out to write something on the blackboard, and on his way back to his seat locked the cupboard door while passing behind the master. All was quiet for some minutes, then we were aware of a gentle knocking on the inside of the cupboard door. The knocking grew more loud and more persistent ; it was evident that the scion of nobility from Balquhidder wanted to come out. Moreover, he wanted to come out rather urgently. Then it dawned on us that he was undergoing slow suffocation in there.

There was a whispered conversation between the boys nearest the cupboard door, and then slowly but steadily one descended from his seat and crept on his hands and knees across the open floor. Should the master turn his head but a fraction he must see him.

We were reading the story of Jael being knocked on the head by Sisera inside his tent ; curiously appropriate. Steadily the drone of the boys' voices went on as they read a portion in turn, but every now and again we watched the creeping figure on the floor. We knew better than all look in that direction at the same time. The door was reached and silently unlocked, and then we watched the return journey—the liberator followed by a very pale-faced and subdued Mac. It seemed to us they took hours, probably it was only a minute or two, but they did it, and the master whom we feared was not one whit the wiser.

Most of the boys were good steady workers, but one or two had a passion for getting into unnecessary trouble. One boy in particular was never out of hot water. A most likeable soul he was, but with the most fertile brain for inventing abnormal forms of amusement. He lived some miles out of Edinburgh, and travelled in by train every morning. For a whole week he skipped school, and spent the entire day in the train travelling backwards and forwards to school, returning home at his normal hour of arrival. I can't recall what the sequel to it was, but what amazes me now is how anyone, even a schoolboy, could find pleasure in sitting in a railway train shunting backwards and forwards on a journey of six miles for a whole week. Some of his exploits were not so placid, however.

One day he brought a baby rabbit to school and kept it beside him through every class. Nor was the rabbit ever discovered, though he had a narrow squeak in one class. I know, for I was sitting next him.

He had taken the tiny rabbit from his pocket to give it a run, as he said. To enable him to do this he erected a parapet of books on the desk in front of him. The communal interest around him in the class drew the master's attention to the fact that something abnormal was going on behind the books. He strode down from the rostrum.

" What have you got there ? "

" Nothing, sir," and it was true, for the culprit had only time to stuff the rabbit up the sleeve of his jacket and push in his handkerchief after it before the master reached him.

" Well, carry on with the translation."

And so the boy stood up and translated, with the baby bunny literally " up his sleeve ". It did not seem to be any the worse when we had our next opportunity of having a look at it.

On another occasion he procured a snake from a shop near the Waverley Steps, and brought it to school in his pocket. It had

had its fangs removed, but we did not know that. He let it loose in the room during the master's temporary absence. Snakes are one thing that boys are really frightened of, and when he heard the master's footstep outside the door and we saw him grab the snake and put it in his pocket, we felt thereafter that, somehow or other, he was different from the rest of us. We felt rather proud of him, but gave him a wide berth for a day or two.

As the years passed at school and I became one of the big boys I found life increasingly interesting. Being in the School Fifteen made a lot of difference to one, even being in the second made life worth living. Though I was probably the fastest boy at school—at least I won the school championship—I never was any good as a threequarter. As a wing forward I found my metier. The thrill of playing for the school is one of the greatest in any boy's life. No old boys' club or rugger of any kind after school gives one quite the same elation.

We had a good fifteen that year and won the Scottish Public Schools Championship. Of the boys in the team several got Scottish caps.

As a curious commentary, in passing on the emigratory habits of Scotsmen, I only know of two of that fifteen who are in Scotland now. I don't think a third of the boys who were at school in my time took up occupations or professions in Scotland. England and the four corners of the earth took the others.

Each member of the First Fifteen had a junior Fifteen to look after. The method adopted for getting them into training was to run them round a football pitch, the hindmost being walloped by the trainer armed with a cricket stump. Even then it always struck me as ludicrous and not unlike a flock of sheep being chased by a snapping collie.

The training for us consisted of scrum practice, and after that more scrum practice. The shades of a winter's night would be gathering over Myreside before we finally took ourselves home. I think it was good for us, but I am quite convinced that we were inclined to be stale for many of our matches.

Rough play was definitely frowned upon at Watson's. I wish I could say the same of some other schools I could mention. The cleanest rugger I have ever known was played by Loretto. They were sportsmen to their finger-tips. Incidentally, there was a curious anomaly about Loretto rugby. Their First Fifteen was always one to be respected. We never suffered from a superiority complex as regards them. But their Second and subsequent Fifteens were, to put it bluntly, poor stuff. At least they were in the times I write of.

Scottish rugby among the F.P.s has one great difference from English rugby. If a boy from any of the leading Edinburgh or Glasgow schools goes on to the University of his native city, he always plays for the school F.P.s rather than have a University blue to his name. The University team was almost entirely composed of colonials, Englishmen and a sprinkling of Scots who have no school team to play for.

This characteristic was the subject of a rectorial address by the late Lord Birkenhead. It always struck me as a blessing for his lordship that he made that speech after his election and not previously. He would certainly never have been elected Lord Rector had he done otherwise.

History for me has always lived. As I walked across the Boroughmuir to and from school I used to picture to myself the gathering of the Scottish army on that same Boroughmuir before they marched away to their deaths at Flodden Field. In the gathering dusk, with the night wind cool upon my brow, I used to wonder if it was here, or here, or here that the old woman burst into King James' tent and foretold the disaster that would rock all Scotland to its foundations.

Or was it here that, in the darkness of the night, young Napier made his way from the Merchiston Castle to the Boroughmuir to meet some like-minded companions and to dig up the body of their hero Montrose, who had been executed that day in the Grassmarket of Edinburgh. I could see in imagination that grizzly exhumation. The limbless body lying on the turf, while the silent group, with white faces and set lips, grimly set to work to cut out the heart of their leader while already the limbs were speeding to the four corners of the kingdom.

But best of all I liked to stand and gaze at the weather-worn old stone let into the wall of the Parish Church of Morningside, into which the Scottish standard was fixed before the army marched south to its death and defeat—but not to its disgrace—at Flodden.

I don't know if it was an undue development of my historical sense, or whether it was merely the sense of " old, forgotten far-off things ", but certainly I did see them as long as ever I can remember.

Let me pass on a piece of historical information which I have never seen in print and which I chanced upon when I was hunting through an old book whose name I have no recollection of in the Public Library in George IV Bridge, which was my mecca even in my schoolboy days.

In the days of one of the James' the King was on a hunting expedition which led him across the flat land below where the Craig House now stands. The land is now occupied by the University and by George Watson's athletic fields—possible even by the school itself. The baron who inhabited the Craig House of that day was a bold, bad man, even for those wild days, and had carried off a fair maiden, who was his unwilling prisoner in the Craig House. The father of the captive maiden came to the King's party on the flat land and told his story and pleaded for justice. The King ordered the bold, bad baron to attend him, and there and then gave him the alternative of handing the maiden over to her father or being put to death. He chose the former. I can't remember where I got the story from, but I am quite sure of my facts even at this length of time.

The old grey building on the other side of the Meadows has now been pulled down and the site of the old school is incorporated into that of the Royal Infirmary. The old school is no more.

A generation ago a tall-hatted and silver-buttoned janitor showed me round the new school which is built on the old playing fields at the foot of the Craig House. The school had not long been opened by a prince of the Royal blood. It was a day of almost tropical heat when the new school was opened. When we came to the baths the janitor, pointing to the spot where I was standing, said :

" Aye, he stood there himsel', and what do you think he said ? He said, ' Man, I could dae wi' a dook fine ' ! "

I would be very surprised if the Royal Duke said any such thing.

Cricket at Watson's, or any of the Scottish schools, never attained equality of place with rugby. Having played golf since infancy, I found it a physical impossibility to keep a straight bat. I don't think I ever got into a higher team than the eighth, and as my size and age made me a pine tree among the shrubbery I decided to abandon the game. I cannot recall having ever made a run in my life.

Golf was my great forte in summer—golf on the big Braids, or the wee Braids—the former threepence, the latter one penny, if my memory serves me aright. Edinburgh is extraordinarily lucky in having the finest golf courses open to the public for a nominal sum. This not only applies to Edinburgh, but to every town and village in Scotland.

There it is a democratic game. Everyone plays golf. The annual subscription to most courses was only seven and sixpence. In England golf is a rich man's game. There, incidentally, it is the social ladder to the man who is making a bit of money. The smoke-room and bar often hold a more important place than the fairway.

There is nothing that irritates me so much as seeing a man dressed to the last tacket of his shoes for the golf course, check plus-fours, light stockings, leather jacket and shining clubs in a bag like a leather pillar-box carried by a perspiring caddie, and taking eight or ten for every hole. Such a man ought to be prosecuted. We all have to learn. Admittedly so, but for heaven's sake let him make himself as inconspicuous as possible until he can hit the ball more or less decently.

The Braids was a grand course, but no place for the feeble-kneed. There was one hole across the valley where you got a full-blooded swipe from one hill top to another. If the swipe did not connect, it was bound to go into the valley far, far below.

It was while returning from the " wee " Braids that I had a narrow squeak from death. Cycling down the very steep hill at full speed with only a cleek in my hand, I dropped the club and it went through the spokes of the front wheel. My head hit the ground with the velocity of a high-speed bullet, and that is all I ever knew about that incident.

Cycling was much safer than it is now. I only remember having one serious accident when I was a boy, and that was not with a car, but a motor-bike and side car.

Near to where I lived there was a triangle of three roads about half a mile in circumference. It was a standing challenge for anyone to break the time record for the lap, and a flying start was allowed. One Saturday morning I felt in record-breaking form, and was being timed by a very great friend of mine. It was the custom for the time-keeper to wave one to stop if anything was approaching the cross roads, which was the winning post. So enthusiastic was my time-keeper about my breaking the record—which I did—that he forgot to keep a look-out.

Anyway, I shot into the cross roads and hit the side-car of a motor-bike clean amidships. The force was so terrific that I was catapulted clean over the heads of the occupant of the side-car and the driver, and landed on the pailings of our family doctor's house on the other side of the road. Marvellous to relate, I did not get a scratch, nor was either machine damaged.

I suppose trick cycling still is popular among school boys. Our biggest thrill was to go down Craighouse Hill—the steepest hill in the vicinity—standing on the crossbar. I wouldn't do it now for all the money in the Bank of England. Trying to force each other off without dismounting ourselves was a fascinating game. I believe I could still hold my own at that, providing I was well.

An occasional Saturday morning in summer was devoted to sitting on the side of the Queensferry road waiting for the passing motor vehicles for a free " hang-on " to Queensferry. That game came to an abrupt end when one of our company, while hanging on to the back of a taxi, found a workman's pit in the road which the taxi negotiated at speed, and he did not.

I think it was under the auspices of the Field Club that we were taken to see certain outstanding places of interest. I remember going down a coal mine at Newton Grange with a party of boys, and I have been a wholehearted supporter of the miner ever since.

Another expedition was to Inchcolm, an island in the Forth, where were the ruins of an old abbey. What interested us much more was a shallow pit we discovered on the island, full of human bones. What a find ! I remember the whole battle fleet going past the end of the island led by the *Agamemnon*. Altogether an excellent day's outing.

Another expedition was to the central fire station in Lauriston Place, where we saw an exhibition of horses and men getting off the mark. The thing that most impressed us was the way they came down from their living quarters by sliding down a greasy pole. Why is this method not adopted in all houses ? Still, I can't imagine any maternal grandmother coming down a greasy pole. I have the feeling that even in case of fire she would rather die in dignity.

Another outside source of entertainment and education were lectures in the Synod Hall by well-known people. I believe these were under the auspices of the Philosophical Society, and so many tickets were allotted to the school. There I heard Shackleton, Sir Wilfred Grenfell and many other notable men and women.

On one occasion the girls from Edinburgh Ladies' College were seated immediately in front of us. I blush to say it, but we surreptitiously tied two girls' pigtails together. The results were fully up to expectations.

Of my intimate friends at Watson's I am now only in touch with one. We have sent each other a Christmas greeting for forty-three years, and though our ways lie far apart, and we meet only once every few years, yet we can resume the unbroken thread where it was last left off. It is a thread which has known no knots, and will last till the scissors of death do their inevitable work.

My great hero at school was Eddie Fry. It is thirty-three years since he was killed in France, but he still remains my hero.

The way in which I came to know him is typical of his outlook on life in general. Our parents were acquainted with each other, but of each others' families we knew nothing. The introduction came this wise. The summer holidays before I went to Watson's our family were spending their annual holiday in Lundin Links, a small seaside resort on the Firth of Forth.

One evening, while watching the pierrots, a note was pushed into my hand by an unknown maiden who immediately disappeared in the crowd. The note directed me to go to a certain spot in the sandhills at a certain hour, and when I saw a red light to whistle three times. Moreover, it warned me not to tell anyone of the appointment. The spot mentioned was a lonely place, and the hour one when darkness would have set in, but curiosity overcame my scruples and I went, telling no one.

On coming to the place I saw a red light flicker for an instant in front of me and I whistled as directed. The next moment two people sprang on me, and after a fierce struggle bound my hands and feet, gagged my mouth with a handkerchief and carried me down to the edge of the sea.

I was laid on the sand by the lapping waves and a gruff voice asked if I would agree not to fight if I were released and not to tell anyone. One must remember that it was pitch dark, and I was only eleven years old. Some instinct made me defy them to do their worst, whereupon my bonds were loosened and I was told I had passed the initiation test and was worthy to be admitted to their friendship. They turned out to be the brothers Eddie and John Fry, who were on holiday like myself and were looking for a boy to play with. Apparently they had seen me and decided to put me to the test, using their sister as the bearer of their note.

Looking back on that episode, I am tempted to think that some boys might have been frightened into insanity by such a prank. Eddie never had any nerve himself, and would have been

47

heart-broken had it been the means of seriously frightening anyone. I certainly never regretted that dramatic introduction. It led me into one of the most exciting holidays I ever remember. We were always tracking somebody or building a new lair in the whin bushes or being mysterious in some form or another.

Eddie lived in a world of romance, though girls had no place therein. As I remember him in later life, he stood six feet high, and was so perfectly proportioned that his size was unnoticed. He had the figure and the head of a Greek God. Not unlike Lawrence of Arabia in appearance, his face was longer and even more sensitively chiselled. Firm-lipped and clean shaven, his blue eyes had generally a far-away look, which gave him a grave and preoccupied expression. His whole being was hedged about with barriers of reserve, which were seldom if ever let down. He had the strongest sense of duty, the most natural cleanness of soul I have ever known in man, and was my nearest approach to Sir Galahad in human form. If ever man lived as man was made to live it was he. Full major at the age of twenty-three, he had the ability and character to achieve greatness. This tribute is not a eulogy ; it is only Eddie as I knew him.

We took things for granted and the religious instruction we received at school was a farce. I only remember one master of those who took us for Scripture, who made any attempt to express to us the realities of the Christian faith. And I am sure the spirit of " Uncle " Shaw will forgive me if I say that it was not the somewhat halting words he spoke to us, but the very obvious fact that he was a Christian gentleman himself, that made us realise what real faith and character are.

Do masters realise what a tremendous influence they have on the boys who sit in front of them ? I have discussed the question with other Watsonians in far-away corners of the world, and we unanimously agreed that it was the same few masters who had influenced us most. Boys have an unerring instinct for sizing up the true character of a master. They know his heel of Achilles even better than he himself does.

The majority of pre-war Watson's masters were fine men, a minority were not. A select few were pure gold.

Sarcasm we hated and one man in particular who continually and cruelly sharpened his wits at our expense was universally disliked. On the other hand, a good-natured banter at our expense we never minded ; indeed, we thoroughly enjoyed it.

Such were the competitions between myself and the inkpot in Mr. Driver's class, where the inkpot got a mark if the answer was wrongly given, and *vice versa* if I were correct. It was a mathematics class and the inkpot invariably won.

Halcyon days ! What an ideal life to go back to.· I think now that I should even like to toy with X and Y. I could even rake up some interest in the unnatural proclivities of those most immoral Greek gods.

I verily believe, yes, I do believe that after all I should like to learn French, on thinking it over. That last is true with a reservation—I should not learn irregular verbs—and I should refuse to sing before my fellow-men " There's a Friend for little children ".

CHAPTER IV

THE CHURCH

THE bulk of Scotland is Presbyterian. It has numerous divisions and sub-divisions, but I was brought up in the " auld kirk "—the Church of Scotland—of which my father was a minister. Throughout the earlier years of my life the Church played a very large part. It was situated in one of the densest populated parts of Edinburgh. In every direction from it were streets upon streets of tenement houses, each becoming more decayed the nearer one got to the church. The church itself was a large one, capable of holding a thousand people, and it was well filled each Sunday morning with a congregation of the better type of working-class people and their families. The actual church membership was in the neighbourhood of two thousand, and it will give some idea of the class they were drawn from if I say that not one family in the church had a maidservant, even in those spacious days of servants.

We lived about a mile from the church because there was no suitable house nearer. My parents were firm believers in that part of the Catechism which states that a person "shall do his duty in that state of life unto which it shall please God to call him ". Since they themselves were the product of the middle classes, their children in turn were brought up as far as was possible in the stratum of society which they themselves had been born into. The consequence was that we lived and moved and had our being among ordinary middle-class folk on weekdays and descended on Sundays to worship among a totally different class of people. There seemed nothing inconsistent in it to us. From our earliest infancy it had been thus and we accepted it without giving it a thought. Certainly no breath of criticism came to our ears.

We were treated with a considerable amount of respect, a respect due entirely to that enjoyed by my father and of which we children shared the benefit. My father came of farmer stock and must have had a very great inherent strength, as he thought nothing of walking to and from the church three times a day when he was well over seventy and starting work when he got there.

It was a curious situation in which we children were brought up. There was the church and there were the people among whom we normally mixed and never the twain did meet, except on Sundays.

As I grew older I came to appreciate more and more the sterling worth of many of these church people. In fact, I knew some of them so well that I used to surprise my father by letting drop some small items of information of which he was ignorant. I remember, for example, letting drop quite accidentally the real reason why Sandy Whitten would not become an elder. Sandy was a gardener by profession and a great pal of mine. A Highlander of Herculean proportions—he augmented his scanty wages by going round the Highland games in summer and winning the prize money for the strong-man events. As a matter of fact he taught me to putt the weight so well that I ended up by becoming the champion schoolboy of Scotland in that particular event. In the winter his Saturday afternoons and evenings were employed as " chucker-out " in a nearby public-house. This was the real reason why Sandy would not become an elder. He thought that the dignity of the eldership was inconsistent with being " chucker-out " at a pub. As soon as he was appointed to collect the gate money at Watsonian rugby football matches on Saturday afternoons, he accepted the responsibilities of being an elder. God rest you, Sandy, and if I hear the drone of the pipes when I approach the Elysian fields I shall know it is you who are playing them.

These Elders were the backbone of the Church. It was their duty to visit that portion of the parish to which they had been allotted four times a year, and to know their charges individually. It is a procedure which the Church of England might profitably follow. There were between thirty and forty Elders, and though I have met many men in all walks of life since leaving home, I have yet to meet a finer body of men. They correspond roughly to the non-commissioned officers of the regular army. They were working men. Their Christianity was not a mere symptom of neurasthenia as it is with so many. They were men whose Christian faith made them finer individuals in every way. They were men who earned their daily bread with the skill of their hands ; men whose only capital was in their labour. Rough hewn, but men in the finest sense of the word. They carried the stamp of manliness and dignity as naturally as noblemen wear the insignia of their rank. I knew them all, and their stature has not grown less with the passing of the years. One or two stand out conspicuously in my memory like gnarled old oaks in a wood with which I have once been strangely familiar.

There was John Sinclair, who on weekdays drove the express between Edinburgh and Aberdeen. John might be seen walking to his engine any day of the week clothed in the pale blue dungarees and glazed peak cap which are worn by those on the footplate. When he wasn't driving the express he was to be found doing some job or other in connection with the church. I have never met any man to whom the immediate presence of Christ was such a reality. His face was always beaming with smiles, and it gave one the impression of having been kept in a state of perpetual polish, just as he kept his engine polished with a greasy rag. The satisfactoriness of a sermon could always be told by the nodding of John's head. He wasn't like another member of the congregation who tried my father's patience considerably. This man invariably jotted down the text on the fly-leaf of his Bible as soon as it was given out, and then composed himself for slumber, which he did deeply and audibly until the end of the sermon. I think we knew John Sinclair best of all because he was most about the house, and my parents depended on him in a multitude of ways.

Then there was Sam Bryson. Sam was what was known as a " thrawn cratur ". He walked in moody silence down to his work at Alder and Mackay's gas foundry. But in spite of his thrawn-ness, I liked Sam. He rather fancied himself as a singer, and I can hear his deep voice coming in at the appropriate moment in that well-known psalm, " Ye gates lift up your heads ".

And then there was John Craw, coach builder, gentleman and Christian. In later life he gave up coach building and became my father's right-hand man. In his extreme old age he is still alive as I write these words, while all the other oaks are fallen to the ground long since.

Then there was Angus Mackinnon, who was a railwayman, a Highlander and a very great Christian gentleman. Angus seemed to have the blood of Highland chiefs in his veins, for in his bearing and in his speech he had that gentle courtesy, that slightly reserved aloofness which is the prerogative of the high-born Celt. He never spoke of Christianity so far as I am aware, but everyone who came into contact with him knew that his Christian faith was a very real thing to him. He was one of the living illustrations of that oft-quoted maxim that the most effective sermon is a silent one.

I could go on for a long time telling about one or another of these Elders, but it would be a pity to pick out some and leave the others unrecorded. I have only mentioned one or two who had a great influence on my boyhood.

The Scottish Presbyterian Communion Service differs very considerably from that of the Church of England. We had Communion four times a year. Every person taking Communion handed a card containing his name and address to the Elder at the door when they went into the Church. In this way a complete check was kept of everyone who communicated. If a person had not communicated for three years, he or she was given the opportunity for explanation or for reformation, as the case might be. If the individual continued to neglect the Communion service then they were struck off the list of membership. This was called " purging the roll ", and every year between two and three hundred members were " purged ". The cards, I may say, were taken along to the members by the Elders on their quarterly visits. The pews of the communicants were all covered with white cloths so that, looking down from my eyrie in the gallery, the whole church gave the appearance of whiteness as of driven snow, and a vast concourse of people waiting solemnly for the " elements " of Communion. It was a most moving and wonderful sight.

In the Highlands they only have Communion twice a year, and it is generally only the very elderly who communicate. It is all due to a too literal interpretation of that verse of the New Testament which states " whosoever eateth and drinketh unworthily, eateth and drinketh damnation to himself ". Regarding this service a most unusual thing occurred—not in my boyhood days—but many years after when I was grown up and married.

It happened that my wife and I were on holiday in the Highlands. When Sunday came round we went to church. It was Communion Sunday, and for some reason or other there was no Elder at the door and we walked in to the church unopposed. The minister's wife leant over from the seat behind and courteously asked us if we would like to stay to Communion. We said we would, so she tiptoed out to the aisle and asked the elderly postman, who was also the senior Elder, for a visitor's card.

Unfortunately, he was very deaf and had no idea that his whispers carried to every corner of the church. " Wae are they ? " he asked. The good lady indicated where we were. He studied us intently for a moment or two and then enquired of her in a loud whisper and with more rolling of r's, " Are they worthy ? "

The Communion Service was when the Elders were on parade, so to speak. My boyhood's memories are chiefly of the length of the service. Later, when I was an actual member myself, which I became about the age of fifteen, it was the haunting sadness of the service which I remember most. I think this melancholy sadness is an intimate part of every true Scotman's pleasure. The long service invariably opened with the hundredth psalm, sung to the tune of the " Old Hundredth ". During the singing of the psalm, a long line of Elders appeared at the church door end of the aisle, each one carrying a silver plate containing small squares of bread or drinking cups of wine, while some carried flagons for refilling the wine cups, and the remainder just walked solemnly up the aisle, the one behind the other. When the Communion Table had been laid they took their places in a wide semi-circle on either side. Then the service proceeded. There were two addresses, one before and one after Communion. At the end of the first address my father left the pulpit and took his place at the centre of the Communion Table. After certain prayers and reading of Scripture, the senior Elder arose and handed to my father a plate containing a large square of bread. He broke off a small portion and, dividing the remainder, handed a portion to the Elder on either side of him. This square of bread was handed from hand to hand up the line of the Elders, the last one rising and placing it on the Table. The same sort of thing happened with the wine. It was given to my father who handed a cup to the Elder on either side of him, and so from hand to hand until each Elder had drunk from it. After this there was a short pause, and then one and another of the Elders would rise from their place and carry the Communion to the congregation. The bread and the wine were passed in like manner from hand to hand with the Elders waiting at the end of each pew to pass them up the line of waiting communicants. In this way the entire congregation partook.

After Communion, and in accordance with the description given in Holy Writ of the Last Supper, a hymn was sung. It was invariably the same " 'Twas on that night ". It was sung to the tune of " Communion ". What sticks in my mind chiefly is of masses of people expressing their thankfulness in this hymn. It seems as though the atmosphere was charged with the emotion of that moment, and I think that even the most prosaic person there was aware of it. I have said there were masses of people, and that is no exaggeration. There was one Communion Service in the morning and another in the afternoon. In the forenoon the church, apart from the galleries, was packed. Fully fifteen hundred people communicated between the two services. I should know, for it was my job as long as I can remember, to keep the Communion Roll. But my earliest memory of that service is of sitting in the side gallery opposite to where we normally sat and watching the slow-moving ceremony down below and wondering if it would ever come to an end.

We were brought up to go to church twice each Sunday. We were not expected to go to Sunday school, largely, I think, because my mother had a fear that we would catch some contagion either of body or speech, a contingency which was quite likely considering the hundreds of children who were crowded into a small area and the natural ability of a small child to pick up the speech of his associates. In later years we taught in Sunday school, though this did not absolve us from regular attendance at church. Actually, I was not a Sunday school teacher for very long, and my chief memory is of pecuniary appeals to aid someone called Moula Bach. Years after, when on my honeymoon, I met Moula Bach in India and conveyed to him personally the greetings of the Sunday school at Tynecastle. I regret to say that he had never heard of it. His imagination was bounded by those who supported his immediate needs, and did not extend to the pennies and the halfpennies of a crowded Sunday school.

It was our custom to wear special clothes on Sunday. I wore a large collar of a type which has entirely gone out of fashion. It was white and it was starched, coming down over my coat collar somewhat in the manner of the dog Toby. It was an abomination to myself and to those who had to put it on for me. From about the age of eight I wore a kilt, the bodice of which was gradually made lower and lower as my height increased, until ultimately a visible portion of black satin bodice appeared below my waistcoat, and it was discarded for long trousers which reposed beneath my mattress during the week-days when they were not in use.

We were very parochial in our outlook, and regarded with the gravest suspicion anybody who did not worship as we ourselves did. We had a strong anti-Popery bias and regarded Episcopalians—or Piskeys as we called them—as halfway to perdition. This was typically exemplified in the course of conversation many years after I had left home and had gone back on a fleeting visit. I was enquiring from a member of the congregation what had happened to a man we both knew.

"He hasna turned out verra weel, ye ken. He's joined the Church of England."

That put our attitude in a nutshell.

This reminds me of an incident in which a relative of mine was involved. He was stranded for the week-end in the mining village of Cowdenbeath. On Sunday night, wanting to go to a place of worship, he saw a light above the door. He entered to find a service was about to commence. On coming out, he enquired of the Scot at the door what denomination they belonged to. The worthy man replied with much rolling of r's and prolonging of a's.

"Hae ye heard of the Church of God in Corinth?"

"Yes."

"And hae ye heard of the Church of God in Laodicea?"

"Yes."

"Well, this is the Church of God in Cowdenbeath."

But it wasn't so narrow a view as was expressed me by an aged Highlander sometime in the early nineteen thirties. It must be remembered that in the far north they consider strict observance of the Sabbath to be almost the greatest commandment of all. We were discussing the shortcomings of the present generation, and he summed up by saying,

"And during the war a Bishop of the Church of England was seen digging his garden on the Sabbath Day."

There were invariably two or three Elders in the porch of the church whose duty it was to welcome strangers and to give a kindly recognition to the regular members. In later years I was not to find their greeting so warm. It so happened that my wife and I, when we first settled in London, decided to worship at the nearest Church of Scotland. We proceeded to church by car, and on the way into the church I noticed a dour-looking Scotsman in the porch. When we got to our seats I turned to my wife and said,

"Have you got any money with you?"

" No," she replied, " have you ? "

It turned out that both of us had come away without any church collection in our pockets. The minister had not come into the church yet, so I tiptoed out to the dour-looking man at the door and asked him if he would lend me any two coins in his possession, and I promised to repay them without fail the same day. He took one long, comprehensive look at me and then he said slowly,

" No, I'll nae do that. But I'll tell you what I will do. I'll pass you by when I come round with the bag."

And he did. He ignored us as completely as though we were two hassocks in the pew.

As I grew older I came to know the church people more and more in their normal settings. Not in any patronising way, but because I genuinely liked them. They took a great interest in everything pertaining to our week-day life and regarded me with a certain amount of tolerant affection. I rather think that most of the congregation took a keen interest in the athletic side of my career and looked upon my doings with a kindly benevolence.

Though my father was a strong Evangelical, he hadn't a great deal of use for those who used the phraseology of the " Unca guid " in their daily speech. I remember his being vastly amused at an incident which occurred in later years when I had been a medical student for some time. A friend of mine, who later was to become my brother-in-law, was taken suddenly ill and was unable to address a religious meeting which was to take place the same evening. I at once thought of a certain " Holy " man who was used to speaking in public, and moreover liked hearing the sound of his own voice. I felt certain he would do it if he was free. I made my way down to the rather depressed-looking tenement where he lived. He answered the door himself in his shirt sleeves. I stated what I had come for, but the " Holy " man insisted that I come inside.

" You'll no mind, but one of the lambs is having a bit bite."

I was ushered into the kitchen. There to my astonishment I beheld a youth of enormous proportions wiring in to a most colossal plate of Irish stew with potatoes heaped up round its sides. This was " one of the lambs having a bit bite ".

Though we did not go to Sunday school, our Sunday afternoons were not wasted. In my earliest days Fox's " Book of Martyrs " was studied assiduously, at least the illustrations were, and I can still see in my memory's eye a picture of an elderly martyr with a large St. Andrew's cross for the background burning merrily on a pile of faggots. These pictures fascinated me.

Later on, I had to learn by heart sixteen lines of a psalm. I found this of the greatest value in later life when the full grandeur of the words came to be realised by me.

On Sunday evenings, when my father would come back tired from the last service, I chiefly remember him sitting back in an easy chair in the living-room singing softly to himself the words of the sixty-fourth paraphrase, " How bright these glorious spirits shine ". It is extraordinary what power of association tunes have for one. I can never hear that tune without seeing the picture of my father seated by the sitting-room fireside.

In our earlier years the Sabbath Day was more strictly observed than it was later on. In these days, all week-day books were put away and only Sunday books were left lying about the house. I had an illustrated copy of " Pilgrim's Progress " with which I spent many happy hours on my stomach on the study floor. Certain things were permissible on Sundays, and certain things not. Going for a walk was permissible, gardening was not. Playing at church was permissible, any other games were not. Playing hymns or classical music was allowable, anything else was taboo. Incidentally, when we were very young we frequently played church on Sunday afternoons. On these occasions one of my sisters generally preached the sermon which was invariably " Peter in prison ", and which sermon resided in an old box in the lowest drawer of her chest of drawers. My job was to take up the collection. There was considerable moving of furniture for this game, and the pulpit was a chair which the preacher mounted by standing on a seat and looking over backwards. The preacher invariably mounted the pulpit swathed in a sheet to represent the Black Geneva gown which my father wore.

The description of church life would not be complete without a word about Sunday school trips. My father was a man among men, but he had no deep understanding of the child mind, still less of children in the mass. And on the occasion of our Sunday school trip it certainly was a case of children in the mass. To my childish mind there were thousands of children, but probably looked at in the cold light of retrospect it would be hundreds rather than thousands. Every other child seemed inherently incapable of standing still in his or her right place, and my earliest memory of this festive day was of my parent marshalling the procession with the aid of a stick. I have often thought since that teachers in council schools of large cities certainly earn their salaries. Ultimately the procession assumed some sort of order and proceeded, literally with banners flying and flags waving, from the church to the appropriate railway station. At an early age I was inspired by a democratic spirit, but even my naturally strong sympathies were never proof of a desire to join in the Sunday school procession. At a discreet distance from the *hoi polloi* we walked along behind them and entered the special train which was waiting. Ultimately we arrived at a large field which was to be the scene of our revels for the day. The great event was the arrival of the tea urns in charge of the Beadle—Jeems. They arrived by road in his charge accompanied by a mountain of bulbous paper bags, one containing our lunch and the other our tea. The former invariably contained a meat pie and an apple tart while the latter contained a bapp, a parkin and a pink coloured cake covered with coconut and surmounted by half a cherry. In the afternoon there were races according to our age and sex, finishing with a teachers' race. The proceedings broke up in the early evening, and it was a tired and leg-weary little boy who eventually got on the " Sunday school special " waiting at the station.

Jeems was a character. His right names was James Aitken and in his early days had been one of the first four Elders ordained by my father. His wife signified her agreement by shaking her head vigorously from side to side, so that when she heard a sermon with which she was particularly in accord her head was more or less continuously shaking. Jeems resigned from the Eldership on being appointed Beadle, but came into his own whenever a christening in church took place.

The majority of christenings in the Church of Scotland took place at home, but on the first Sunday of every month a few bolder spirits succumbed to clerical persuasion. Personally, my sympathies were all with the parents who had it in the privacy of their home. The sequence of events which took place in the church was as follows.

First of all, an uncomfortable and self-conscious father was seen sitting in a seat near the front which was not his normal one. Then at the end of the sermon a hymn was given out which was called the Baptismal Hymn. During the singing of this hymn the door leading to the vestry, and which was right in front of the congregation, was thrown open and two ladies entered preceded by Jeems. One of the ladies carried an infant who was sometimes quiet but generally not. The mother and foster mother took up their stands beside the font while the perspiring father left his seat and joined them, literally before the whole congregation. At this moment Jeems came into his own, and grasping the already nervous parent by the coat dumped him down like a sack of flour at the place where he was to stand. I do not propose to go through the various stages of infant baptism in the Church of Scotland, sufficient it is to say that it was a much relieved male parent who eventually reached his seat, while the two ladies, accompanied by the now certainly squalling infant, clattered out into the privacy of the vestry.

When my father had his first grandchild it was only right and fitting that the ceremony should be carried out in the church. My brother-in-law was a member of the Church of England, and not well versed in Scottish ways. When the Sacrament of baptism was over and the two ladies were going into the vestry, instead of returning to his seat he gave one panic-stricken look round and then bolted like a rabbit after his wife.

It was little wonder that ministers had a considerable difficulty in persuading fathers to have their children baptized in church. The marvel to me was that any came at all.

In connection with this an uncle of mine who was a minister of the Church of Scotland had a most amusing experience. He had a great friend who was also a minister in Edinburgh, and one day he had occasion to call on his friend. An altercation was taking place in the latter's hall between the minister and a typical British navvy. It turned out that the navvy—or rather his wife—had had many children who had all been christened at home because the father refused to have the Sacrament performed in church. His wife had recently presented him with another, but this time the minister was firm. No church—no baptism.

" All right," said the angry navvy, " I'll nae gang to the kirk, and what's mair I'll be leaving the church because I dinna care a damn for it."

Now when a person leaves the church he takes with him his " lines," which is a certificate reading that so and so, residing at so and so, leaves this church in full communion. The minister had told the navvy to call for the " lines " that same evening on which my uncle called on his friend, but the minister, instead of stating that he left the church in full communion had amended the certificate to read, " So and so, residing at so and so, leaves this church because he doesn't care a damn for it." This was the altercation that my uncle had seen when he walked into his friend's hall. A pleasant sequel to the story is that the navvy decided to have his child baptized in church and not to " lift his lines ".

The church was open during the hours of service, but neither Easter Day nor Christmas Day was marked by any special services. In these respects the Church of Scotland has got a lot to learn from her sister church south of the border. It is the same with church architecture. The Scottish Presbyterian churches are buildings built primarily for utility rather than beauty. It is seldom one comes across a parish church in Scotland that has that aura of loveliness which extreme age gives to a place—more especially when people have worshipped in it for many hundreds of years. There is an historical reason for this. Scotland has been so often fought over and ravaged that few of its pre-Reformation churches have survived. It must be remembered also that the Reformation in Scotland was much more violent than it was south of the Border.

Our own church of Tynecastle was no exception to the rule. It was the third which had been built in ten years, and it only cost four thousand pounds. The previous ones had all proved too small. The people couldn't afford any more, and they had no money to spare for beauty. It was a large church with buffy-yellow walls and deep galleries which lined three sides. The pulpit was very high and was placed at the end. The church was merely the place of gathering together and the people who met in it were infinitely more important than the building where they worshipped.

For a very brief few hours I was tempted to think that a minister's job was one that I could take in my stride. It happened this way. My uncle was the minister of the parish of Benholm in the Mearns.

There were two churches in the parish. One, inland beside the manse where the morning service was held and the other, called the chapel, where the evening service was held in the fishing village of Johnshaven. The churches were about three miles apart. It so happened that my uncle was spending a few days with us in Edinburgh, intending to return to Benholm on the Saturday with a view to taking the services on the following day. Most unfortunately he contracted influenza, and when the Saturday came round he was still in his bed with a temperature in the neighbourhood of 103. There was no one whatever to take the services.

In his extremity he sent for me. I was then in my final year as a medical student, but had no experience whatever as a clergyman.

"Jim, there's only one thing to do, and that is for you to take the services yourself."

"Don't be silly, Uncle Jack, I've never preached a sermon in my life."

"Well, you'll have to start to-morrow. Luckily, I've got a couple of sermons with me which you can read over in the train. All you have to do is to deliver these sermons to the congregation. You'll manage all right."

I have already stated that I am a kindly individual, and at the moment my good nature overcame my discretion. I agreed to go. I recall vividly the dimly-lighted carriage in which I tried to peruse my uncle's sermons. They were probably very good sermons, but as I could not understand my uncle's handwriting any attempt to read them next day with any intelligent understanding was doomed to failure. As my journey drew to a close I made up my mind what course of action I would take. The only sermons I would preach would be my own sermons. That night, in the quiet of my room, I prepared two sermons entirely of my own composition. I sat up with relays of coffee and wet towels. In the end I was pleased with them, though I say so myself. My *modus operandi* was to write out in full the complete exposition and to make a synopsis on one sheet of paper on which were written only the bare headings of my subjects. It took me a long time, but ultimately I got to bed very late—or was it very early?—to get some sleep before facing my congregation on the morrow.

The mode of service in the Presbyterian Church is vastly different from that in the Church of England. In the latter church the incumbent has only to stick to the Prayer-book to achieve a modicum of success. In the Scottish kirk it is different. There is no Prayer Book and the clergyman is thrown back on his own resources altogether. One of the main features of the Scottish service are the prayers. These are extempory, or, as the saying is, from the heart. (I have heard one nervous assistant of my father's struggle to find words for many minutes, but no words whatever came to his lips. The silence which ensued was profound and prolonged.)

I scored in that, being a minister's son, and having been brought up to attend church regularly in my youth I could repeat the prayers practically word perfect. As the prayers—there were two main ones—were of about ten minutes each in length, it was no mean achievement.

In the morning I followed the beadle up the pulpit steps with a certain amount of trepidation which was not lessened as the assembled worshippers gazed at the minister's nephew in much the same way that a cow might look over a fence at a flock of sheep. As I gave out the psalm my confidence returned, and by the time I had coped successfully with the prayers I gave out my text and preached a sermon that the Archbishop of Canterbury might envy. By the time I had come to the end of the service I thought that a minister's work was an easy job. Alas! I was soon to find out how very true it is that " pride goeth before a fall ".

In the evening I made my way down to the chapel in the little fishing village. I knew the church well. I knew more than the church, I knew all the folk in Johnshaven and I knew full well that by now the fiery cross had gone forth and that the village would turn out to a man to hear me preach.

Things went wrong from the very beginning. The vestry in the chapel was beside the door. There was a plate near the door, and I started to get stage fright. Every penny that tinkled brought a fresh bead of perspiration to my brow. Shortly before the service started the beadle appeared. I was standing ready to follow him into the church and was wearing the dark suit which I reserve for special occasions. He took one look at me and shook his head.

" You maun put on the gown," he said.

It must be realised that in the Scottish Presbyterian Church the black Geneva gown is worn by the minister. It is composed of heavy brocaded silk. My uncle, unfortunately, was a short man, and I stand six feet two, so the result was not only ridiculous, but painfully uncomfortable. The bottom of my gown reached to somewhere above my knees, so that it gave the impression that I was wearing what the ladies of to-day call a coatee. I was not well versed in church law, and the beadle stated with such authority that the gown must be worn that I submitted to be overruled by his authority. The procession made its way up the aisle, and I was dimly aware of an abnormally large congregation as I followed the beadle up the pulpit steps and he deposited the books in their appropriate places. I gave out the opening hymn. I was only too well aware of the deficiencies provided by the gown. The amazing thing is that the congregation did not take a humorous view of the proceedings, but whatever their inward thoughts they sang lustily and gazed at me with an expression of interested expectancy.

The chapel was lit by oil-lamps and the heat provided by these, along with the weight of the gown, was almost overpowering. As the hymn drew to a close I felt in my pocket for my sermon. Unfortunately, in the excitement of my interview with the beadle, I had left the manuscript and the synopsis in the vestry. To retrieve it I would have to walk the whole length of the church, a prospect which filled me with dismay. I do not know how I survived the first part of the service, but when it came to the hymn before the sermon I could endure it no longer. I bent down behind the book-board out of sight of the congregation and took off the gown which I rolled in a bundle and deposited at my feet. The congregation must have been somewhat startled to have seen the preacher disappear from view wearing the gown and reappear clothed in his normal garments. Luckily I remembered the text. I don't know what I said, but I am certain that it had no connection with the sermon which I had written out so carefully the night before. Somehow or other I staggered through a few sentences before I drew the proceedings to a close and gave out the final hymn. I can only remember throwing myself in imagination on the goodwill and understanding of these kindly folk. I was never again tempted to think that my gifts of oratory had been wasted by not going into the church.

I was all my life very keen on impersonating other people. One day, when I was in my late teens, I sallied forth one summer afternoon in my father's clothes. My father could not be described as a stout man, yet he was considerably stouter than I was. To fill in the normal contour of his garments I inserted a pillow, which in the course of time became very warm. It was a summer's afternoon. The road adjacent to our house was long and straight, and when I entered it the only person in sight was a well-known professor of theology who lived near our house and who was an acquaintance of my father. My way led directly past him, and as we drew level on the same pavement we eyed one another in the approved manner with which clergymen look at each other in Scotland. I gave as good as I got, as I well knew the looks which ministers give to each other. We looked for all the world like a couple of strange dogs which eye each other suspiciously as they meet. At that precise moment a gust of wind caught the false moustache which I was wearing, and which was attached by spirit gum to my face, so that it hung down at right-angles to its normal line of attachment. I hurriedly blew my nose, but the damage was done. I looked back at the next street corner; the professor was still standing at the spot where I had passed him. He seemed rooted to the ground. Apparently the ministerial look had got more than it bargained for.

On another occasion my propensities for dressing up had an unfortunate sequel. Once again I was in my father's clothes. It was a winter's evening, and I called on a maiden who shall be nameless. I knew the church which the young lady's father attended, and I decided to impersonate a mythical assistant minister at her church and get her to join a mythical Bible class. The night was dark and I boldly marched up the garden path to the front door. A maidservant came to the door in answer to my ring, and to my inquiry as to whether Miss X was at home she replied that she was out. Just at that moment her father came down the staircase and came forward to the front door to see who the visitor was. I introduced myself as the new assistant minister at his church, but refrained from mentioning the Bible class or his daughter. With true Highland hospitality he pressed me to come in. Reluctantly I entered the house and followed him through to the drawing-room. Hesitatingly I sat on the edge of a chair and made conversation about his church. For an hour I spoke to him and ultimately took my departure thankfully and tactfully. The fabrications I gave vent to in that time would fill a large volume. I often wonder what the worthy man must have thought when he discovered that his particular church had no assistant at all.

The whole spirit of the church centred round my father. He was a man of few words, but his Christianity was strongly spiced with common sense and a shrewd understanding of human nature. The people of the parish respected and had a deep affection for him. He was not a brilliant preacher and words did not come readily to his lips. Long after he was dead I was travelling somewhere in a railway train. The only other occupant of the compartment was a gentleman in clerical garb. We started talking and he turned out to be the brother of the late Archbishop of Canterbury. He asked me about my father's success as a minister.

" Was he a brilliant preacher ? "

" No."

" Was he a wonderful organiser ? "

" No."

" Was he gifted in ways in which ordinary men are not ? "

" No."

" Well, what on earth made him such a success ? "

" I can only reply by using a Scriptural phrase and saying that ' he walked with God '."

He was a real Scotsman and his speech was broad and sometimes lapsed into the broad Doric of his boyhood. He had a pawky humour which expressed itself in odd ways. I remember four of us playing golf on the course beside the river Tay at Aberfeldy. It was my eldest sister's turn to drive, and she was standing to put the ball plumb into the river. I was standing beside my father, and as she lifted her club I overheard him murmur a little prayer :

" May the lassie no hit the ball."

His prayer was answered.

I cannot do better than quote an article by the late Dr. Norman McLean which was published in *The Scotsman* shortly after my father's death. I reproduce it by kind permission of the proprietors of *The Scotsman*. It is a description of his funeral and is entitled " James Bell Nicoll, the man who solved a problem and said nothing " :

" There is an Irishman who sells evening papers at a point where three streets meet, and who has time for a sentence or two when I buy a paper from him at the end of the day. When the temperance polls were being announced he was full of excitement. ' Wat div ye think of it noo ? ' he would exclaim, dancing on the roadway ; ' isn't it a graand climate ; getting wetter and wetter every day ? ' And his laugh was truly infectious. But the other evening he didn't dance or laugh. He produced the paper from under his arm, and leaning forward solemnly, he said ' Bell Nicoll is gone.' ' What ? ' I asked abruptly, not grasping his meaning. ' Bell Nicoll is dead,' he went on, the smiles all gone ; ' Eh ! but mony will miss him in Gorgie.' That was how I heard that the most successful minister in Edinburgh had entered on his rest and on his reward. Without pain or waiting, in the front of the battle, he died as a soldier would choose to die. And he was a good soldier this man—tireless, eager, hopeful, never discouraged, certain of victory—and achieving it because of his certainty.

" On Saturday I went to the Tynecastle Church to say farewell to James Bell Nicoll. There are folk who are sore perturbed about the working classes, and who like to hold conferences about the church and the working man. (If this old world could be saved by conferences, the millenium would have arrived long ago !) I only wish these tremblers for the Ark of God— these preachers of the gospel of wail—could have been brought to Tynecastle Church, where the dead minister lay in his coffin in front of the Communion Table. The conductor on the car knew without any telling where I was going. When I prepared to dismount at the nearest station he beckoned me back to my seat. ' Ye're going to Bell Nicholl's funeral,' he said. ' I'll let you out at the church itsel'.' And so he did, stopping his car at the church door contrary to all usage. Though I was early, yet already the church was packed. What a congregation of working men and of working women ! I was squeezed into a seat in the transept, and from there I could see the vast crowd below and the packed galleries and the men standing against the walls. Three ministers came and took their places, and then came elders ; each a worker with his hands—skilled craftsmen and labourers, with the stamp of manliness and dignity. And then the service began by singing ' The Lord's my Shepherd.' Now, the atmosphere of that moment defies language.

> " Yea, though I walk in death's dark vale,
>   Yet will I fear none ill." . . . .

The great crowd sang with a sort of rapture. But there is no language to express it. That defiance of death ; that triumph of faith ; that certainty that the end of all toil is not dust and ashes ; that assurance which welcomes the last shadow as the gateway of the Celestial City—all that and far more rose, throbbed and winged, heavenward. And the dead preacher lay still there in his coffin.

" The elders carried the dead minister out of the church, and as the slow procession moved to the door the church was like a field of corn which the wind stirs so that you can see the wave pass from end to end. It was like that as he passed out for the last time—the dead minister, who had shared the joys and sorrows of these people for thirty-three years, and when we came out there was a greater crowd outside than inside. On the pavement, facing the door, the children massed—such a multitude of children. All the children in Gorgie seemed to be there! Up and down the street they stretched. And then these working men marshalled the procession. At a sharp turn of the road, as the procession turned to go up Ardmillan Terrace, I saw at once before and behind. Up the slope went the elders, leading the way, before the dead minister, and behind, all down the Gorgie Road, far as the eye could see, there was the dense crowd following—men and women and children. Since the day we buried Hector Mackinnon at Shettleston, eleven years ago, I have not seen anything like it. . . . And at arid conferences the wise shake their heads and discuss the problem of the working classes and the Church. There is no such problem. The only problem I know of is the problem of war profiteers and the Church. And as the war profiteers are vanishing rapidly, why, to-morrow, there won't be even that problem! To-day it is the working man's family that is keeping the torch of faith burning most brightly.

"And so we came to the churchyard (only it is not called that here)—that is too beautiful a word for these days—and the clerk, seeing the children and feeling the atmosphere surcharged with feeling, turned to me and said, 'You should write about this and try to make people see the meaning of it.' 'Nobody could write this down,' I replied, 'for there is no tongue, no language, no material in which to express this. It is just an ache, a dull pain, a sense of irretrievable loss; it defies expression.' 'You try,' persisted the clerk; 'Perth is the best town in Scotland for a minister to die in; but Perth never showed anything like this.' 'Perth!' I objected; 'not for ministers to live in.' 'I did not say live,' replied the clerk; 'I said the best to die in . . .' And so we came to the grave. . . . When Norman Macleod was buried an old woman in the crowd, watching the procession, said to her neighbour, 'Eh, but Providence has been kind to Norman, giein' him sic a grand day for his funeral.' And Providence was also kind to Bell Nicoll. The pale wintry sunshine shone into his grave, while the multitude stood with bowed heads. It was as if all Gorgie stood around.

"It is strange how parochially-minded long stretches and areas of a great city can be. There are wide spaces in Edinburgh where the name of Bell Nicoll was unknown. But everybody who knew anything about the church knew that in the heart of a great working-class district in Gorgie this man had his church filled with working folk—nearly two thousand members ! How he did it I cannot tell. In every theological college you will find some unsuccessful preacher in the guise of a practical theology lecturer, explaining to weary students how they can become successful preachers ; but the successful preacher himself can never explain why he is successful. If one asked Bell Nicoll why he was so successful he would deny the fact, and then say that there was no explanation. And there is no earthly explanation. But one thing at least is certain—that along the road of intellectual gymnastics there is no successful ministry. This preacher had no stock in that. He knew nothing of the doubts and hesitations which many propound in the guise of religion, but which is really only a nervous complaint, and not religion ! This man knew only one thing—what it was to live close to the very heart of fire, which is the love of God. And that fire of love he proclaimed. And as he went up and down the endless weary stairs he made the weary and sorrowful realise that love was supreme—for love shone through him. If the Church is to have any power to move and stir and enthuse men, it must know what its message is. And this man's power was that he knew. ' I know Whom I have believed,' he would say ; and so men and women gathered round him and learned his secret. He was the humblest and kindest of men. I remember after a sparsely-attended meeting, addressed by a wandering Evangelist in the Assembly Hall, his expressing his wonder and disappointment at the smallness of the audience. ' I can't understand it ; there has come a change over people's minds,' he said. But I think I can understand. When people have evangelists like this man, living epistles, in their own midst, they have no use for transitory spellbinders. It was goodness that gave James Bell Nicoll his unique power. It was no common gift that enabled this man to make his church so great a centre of life that for a vast multitude life seemed suddenly poor and empty when they heard that he was dead. . . . I have said that he was the most successful minister in Edinburgh. By that I mean the souls he got for his hire—the love and gratitude he won. . . . And he never made a speech in the Assembly, and never opened his mouth in the Presbytery."

CHAPTER V

THE UNIVERSITY

IN due course I found myself a student at Edinburgh University. The University has got its several departments scattered throughout the length and breadth of the city. The headquarters of the Botany Department is at the Botanical Gardens, which are situated on the north side of the town. As we had to be there every day at eight o'clock, it meant leaving home at an uncomfortably early hour to anyone who, like me, lived on the other side of the town.

Sir Isaac Bayley Balfour was the presiding genius over this Mecca and he was a man whom we feared greatly. Sir Isaac was a character and only the very great can afford to be "characters". He invariably wore a broad-brimmed straw hat when outside. The hat was of a bygone vintage and looked like some relic that Queen Elizabeth had cast aside. His lectures were like the Burial of Sir John Moore at Corunna, "Not a drum was heard, not a funeral note." A story was handed down to us partly as a warning and partly as a reminder of what giants there had been in the past.

In the years before the first World War it was the custom for the Professor of Botany to take his class out for a botanical excursion on Saturday mornings. One day he was standing beside a hillside pond on the Pentland Hills near Edinburgh demonstrating the peculiarities of algæ. The class were crowding round him on the landward side, when one youth, with more brawn than brains, gave the class a shove. The professor lost his balance and was pushed into the water. The moral of the story is this, that particular student never passed his professional examination in botany. Ultimately he joined the army on the outbreak of war and went to France and was killed.

Anyway, we took no liberties in the botany class. I never found any need for botany during the twenty-five years I was a doctor, and my knowledge of that subject departed with the textbooks which I sold as soon as my name appeared on the list of those who had passed.

The other subjects which we studied that first term were zoology and anatomy. The former was taught at the old quad —the original University building—and almost on the site of where Darnley, the husband of Mary Queen of Scots, was murdered long ago. Zoology was taught after lunch to an audience of sleepy and lackadaisical students. Cossor Ewart had an affliction of his lacrimal glands which made him weep copiously during his lectures. The class was not slow to observe this fact and a rain of handkerchiefs would descend on his desk whenever he turned to the blackboard behind him. Practical zoology stands out chiefly in my recollection for the atmosphere of the slaughterhouse which pervaded its dissecting rooms. I believe I could even now dissect the internal organs of a frog or the cranial nerves of a skate. A most amusing situation arose over my dissection of the skate.

At the end of the summer term my family had gone on their summer holidays, whence I followed them, having been delayed by my written examination. It was my intention to come back for the practical part of my examination and with a view to improving my knowledge I purchased a skate at a shop in Fountainbridge on my way to the train. I explained to the shopkeeper that it was not required for eating but only for dissecting purposes. Probably that was why I got it cheap. The day was very warm and when I got to the Caledonian Station I deposited the paper parcel containing the skate up on the rack of the carriage. The carriage was crowded with people but there was no escaping the aroma of the skate. The windows were let down to their fullest extent but at the train's first stopping place everybody got out. I stuck my head out of the window to see where they were all going and to my surprise saw them all rejoin the train at another carriage farther up. I was left severely alone to finish the journey in peace.

Every afternoon was devoted to anatomy. The pungent smell of formaline will always bring back to me the atmosphere of the dissecting room. It was a very large room containing four fireplaces and had a gallery running along one side. Dr. E. B. Jamieson, "Jimmy" to many generations of medical students, sat in a little glass house at one end of the room rather like the umpire at some athletic contest.

At the beginning of the term there was a neat row of white bodies lying awaiting dissection. But as the term progressed the limbs were dissected from the trunk and carried away to separate tables, much in the manner of a vulture carrying off a carcass to enjoy it in solitude. At the end of the term there was nothing left but some bones with some leathery-looking muscles attached to them.

It was the duty of Charles, the attendant, to gather together the separate portions and to see that each corpse was supplied with the requisite number of limbs, etc. It was more by luck than anything else that limbs and torso which were ultimately buried with the head were those of the original owner. As Charles used to say resignedly :

" This 'ere Resurrection won't half be a muck up."

An uncle of mine had apparently had a great desire to see the inside of the anatomy room although he was a theological student at the time and it was against the law for anyone other than medical students to enter the dissecting room. My uncle, however, got his much coveted visit. It was the beginning of the term and the first corpse he came to had a ticket around the neck stating that it belonged to "John Nicoll". By an extraordinary coincidence that was his own name. He rushed from the room and was violently sick. He told me that he never again expressed a wish to enter the anatomy room.

I remember another extraordinary coincidence occurring in connection with that room. At the beginning of the term one was allotted a partner with whom to work. During my first term in the anatomy department I was given an arm to dissect. I was assigned to work with a student whom I had neither seen nor heard of before. We became friendly and one night I was seated in his digs and was twitting him about being an Englishman and coming to Scotland for his education.

" Oh," he replied, " I'm only half an Englishman. My mother's people came from Dundee. Indeed we have still got some property there which was handed down from my great grandmother."

I enquired where the property was.

" Then your great grandmother's name was Jean McKenzie."

A look of blank amazement came over his face.

" It was, but however did you know that ? "

" Because it was the name of my great grandmother too."

We were second cousins and neither of us knew of the other's existence. By a fortuitous chance I knew that my great grandmother had owned most of the property in that street and that she had established a trust with it for her children's children—until the third and fourth generation.

In the anatomy department was the grimmest room I have ever seen. Round every one of its walls were row upon row of skulls. They stretched from the ceiling to the floor, Bantu skulls, Polynesian skulls, European skulls. They spent their last years grinning across to each other, each one seeming to say to the one opposite,

" I've got better teeth than you have."

The Chamber of Horrors at Madame Tussaud's had nothing on the anatomy museum for sensationalism. It had a murderers' corner containing the skeletons of those who had been hanged for their crimes. There was also the skeleton of " Bowed Joseph "—a cripple who led the Edinburgh mob in the days of long ago. There were dissections of human bodies made by the alchemists of the Middle Ages. It was a curiously silent museum ; a place where one walked on tiptoe ; where the dead ceased to be dead and became mere exhibits in glass cases ; a room of shadows and ghostly half lights.

I demonstrated in anatomy for some time after I had passed my professional examination in that subject. The demonstrators wore a long white coat to distinguish them from the other students and generally stood near one of the fireplaces in a nonchalant attitude until some student should come and ask them a question. Occasionally " Jimmy " would come forth from his little glass sanctum and a knot of students would gather round him, for he was an expert teacher on his subject. To see him in action, with a long white coat and black velvet skull cap on top of a clean shaven, putty-coloured face devoid of colour or expression, was a sight never to be forgotten.

This remarkable man had a remarkable memory. I remember one nondescript student going up to him on his return from the war. " Jimmy " took one look at him and said in his expressionless and slightly nasal voice, " Brockshaw P. J." Brockshaw P. J. was only too glad to congratulate the famous man on remembering him.

" What a remarkable feat of memory, sir."

" You have a very remarkable face," was the devastating and unexpected reply.

In the last two terms of the first year we studied chemistry in addition to physics and anatomy. Chemistry was taught by Sir James Walker, a man who had a complete knowledge of his subject and a complete control over his class. It is a tribute to his memory that I still retain a modicum of chemistry.

I nearly came down in my viva in zoology. Vivas have always

been nightmares to me and I had an unfortunate habit of saying things which I would never have said in cold blood. I knew I had done a good paper in zoology and certainly my paper saved me. The "spots" were ones I had never seen before. One was of a certain fish attached to its yolk sac by what looked like a bit of rubber tubing. The examiners were Cossor Ewart and an outside professor of zoology. I got the outside professor. He asked me what the exhibit was. On any other occasion I would have been glad to have learned what was inside the bottle, but as a matter of fact I didn't know that fish had yolk sacs. I was driven into a corner and it was obviously up to me to say something.

"It's a little fish," I ventured.

"Don't be a fool," was the reply. "What's that?" pointing to the valve tubing.

It looked for all the world as though the fish were speaking down a telephone. It certainly wasn't that, however. I floundered.

"It's a bit of seaweed that has got stuck on to the fish," I replied.

His answer was devastating in its simplicity.

"Don't be a damned fool," he replied.

I was not done yet, however. He handed me the upper jaw of a sheep. Any farmer would have recognised it. Unfortunately he handed me the bone upside down, so that my bemused brain thought it was the lower jaw of some obscure animal. I turned it over and over. A gleam of intelligence came into my eye.

"It's the lower jaw of a snake," I said.

This masterpiece left the great man speechless. We turned to worms. Worms saved me. I could even recognise them down the microscope.

While I am at it, I might as well describe my tribulations with vivas. My worst experience was in pathology. On a warm summer's day those unfortunates about to be examined were locked in a small room and let out one by one as their turn came to cross the passage into the professor's room. My turn came to be let out. I met a studious youth of the class face to face while he was emerging from the professor's room. I just had time to mutter, "What did you get?" and have his answer, "A brain with G.P.I." before we had to go our respective ways. I cudgelled my brains to think what a brain with G.P.I. looked like. I was unable to remember, so I determined to face the situation with a mixture of cunning and deduction. The day was very warm and I calculated that the professor would be unwilling to make the necessary effort to lift more than one bottle from the shelf. That bottle would contain the brain with G.P.I. and was presumably the one shown to my predecessor. The professor knew me personally and I had always found him the soul of geniality and kindness. In fact he was more like a minister of the Free Kirk than a professor of pathology.

" Well, Nicoll boy, sit ye down and tell me what this is."

I looked him straight in the face but unfortunately omitted to look at the bottle first.

" It's a brain with general paralysis of the insane."

I thought Lorraine Smith would never stop laughing. He laughed so much that out of sheer politeness I had to laugh too, though I hadn't the faintest idea what the joke was.

" It's a heart with pericarditis," he said when he could speak. He knew perfectly well how I had arrived at my answer. " Now," he said, " pull yourself together and we'll start again." And so the kindness of the professor saved my life in the pathology oral.

The last time an oral examination nearly finished me was in my surgery finals. A question on the paper was one of these " compare and contrast " things. It actually was " compare and contrast the deformity resulting from cervical Potts Disease with that arising from congenital torticollis." Now I knew a good deal about T.B. of the bones of the neck which is what cervical Potts Disease is but I found it a little difficult to describe congenital torticollis, or in other words " wry neck ". Then a brilliant solution struck me. Alexis Thomson was examining. He liked originality. I would risk it. I merely wrote " The deformity resulting from congenital torticollis is typical, and is said to resemble that of a pelican thinking hard." I handed in my paper and in due course my name was put up to attend the oral examination. Alas ! In the interval Alexis Thomson was taken seriously ill. In fear and trepidation I was ushered into a room where a well-known surgeon from Glasgow sat on the other side of the table. I gave my name. He looked as though he had been expecting me.

" Nicoll, ah yes, let me see."

He ran through a pile of papers on his desk. With a horrid feeling in the place where my stomach ought to be, I recognised my paper. He folded it open at the damning words.

" What made you say this ? " he asked.

A sickly grin spread over my face.

" I'm afraid my sense of humour ran away with my surgical knowledge at this point, sir," I replied.

"Well," said that remarkable man from Glasgow, "I think it so original that I intend to incorporate it in my lectures."

I was bowed out like an Emperor and never asked another question.

To return to the first year. There was a considerable amount of ragging when opportunity presented itself. After the first year either the student had reached years of discretion or else he was too keen on his job to bother with the lighter side of life. The class of physics was the one where ragging was carried out in excelsis. The class was like Bedlam. High up behind the lecturer and running along the wall was a narrow gallery in the staircase of which it was possible for a student to conceal himself before the lecture. The lecturer in physics was a man of gesticulation and many expressions. A student who had a considerable gift of mimicry spent the lecture hour in the gallery above the lecturer's head and followed faithfully his every gesture.

I did not realise however, that my halcyon days in the physics class were coming to an end. It was the custom, when a student was asked to leave the room, for him to leave a card bearing his name on it. Many and varied were the fictitious names which the cards bore. On a certain day it fell to my lot to be asked to leave the room. I did so and left a card with the name " C. G. Knott " on it. C. G. Knott, I may say, was the name of the lecturer in physics. By some inspiration, probably not unconnected with previous flights of imagination in the same direction, the lecturer picked up my card and read his own name on it. My doom was sealed. I was told to come to his private room after the lecture. It was a command I dare not disobey. I don't propose to relate what was said to me in that room, it is sufficient if I say that I found the lecturer in physics to be a gentlemen and a Christian. When I left that room it was with a lump in my throat, and I had given my promise not to take part in any more rags in the physics class. I went back once more but I could neither enter into the pranks of the class nor could I bring myself to sit in the front two rows of seats with the studious section. I was neither flesh nor fowl. I never went back. C. G. Knott died shortly afterwards.

At the end of my first year I left to join the army and when I came back to take up the threads once more I found myself a second year student studying anatomy and physiology. The latter I found as unpleasant as I found anatomy interesting. Physiology was taught by Sir Edward Sharpey-Schafer, the originator of the well-known method of artificial respiration. Practical physiology is divided—like Cæsar's Gaul—into three parts, experimental, chemical and histology. Experimental physiology was chiefly an affair of frogs muscles, tracings and electric currents. It was taken by Dr. Elsie Walker, the only woman lecturer in my experience. Chemical physiology was under the lectureship of Dr. Taylor in whose class there was a certain amount of ragging. We had not yet assumed the stature of men. Histology was taken by a Chinaman —Dr. Lim. I, however, seemed congenitally unable to distinguish the different organs of the body as they appear under the microscope —which is what histology is. I did not shine at histology therefore.

I enjoyed an undeserved reputation at the University for being clever. I seldom attended lectures and yet I generally knew the subject reasonably well. The answer was twofold. In the first place, I soon gave up taking notes for the simple reason that I couldn't read my own writing. Secondly, I attended comparatively few lectures after the first year. For example, out of one hundred lectures on materia medica, which is the study of drugs, I think I only attended four. The reason is simple. I have always had an excellent memory for seen words but a very poor one for heard words. There were excellent books on the subjects. In fact, the majority of professors had published one themselves which their classes were expected to read, thereby incidently, considerably augmenting their income. It struck me early in my University career that I could spend the time more profitably and certainly more comfortably in the library of the University Union than on the hard benches of a lecture theatre. It was necessary for a student to be present at seventy-five per cent of the lectures so far as I remember. A silver-braided and top-hatted servitor stood at the door of the lecture theatre with a box in his hand into which the student had to drop a card containing his name. It was a simple matter when the room had two doors—one merely went in at one end and out at the other, but when there was only one door the matter required a certain amount of finesse. The silver-braided one was engaged in conversation and a card surreptitiously dropped in the box, or possibly someone going to the lecture might be persuaded to drop in more than one card. If the worst came to the worst one could always attempt to explore the murky avenues of bribery and corruption, though the servitors, as a body, were quite beyond the appeal of any pecuniary consideration.

In any case the other students thought that I was slacking in the

Union, a delusion from which I took good care not to disabuse their minds.

There were large numbers of coloured men in our year. There was no colour bar, as such, and yet the invisible colour bar in the Union was very strong. One could have drawn a line through the large smoking room with coloured men on the one side and white men on the other. In my time at least none but white men were elected to the Union committee and no coloured man was appointed to the residency in the Royal Infirmary.

Of course, during these war years the proportion of men from home was much less than they normally would have been. In later years the proportion of ex-Servicemen greatly increased. In the years when the men returned from the war we not infrequently had ex-lieut.-colonels and majors in our class and it was most entertaining to see one of them making a fool of himself just like an ordinary mortal. It was a constant joy to hear the lecturer question one man in particular who never forgot that he had been a lieut.-colonel. One day the lecturer asked him for the classical symptoms of a " cold abscess " which is another name for a tubercular abscess. The ex-lieut.-colonel hummed and hawed. He stood on one leg and then on the other, at last came the amazing reply from the depths of his military throat, " Goose skin, sir." Hoots of derision from the rest of the class !

When I am referring to coloured men, I mean everybody who was not white. They ranged from the fuzzy-haired negro with lips like bicycle tyres and the parting in his hair made with a razor instead of a comb, to the slightly saffron-coloured man whose grandmother probably was an Indian and whose grandfather probably was a British officer. Looking back on it from afar, I can find no personal antagonism to coloured men such as some Americans have. Rather, we were specially polite to them. But the fact is that we tended to mix with the fellows we had been at school with. We just didn't have anything in common with the coloured men and so the white men tended to stick together and the others to do likewise.

There were ample opportunities for us to broaden our minds by contact with men from overseas and also to meet men with different backgrounds from our own, but the fact was that we had little time for anything but our work. The five years hard labour which medical students endure is not a period of ease, nor a time when the Cultural side of the University makes itself felt on a medical student's life. Learning medicine was a full time job and probably the chief reason why doctors have no outside intellectual interests is because their work is so time-absorbing that they have no time left to enjoy other forms of culture.

In my third year I started to attend the Royal Infirmary. The lay world calls it " walking the hospitals "—a phrase that I never heard used among medical men themselves. Every morning from eleven to one was spent in some form of hospital activity—ward rounds, clinical lectures, maybe actually assisting oneself in the multitudinous activities of the ward. There was one chief and one junior chief attached to each ward. This system applied to both physicians and surgeons. These men were at the head of their professions and they had the twofold job of treating their patients in the wards and of teaching us medical students.

I remember the first time I was assisting a surgeon at a small operation. In my zeal to do well, I dropped an instrument on the floor and started to retrieve it. The surgeon let me have it with the full force of his foot and that kick taught me more surgery than a bookcase of tomes.

It was necessary for us to have three terms with a physician and three with a surgeon. We could choose whoever we liked and generally we chose three different men from each branch of the profession in order to skim the cream from the brains of each. I was never missing from any of these activities if I could possibly help it. We spent a considerable portion of our day in the company of those who taught us and all the time they were teaching us about the patients in their charge. A ward round meant that we walked round with the chief or his junior and they would tell us why they had come to conclusions which they had in their diagnosis, the treatment and what the outlook was likely to be for the patient.

Let me describe one or two of these men. There was Professor Alex Thomson. Typical Corinthian, but born one hundred and fifty years after his time. He was a brilliant surgeon, a colourful personality and his knowledge was profound. Alexis made no secret of his dislike of lady medicos and lost no opportunity of showing it in a genial and witty way. He truly was a knight of the scalpel, and his lectures were peppered with gems of pungent humour and original wit. He was an excellent lecturer, and he knew no bounds to his surgery. He would tackle anything before which ordinary mortals would quail, and he would achieve triumphant success. During the term I was in his clinic he had a stroke. When he recovered he went down to Algeciras in Spain to recuperate. He never came back. It is a curious thing that a brilliant surgeon should be the direct successor of Drake and of Grenville.

Then there was the other Professor of Surgery, Sir Harold Styles. Sir Harold was a striking illustration of the maxim that genius is an infinite capacity for taking pains. He took pains—infinite pains—and he got the reward of his thoroughness. If any student wasn't sure whether the pain in his stomach was appendicitis, he would generally go to Styles. Sir Harold was not a tall man, and like many men of his build he had no small opinion of his capabilities, nor had he a highly developed sense of humour. But he had every right to have a good opinion of himself, for he was a great man. One could not be in his presence for five minutes without being aware of this fact. It has been my lot to meet few of the so-called great of this world, and I have been consistently surprised at the qualities that these few possess. I have never had the least doubt that Sir Harold Styles was naturally a great man.

Sir Harold had a great reputation in the States, and the front row of his audience was usually composed of Americans. One day he was lecturing on " Tumours of the Pituitary Gland."

" I have operated on three," he said. " They all died, and here are the tumours."

With that, there were passed round three specimens of pituitary tumours for examination.

" There is only one man in the world who can successfully remove these tumours. Who is he ? "

With that he pointed a finger straight at me. Now at that time the Professor of Clinical Surgery had a house surgeon who was not famed for his modesty. Let's call him Mr. Bumptious. Sir Harold obviously wanted me to say the name of Harvey Cushing, partly as a graceful compliment to the Americans present as he was a well-known American surgeon. Instead of saying the obvious thing, I answered,

" Mr. Bumptious."

To make my sin doubly heinous, Bumptious was in the theatre himself. Sir Harold, like Queen Victoria, was not amused.

Gradually, unknown to ourselves, we were being hewn into the shape of doctors. When first we started medicine, we had been callow youths, now we were grown men. Medicine is an art, not learned from books. It is an inborn skill learned from men who are themselves masters in the art. Mere facts are but the cement which binds the skill together. These wise old men sought to pass on to us the wisdom that they themselves had. Above all, they sought to pass on to us their habits of thought and the accumulated experience of a lifetime which guided them to their conclusions.

One of the most famous surgical text-books in Britain in my days was " Thomson and Miles' Manual of Surgery." If Alexis Thomson was at one end of the scale, his collaborator in the " Manual of Surgery " was at the other. Miles was a canny Scot who was a born teacher. He had the gift of explaining how he arrived at his conclusions—a gift which is not given to all who profess to teach. Some men arrive at a conclusion by a process of reasoning, some by intuition. It was the former with Miles. There is many a doctor scattered throughout the length and breadth of the British Empire who looks back on Sandy Miles with affection and regard, and there is many a patient who has to thank God for the clear insight of their doctor, an insight which came in the first place from that quiet, efficient Scot, Alexander Miles.

Of the physicians who made an impress on my youthful mind none stand out such giants as the surgeons. Each one, however, was a man of outstanding calibre. I was with Fleming and John Comrie and Professor Bramwell. I remember an incident in which Comrie figured which caused us much amusement. He was taking medical out-patients at the time. Comrie had a great admiration for his predecessor, Dr. Joseph Bell, and tried to copy his methods. One day a woman who was suffering from asthma was shown into his clinic.

" What is your work ? " Comrie asked.

" I work in a butcher's shop, doctor."

" I suppose you keep rabbits and fowls in the butcher's shop ? "

" Yes, sir."

" Then, gentlemen, the case is obvious. She is allergic to fur or to feathers. Change your job, my good woman, and your asthma will disappear."

" But I had asthma years before I worked in a butcher's shop, doctor."

The mantle of Dr. Bell had not fallen on his successor.

These doctors, like our masters at school, had soon their inner-most thoughts laid bare, so that we saw the naked truth of their minds. We saw them exactly for what they were. If a man was judged in the eyes of the world to be clever, such a reputation counted for nothing with us. The attractive exterior was penetrated and the real man emerged. We students knew the exact worth of every man that taught us. Cover it up how they would, we instinctively knew the truth. Money counted for nothing here. All the weaknesses of a man were ruthlessly exposed. Little did he realise that every individual in his class was sitting in judgment on him—a judgment just as certain in its way as that last assessment when a man is known for what he really is.

But all our days were not spent on work ; occasionally the animal spirits which lie latent in every medical student's breast burst its bonds, and we would take part in a rag.

I remember, for example, the affair which I might call " The incident of the policeman's boots ". Some important person was receiving an honorary degree at the McEwan Hall, and a few scattered policemen kept the pathway clear from the University Union to the Hall. One was an enormous man with a girth that gave him the appearance of a happy event shortly to be expected. At a prearranged signal a mob of students surged around him and cut him off effectively from his fellows. He was then hustled into the Union and locked in the smoking-room along with a decanter of beer. His boots were then forcibly taken off him and ultimately hung suspended from the highest pinnacle of the Union. We found that a policeman without his boots is as helpless as a babe without its nappy.

On another occasion, a rag didn't end quite so happily. It was on the occasion of the opening of the electric car system in Edinburgh. It had previously had the cable system in operation —a system which was famous for its inefficiency and breakdowns. The first electric car was to go from the Register House to Liberton, and would therefore have to pass the old University. A section of the Town Council was on top, with the Lord Provost sitting in front. The car had no covering to its top. The Councillors and the Lord Provost were all arrayed in black frock coats with shiny toppers. As the car approached the old University it drew to a halt before several hundred students gathered in front of it. The Councillors took it as a mark of personal esteem, and the Lord Provost got to his feet and took off his topper. In a moment every hat on the top of that car was the target for little paper bags each containing a quantity of flour with which we had armed ourselves. In a moment the black-coated Councillors resembled a group of Arctic explorers. When the car came to a standstill, it was boarded by scores of students who proceeded out to Liberton with the Councillors. In fact, the car was festooned with students who clustered on it like a hive of swarming bees. When they got to the terminus they were ordered off. One student unfortunately had a scuffle on the running board of the car when it was going. He fell off and was killed instantly. It was a terrible tragedy, and was no fault of the Councillors who behaved like sportsmen throughout.

It must have been about this time that I developed a wish to be a surgeon, and one moreover who specialised in surgery of the heart—a subject which in these days was a practically undeveloped branch of surgery. My enthusiasm led to unfortunate results. I decided that a heart was necessary for me to pursue my investigations. I was still demonstrating in anatomy in the afternoons, and I determined to take a heart home with me from the dissecting room. Such a procedure was strictly against regulations, but I considered that in the interest of science mere rules and regulations should be ignored. Anyway, the heart duly arrived home in a paper bag and in the privacy of my room I proceeded to dissect it. Both sanitary and ethical conditions compelled me to put it outside when I was not working on it. I decided on the meat safe as a suitable place for hiding it temporarily. Our meat safe was one of those affairs not unlike bird cages which are attached to the side wall of the house in the manner of a nesting box, and was not in use at the moment. Like many another beginner my enthusiasm waxed and then waned, until ultimately—I forgot all about it. Some time later the family complained of an unpleasant smell which came from the back part of the house. They came to the conclusion that it was "the drains". and on the strength of being a medical student I was called into conference. I decided upon personal investigation, and so the family, with me at their head, set out on a tour of investigation. There was no doubt whatever about the smell. It was one of these all-pervading, offensive, penetrating smells which would shortly make the house uninhabitable if it were not dealt with forthwith. My sister, with unerring perception, tracked down the source of the smell to the meat safe, and drew out a plate containing the decaying remnants of my heart. The family were gathered at a suitable distance, and as I bore my trophy towards them and explained what it was, they turned and ran. I saw no warm gleam of understanding come into their eyes. Solemnly and alone I carried out the last rites of burial among the cabbages at the top of the garden. I have always thought that the owner of that heart did more to make his presence felt in death than ever he did in life. Thus came to an inglorious end my attempt to become a heart surgeon.

It was in those years that we got to know our patients as individuals, not as mere cases in a text-book. Some of them had an amazing knowledge of their own illnesses. Such a one I luckily ran across in my final examination in medicine. We had one " case " to do, and we were expected to do it thoroughly. I was allotted a patient. I approached him in the half-familiar, half-soothing manner in which one might try to make friends with a difficult child.

" And what's the matter with you ? " I said.

" Corium bovis," he replied, to my astonishment.

He then proceeded to give me every possible detail about his condition. He had been lectured on so often that he knew his condition by heart. Professor Bramwell was examining me. He subsequently asked me if I would care to be his house physician— an offer not unconnected with " corium bovis " in my opinion. I declined, as I had no wish to spend a good part of my life among the nerve cases which filled the majority of his beds.

I don't think I ever saw a student faint at an operation, and all the stories about people fainting at their first operation are sheer nonsense. They are much more likely to faint at their first post-mortem. If it is a bad one their first experience can be really devastating.

A youth of our year, who is now one of London's most fashionable doctors, undertook to spend the night alone in the postmortem room at the Royal Infirmary, with a view to proving that his nervous system was stable. He emerged the next morning pale but triumphant. The same youth took many years to get through medicine, chiefly through an inability to attend any lecture before ten o'clock in the morning. I had occasion to go round to his digs one morning early. A most extraordinary sight met my gaze, and a yet more remarkable noise my ears. He had tied a thread to the trigger of an alarm clock and thence to the starter of a gramophone record ; another thread went to a hammer which had been precariously balanced over a tin basin ; yet another string led to the window, and another to the door. The alarm was set for eight o'clock. At that hour the alarm went off, the gramophone started playing, the hammer fell into the tin basin, the upper part of the window fell down and the door opened. The main point was that the sleeper had to get up to turn off the gramophone. Unfortunately, when I visited him, he was sleepily making his way back to bed. His efforts had proved unavailing. I maintain that such an inventive genius deserves to become one of the most fashionable doctors in London.

In my third year occurred my first case in private practice. As it was so unusual I propose to describe it in some detail. My sister was convalescing after some illness, and I had taken her to recuperate to a small village near the foot of the Pentland Hills some miles from Edinburgh. Somehow or other the house-keeper of the local doctor had heard that I was a medical student. One afternoon I had a note from her stating that a message had come for the doctor saying that a woman was choking at a farm up in the hills ; that the doctor was fully an hour's run in the opposite direction, and finally that it was a matter of life and death.

I had no means of transport whatever. However, I stopped a motor-cyclist on the street and explained to him that it was a matter of life and death. I remember that the bicycle was an Levis two-stroke. I sat on behind. I spent most of the time regretting that I had mentioned to him that it was a matter of life and death, as there was every indication that the first death would be mine. Eventually we got there, a lonely farmhouse far up in the hills. It appeared that the farmer's wife had been eating an orange. Now there are several ways of eating an orange, and this woman had chosen the worst method of all. Most people discreetly discard the stringy part of an orange. She had swallowed it entire. Not that she had meant to do so, but it slipped down her throat, and was now lodged between her gullet and her wind-pipe. In consequence she could neither swallow nor breathe.

When I got there the woman was lying on the floor of the room, and was obviously *in extremis*. When I tried to hook out the mass with my finger I merely succeeded in thrusting it further down. I tried to give her an emetic to make her sick. It merely came bubbling back. The relatives looked at me and obviously ex-pected me to do something to restore the woman. Little did they know that I knew very little more than they themselves. I tried massaging her throat. I could feel the mass but could not move it. Then suddenly I remembered a drug which makes one sick if it is injected under the skin.

I hastily wrote a prescription for it and for a syringe. The motor-cyclist was still waiting, but I knew of a certainty that the patient would die before his return. I went out with him to give final instructions, and outside I chanced to look at the motor bike. That glance saved the woman's life. It was the days of acetylene lamps, and a piece of rubber tubing ran along the tank connecting the front and rear lamps. It was work of a moment to pull it off and rush back to the house. I opened the woman's mouth and pushed the tube down her throat. I felt the obstruction give in front of the tube. I might, of course, have passed the obstruction into the woman's lungs. As it was, I pushed it into her stomach. She gave a few gasps and in a minute or two was restored to her normal colour. I thought that if this was a sample of general practice, I had surely chosen the worst job on earth wherewith to earn my living.

As I have indicated, some of the men took many years to pass their final examination. The most outstanding case when I was there was that of an elderly man who was so advanced in years that he had been a student when the fathers of several of my friends were themselves students. He had seen at least two generations come and go. It happened this way. During his first year as a medical student a relative had died and left him five hundred pounds a year as long as he was a medical student. He had a small income of his own, and this—combined with the relative's legacy—was sufficient for his needs. Each year he paid one guinea as his matriculation fee, and was four hundred and ninety-nine pounds to the good.

It was when I was in the ear, nose and throat department that I had an experience which shook me to the core. A man was suffering from a quinsy or abscess above the tonsil. The abscess was going to be opened before a small group of students to demonstrate the case to them. We all gathered round the shoulder of the surgeon in the darkened room. The surgeon was wearing a head mirror, and was showing us exactly where he proposed to thrust the knife into the abscess. The patient was seated on a stool in front of him. The surgeon made his incision. Instead of pus there came out blood—pints of it. It flowed from his mouth like a cataract. The surgeon had opened one of the main branches of the carotid artery by mistake. In this man's throat it ran abnormally just underneath the abscess. The surgeon was excellent at his job, and he was not to blame. In a few seconds the man was lying unconscious at our feet. The presence of mind of one of the students saved him. He grabbed his carotid artery and hung on like grim death until the artery was securely tied. Let anyone who has a quinsy take heart from three things. The abnormality of the artery does not exceed one in a million. Secondly, the vast majority are cured nowadays without operation by means of penicillin. Thirdly, it is the universal practice now to guard the blade so that only the tip penetrates the quinsy, and does not injure any blood vessel underneath.

During our years as medical students we learned many other things beside those taught in the Royal Infirmary. For example, there were a series of lectures on public health, or public filth as it was called, but by far the most entertaining, the most dramatic and the most interesting were Harvey Littlejohn's lectures on forensic medicine, as the law relating to medicine is called.

I don't know whether the subject made the lecturer or the lecturer the subject, but the class was the most popular in the whole medical curriculum. The lecture theatre was always packed out with students—a considerable number of whom were not medicals at all. Harvey could squeeze the last drop of drama from any given situation. Bristling moustache, immaculately groomed and with that inability to pronounce the letter " r " which some great orators have, he would stride up and down behind his desk with a wealth of gesticulation and posture. At one moment he would be reclining in an arm-chair, at another seated on a kitchen chair, and yet again seated on a three-legged stool—all three were ranged behind his desk.

I can hear him as he tells the story of how a murderer was caught after having sought to make it appear that an accident had occurred.

" I caught the murderer, gentlemen. Yes, I extracted the cork from the victim's throat. The cork was to make it appear that he had extracted it with his teeth. But gentlemen, but . . . the cork was upside down."

To say it was as good as a play is to under-estimate Harvey's capabilities as a lecturer. It was better than a play. It consisted of potted thrillers served up hot. Though his tongue might be brusque in private, Harvey was an ornament to any University.

Rivalling Harvey's popularity were the series of lectures on hypnotism. It was unquestionably the subject here that was the attraction, though the lecturer was good and always interesting. His subject was a small, undersized man who did the most amazing things when under the lecturer's hypnotic influence.

I remember three office stools being placed in a row and the subject of the experiment told to lie down on the top of them so that the back of his head was resting on one, his hips on another and his heels on a third. The patient was told to hold himself quite rigid and the centre stool was taken away. He lay as stiff as a board resting only on the back of his head and on his heels. It is an impossible feat even for a person with a highly developed muscular system.

But the most striking thing that I saw performed—at least it made the biggest impress on my mind—was this. When under the influence of hypnotism, the patient was told to look at his watch—to write down the time on a piece of paper and give it to the lecturer. He was to do this in a certain number of seconds —several thousand. We students worked out the time for ourselves to see when the experiment would come into action. The hour was a quarter past three in the morning. It was exactly like a delayed action mental bomb. The patient came out of his trance with no recollection whatever of his instructions. The next time the class met, the lecturer asked the man to tell us just what had happened.

" I woke up at a quarter past three in the morning. I looked for some paper and a pen. I then wrote down the time—3.15 a.m., and though it was a long way to your house, I walked, as of course there were no cars at that time of night."

The lecturer asked him why he did it.

" I don't know," he said. " I woke up and something just seemed to tell me to do it."

It is no wonder that the class were not merely earnest believers ; they were disciples of the gospel of hypnotism.

As I have said, we were taught many other things during our five years at the University. Gradually the years passed, each one with a group of professional examinations at the end. We were always looking ahead at the next hurdle. We worked really hard during our five years there. Looking back on it all, I don't think I would face my five years at the University again. I am sometimes asked whether I preferred my years at school or my years at the University. At school, my brain was unruffled by a thought ; at the University, I worked hard—very hard. I think I am naturally lazy. My brain likes being unruffled. I preferred school.

It was a constant grind for us to keep abreast of our work. The only free time we had was in the evenings, and all our reading had to be done then, except for that select few who, like me, read during lecture time. Even then, it was necessary to work on most evenings. In the latter years it was frequently necessary for us to go back to the wards, so that little, if any, reading was done on these evenings. A few had phenomenal memories, and before exams they would sit up all night drinking coffee and with damp cloths around their heads. A certain number of them passed their exams. A select few even achieved distinction. But the knowledge thus gained did not last. I met one of the owners of these phenomenal memories recently. He had forsaken medicine for literature.

" I can't even remember the dose of castor oil," he confessed.

No, it was the steady worker who turned out the best doctor in the end.

Gradually the finals loomed on the horizon. As regards work, the heat was turned on to boiling-point. Eventually on a raw November evening one of the servitors pinned up a small piece of paper containing a list of names. There was a small knot of students gathered under the arch in the new quad. We crowded forward to see if our names were on the list. There was much hand-shaking and cheerful banter. A certain few looked in silence at the board and faded away into the night. Their names were not posted as having passed.

The graduation in the McEwan Hall came as a sort of anti-climax. We all had hired gowns and hoods for the occasion, I have never had one on since, which I sometimes think is a pity as my hood was a gorgeous affair of pink silk and white fur— probably from a rabbit. The graduation ceremonial was carried out with all its usual pageantry and ceremonial. The procession of professors in their robes proceeded slowly up the aisle while the next generation of students in the gallery sang " See the robbers passing by ".

Already we felt that a softer generation was succeeding us. The proceedings were not enlivened this time by a live cock who crowed lustily whenever his tail feathers were stimulated which, I regret to say, was frequently. There is a legend in Edinburgh that the black hat whereby the degree is conferred is made out of the seat of Geordie Buchanan's breeks. Geordie, I may say, was a well-known Scottish Divine of the time of John Knox. Be that as it may, I was well and truly capped and outside the hall proceeded to shed my finery for the first and last occasion. I felt much as a woman does when she changes her name at the marriage ceremony. For ever after I would be Dr. Bell Nicoll—plain Mr. disappeared. But all the same I took some time to become accustomed to my new title. All the world was at my feet, all the drudgery behind me.

CHAPTER VI

HOUSE SURGEON

I SOUGHT a solitary place in the Union along with the current copy of the *British Medical Journal*. My method of seeking a job was simple. I folded it open at the page advertising vacancies for house surgeons and ran my finger down the list. I stopped it at the one which offered the highest pay. It turned out to be " Resident house surgeon and house physician at Auchterkirk Infirmary ".

I wrote and applied. To my surprise, it was answered very speedily, and I was told to appear at the hospital with copies of recent testimonials. I duly appeared, bulging with statements regarding my proficiency, my character, and what a good fellow I was. I remember reading them over in the train and being in some doubt as to whether it was I they referred to.

The outside of the hospital was certainly not imposing and the inside was not much better. Apparently a new and up-to-date hospital was about to be built, but at the time it was in a " make-do-and-mend " sort of state. I was interviewed by the leading surgeon of the hospital and handed him a few of my hard-won testimonials. He waved them aside, saying :

" I've written too many myself to lay the slightest stress on what they say. Tell me, what games do you play ? "

I told him " golf and rugby."

" What's your handicap at golf ? " he asked me.

" Eight."

" And what club did you play for at rugby ? "

" Watson's."

" How long did you take to get through medicine ? "

" Five years."

" Write me out a prescription for tape-worms. Do you know anything about X-ray work ? "

" No."

" Can you learn it by the first of January ? "

" Yes."

" Well, start here on that date."

There were a few more questions, and that was the end of the interview. I found myself on the road to the station not knowing whether I stood on my head or my heels. My dearly-bought testimonials remained unread in my pocket.

I bought a book on X-rays and arranged to have an immediate course on the subject. Alas! the instrument on which I was taught was a modern one. The vintage of that at Auchterkirk was that upon which the earliest experiments in X-ray work had been carried out. The only thing I learned which was of real use to me was that it was absolutely essential to be protected when working the machine. The instrument at Auchterkirk was as devoid of protection as a rhinoceros without its hide. The risks which my predecessors had run in the X-ray department seemed to me like a child playing with a fire.

Incidentally, the X-ray machine provided me and my friends with many minutes of pleasurable excitement. It was situated at the top end of the little corridor that led to my own suite of rooms. The room was as dark as the tomb and I used to entertain my friends who came out to visit me by giving them momentoes of their visit in the form of X-rays of their bones to take home with them. I found that one of the most popular forms of entertainment was to see their own hearts beating, and I had the greatest difficulty in drawing the proceedings to a close on these occasions in spite of explaining the danger to my health as well as to their own.

The X-ray room, however, had other uses. Occasionally I was visited by colleagues for whom I felt no bonds of affection. It was my custom to take these men into the X-ray room and plant them firmly on one spot, telling them that they moved from it only at dire peril to themselves. I then pressed the switch and sparks began to fly about the room with the rapidity of a lightning storm. The room speedily took on the appearance of Dante's Inferno, and when a large spark was snapped right in front of the observer's face, he could usually stand it no more, but cried to be let out. My bathroom was also the place where I dried my X-rays. It had a multitude of strings with films suspended from them, running in all directions. In fact, it was more like the pictures one sees of a Chinese temple with its flags fluttering, or the drying-room of some laundry, than the bathroom of a respectable house surgeon.

It was a work of art getting into the bath, and much the best thing when one had achieved one's purpose was to stay there and contemplate the X-rays one had taken during the day. As I usually took about half a dozen different exposures of varying length, in the hope that one would be readable, the number of films which I used during the day and which were drying in my bathroom at night-time, was considerable.

My chief would then be about forty-six years old, clean shaven and ruddy-faced, his hair parted in the middle and greying at the temples. Inclined to slight stoutness, he had that direct look and set of head which is the heritage of only a few men. I have never seen him ruffled. I have never seen him treat a patient with other than perfect courtesy, be he rich or poor. I have never seen him lose his sense of humour even in the most trying situations. He was a first-rate surgeon, with a knowledge which enabled him to cope with any eventuality. He was confident of himself, thorough and painstaking. But I could go on for many hours describing his qualities. It would only bore the reader, however. He was quite a different type of man from my father, and yet these two men left the biggest impress on my life. I can only sum him up by saying that he was a natural gentleman, a really brilliant surgeon and a man who was a sportsman in the cleanest sense of that much-abused word.

He had his eccentricities—what great man hasn't? I think he slept in his arm-chair every night. A cold bath in the morning seemed to be all he needed to freshen him up for the day.

Another eccentricity was his dislike of motor-cars. He used a Douglas motor-bicycle and seemed to be perpetually taking off or putting on a pair of waterproof trousers, which he wore to keep his clothes clean. He was no fool and didn't suffer fools gladly. An air of good fellowship might lead an unwary observer to miss the steel behind the genial exterior. He got a great deal of satisfaction from things that might appear childish to an observer.

For example, I remember a doctor bringing in a patient who was practically moribund. The woman was suffering from a ruptured cyst in the abdomen, and the doctor inquired in a patronising way whether my Chief felt competent to do the job. Normally it would have been my job to give the anæsthetic, but, partly because he needed an assistant and partly because, in the event of the woman dying on the operating table, her own doctor would have the responsibility of her death, he asked him to give the anæsthetic while I assisted. The doctor couldn't very well refuse. In the course of the operation he left his post with a view to seeing how the operation was proceeding. To make his sin doubly heinous, he had no mask over his face. While he was breathing into the wound I distinctly saw my Chief give the cyst a squeeze with his gloved fingers so that its fluid contents went over the clothes of the anæsthetist. To say that he was soaked would have been an under statement. Amid profuse apologies for his carelessness, the surgeon finished the operation. The patient was lifted off the operating table alive, recovered from the operation and left the hospital vertically instead of horizontally. When I saw my Chief afterwards in the privacy of my sitting-room and congratulated him on the success of the operation, he looked at me with a twinkle in his eye and said :

" Yes, it was a most successful operation, but the most satisfactory part was the way the cyst was evacuated."

That was typical of the man.

The hospital, as I have said, was an old building. Most of the administrative rooms were to the front and the wards stretched out, like the fangs of a tooth, behind and most of them were overcrowded with beds.

I arrived after lunch and my first emergency arrived soon afterwards. I think it was a fractured collar-bone. Anyway, it was one of Auchterkirk's leading football players. That same night an emergency was admitted and thereby hangs a tale, We had an honorary anæsthetist on the staff of the hospital. but he only attended on operating days. When emergencies came in it was my duty to give the anæsthetic. I was naturally anxious to do well as it was my first case under the eyes of my Chief. The porter was off duty, so I got the man on the trolley and pushed it along to the operating theatre. Unfortunately, the operating theatre was at the other end of the building from the ward, and I arrived considerably out of breath. Having got the patient on to the operating table, I seated myself on the little white revolving stool at the patient's head. I had not administered a drop of anæsthetic when the Chief, who was washing his hands, turned to me and asked :

" No false teeth and bladder empty ? "

With that I rushed out of the theatre and across the hospital to the ward from which I had brought him. The sister assured me that both functions had been attended to, and I carried the information back to the theatre with the celerity of a sprinter at the Olympic Games. When I arrived there the Chief was still washing his hands. He looked up with a twinkle in his eye as I entered.

" It's all right, Nicoll. He has."

" How on earth do you know ? " I replied.

" Oh, I just asked him," he answered.

There are various ways of feeling a fool, and I had probed one of them to the depths.

My last duty at night was to make a round of all the wards. It was generally a late business and conducted with the minimum of formality towards both nurses and patients. I had an experience at that time which nearly terminated my career as a house surgeon at Auchterkirk. I was preparing to go to bed one night when the bell to my apartment was rung. It was the night sister. It appeared that a stray cat had stolen the night nurses' meal for several nights running. They had caught it in the very act. It was now being held in the kitchen of the women's ward, and would I come along and put it to sleep ? I assured her that I would come right away, but it occurred to me that, purely in the interests of science, it would be instructive to put the cat to sleep with an overdose of morphia. The normal way was to give it an overdose of chloroform, but I was determined to try something new.

I filled a syringe with enough morphia to put several human beings to sleep permanently, and we made our way along to the women's ward. When we arrived at the kitchen a nurse was holding a moth-eaten cat by the back of the neck. I jammed the needle into its thigh and we all stood around to see what would happen. Unfortunately, the nurse who was acting as prisoner's friend to the cat stood up and joined the expectant circle. We watched, fascinated. Personally, I expected the cat to curl up and die, but I wanted to see how long it would take.

The cat did nothing whatever for some seconds, then it spun round like a top. Suddenly it dashed off at at tangent and hit its head violently against the kitchen wall. It cannoned off that and shot out of the kitchen door. I should add that during all this performance it was giving vent to the fierce cat-like noises and hisses with which a tom cat can make the night hideous.

The door into the ward consisted of two halves, one of which, unfortunately, was open. The cat went through the ward door like a rocket and then took a flying leap. It landed right on the stomach of a woman who was lying asleep in the first bed. The cat, whose vocal chords also seemed inspired, proceeded to hurdle from bed to bed up the ward. If a time bomb had fallen in the ward the women couldn't have got out of bed quicker. Soon the only horizontal forms were those with broken legs. Not the least part of the entertainment was to see long lines of women, each one clutching her nightdress and trying to make herself as inconspicuous as possible.

I had followed the cat into the ward and now I proceeded to make two radical mistakes. In the first place I stood at the end of the ward and simply howled with laughter. I did not know then that no woman likes to be laughed at, least of all when she has had no time to put her teeth in.

My second mistake was to speed the departure of the cat by throwing something at it. What I threw was a book. The book missed the cat, but struck a syphon of soda water standing on top of a locker. Now a smashed syphon of soda water is a thing to remember—even in the day time. In the silent watches of the night, with the cat providing a background of fire and brimstone, the noise was like the last trump, as doubtless many patients in the hospital thought it was.

It only remains to be told that the cat disappeared into the bathroom at speed. The window was open, though the ward was not on the ground floor. A cat with such indomitable vitality would certainly have landed on its four feet. Anyway, the cat was never seen again.

But there was a sequel. It arrived next day in the form of a note asking me to attend a meeting of the managers to be held in the hospital on that afternoon and to explain my conduct in creating a disturbance in the women's ward on the previous night. When the Chief arrived I showed the letter to him and asked his advice.

"I should tell the truth, the whole truth and nothing but the truth," he said. "But first let's look up the book for the effect of morphia on cats."

We did, and to my consternation I found that morphia only sends cats out of their minds. It, unfortunately, doesn't kill them.

The managers met around a horsehoe table. The chairman sat at one end and I stood at the other. I told my tale as simply as I could, and I explained to the managers how circumstances had arisen which compelled me to cope with them from time to time.

When I came to the point about the cat jumping from bed to bed, I noticed that the chairman dropped his pencil on the floor and bent down to retrieve it. When I came to the bit about the soda water syphon the chairman bent down to tie his bootlace. I was asked to leave the room while they considered their verdict. I was never in any real doubt about the result. I was reprimanded and told not to do it again.

Things, however, were only warming up. That first month we generally had at least one emergency each night. Night after night I phoned the Chief and never found him in bed. He told me that never in the history of the hospital had there been a time like it. I slept at any odd hours I could. It was constant unremitting toil. I worked literally night and day. The hospital got an unwelcome publicity in the obituary column of the local paper, for many of those who were sent in for immediate operation were too far gone to have any hope of recovery.

In the middle of the first month I was called to the 'phone one evening. It was a doctor speaking from Edinburgh to say that my father had died suddenly. I had paid a flying visit home on the previous Saturday afternoon and he had seemed in his usual good health. I had arranged for my sister and him to visit me at Auchterkirk the following week-end. That night I 'phoned my Chief and with a heavy heart caught the train for Edinburgh. I remember sitting alone in the dimly-lit third-class carriage as the train crawled along, stopping at every station, and realising that I was alone now. There was just sheer misery in my heart. The world that I knew and had been brought up in had come to an end. Henceforth my home would be wherever I chanced to be.

I listened to the wheels going round and the rhythm seemed to beat a refrain into my brain, " He's dead, he's dead, he's dead ". I remember making my way down to his brother's house, where he had died. I remember walking in the funeral procession beside that same brother. I remember going home afterwards to four walls and heavy, old-fashioned furniture. It was no longer home. The light had gone out.

I went back to Auchterkirk to carry on with my work. I had so much to do that when I had finished my last operation for the day I just tumbled into bed in the " wee sma' hours " and slept the sleep of utter exhaustion. Probably the hard work prevented me from thinking too much.

A fortnight after my return I was summoned to the 'phone again. My father's brother—at whose house he had died and with whom I had walked to his funeral—had been found dead in bed at Wemmys Bay, at the mouth of the Clyde, where he had gone on holiday. I was his only surviving male relative. I went to Glasgow and thence down to Wemmys Bay and had the miserable business of identifying the body. Later I went up to Benholm for the funeral, to where I had spent so many happy holidays. Now Benholm would pass into other hands. An old generation had passed away and a new and untried one was to take its place. That chapter was not only closed. The covers were shut and the book put away.

" And there were giants in the land in those days . . ."

I didn't get up very early ; probably no house surgeon does, as he is in the habit of going to bed late. It was my custom to go round every bed in the hospital in the early part of the fore-noon and decide to what I would draw the Chief's attention and what could be safely left over. The Chief usually appeared between eleven and twelve and the two of us did the same round all over again. He missed nothing. His examination of a patient from a workhouse was as thorough and conscientious as it would be for a millionaire.

The afternoons were my least busy times, and I was supposed to get some time off then for recreation. I seldom did.

Once a week was operating day. On these days the Chief would appear earlier and we would commence operating at ten o'clock. We worked steadily through the operating list and frequently I did not get my lunch till four or five o'clock. As the months passed the Chief would leave more and more of the work for me to do—a sure sign that his confidence in me was getting stronger. I think he thought he would make a surgeon out of me, but I had no ambition that way. I came to the conclusion that surgeons earned their money dearly, for I was as limp as a rag at the end of a long operating day. It may have been standing so long ; it may have been the humid heat ; it was maybe the intense concentration for a prolonged period. Anyway, I decided that I was not cut out for a surgeon.

Part of my duties was to see the relatives, especially of those who were seriously ill. I well remember interviewing a man who had been recently married and whose wife was dying of kidney trouble. I can't remember what his surname was, but I remember that the wife's name was Jeanie. Every night, when he came home from his work, he would sit by the bedside of his wife. She was on the danger list for a long time.

Every few days he would come to me and he would say :

" Well, how's Jeanie ? "

And I would say, " I'm afraid there's no hope for Jeanie, and the only thing we can do is to ease her passing as much as possible."

The silence grew more profound. I noticed that at the end of a long day's work he would be inclined to doze as he sat by his wife's bedside. I had a strong suspicion that he was missing the comforts of home. My suspicions were justified. One day he came to me as usual and asked how Jeanie was. I gave him the usual reply and a sigh came from the depths of his being.

" Aye," he said, " we'll need tae tak a hammer tae Jeanie."

There was no lack of love in his voice. It was only the cry of a man who was utterly tired out and who was at his wits' end to cope with the long drawn-outness of death. Jeanie ultimately died, but her passing was like that of King Charles. She was " an unconscionable time adying".

A kaleidoscope of faces ; a long line of beds ; each one containing a world of suffering ; each one with an experience peculiar to that one alone. Out of these many faces stand out two or three who, by reason of some peculiarity of their illness, have stayed in my memory.

Auchterkirk was the centre of a large coalfield. When a mine accident occurred it was the custom for all the mates of the injured man to accompany him to hospital. If the accident happened at night it was quite common to see black and grimy men with only their coats covering their naked chests, festooned round the ambulance like so many bees settling after a swarm. One night I was informed on the 'phone that a man had been injured by a fall of rock down at the collieries. I was at the front door awaiting the ambulance. It was quite a sight as it drew up to the main door of the hospital. The lamps in the men's caps had been extinguished, but they were still in position and, with the exception of having put on their coats, they were just as they had come off work.

They insisted on carrying the injured man themselves, and put the stretcher down on an examination couch in the dispensary. This room had actually nothing to do with dispensing, but was used for out-patients and for minor surgery. It was littered with the impedimenta of the out-patients' department, and had the usual glass cases of instruments ranged against the walls. The man, a young and powerfully-built fellow, was suffering from a condition of cerebral agitation. He was quite unaware of what he said or did, or where he was, and was extremely violent to everyone, lashing out with his fists in all directions and liable to severely injure anybody within reach of him.

I gave him a strong injection of morphia to keep him quiet. I might as well have given him a drink of water. I tried lots of things, but they were not of the slightest avail. The man merely continued to fight like a tiger, and it took all the strength of his mates to hold him down. In the end I had to chloroform him. It was the only way, and I soon had him unconscious and relaxed.

While he was quiet, I stole away and 'phoned my Chief. He said he would come down immediately. I met him on the door-step, and we walked up the corridor together. I described the man and his symptoms. He asked me what I had done.

"As everything else had failed, I chloroformed him."

"Mm," he said. "A little drastic, wasn't it?"

Now such a remark from the Chief was the equivalent to a severe ticking off from anybody else. He was a man who consistently played the light pedal, and the slightest touch of the heavier one made his words sound severe. I did not answer back or even attempt to justify myself.

When we reached the dispensary the man was still quiet. Actually, he had fallen asleep after the chloroform and was just waking up. The Chief went forward in his usual courtly, old-fashioned manner and laid his hand on the man's shoulder.

"How are you feeling now, my good man?"

The Chief bent down to catch the man's reply. The next moment he was catapulted through the air and landed in a show-case opposite. He had got a blow between the eyes from the miner which would have laid out anyone less strong than the Chief. When he had picked himself up and shaken the glass out of his hair, he turned to me and said, "A little more chloroform, I think, Nicoll; a little more chloroform."

The following story is one which was broadcast recently, and it is reproduced by kind permission of the B.B.C.

It happened twenty-five years ago, when I was a house surgeon in a town in a big industrial area. Now, to be a house surgeon is the goal of every medical student's ambition, but looking back on it from the heights of general practice it seems the lowest form of animal life. Anyway, I want to take you step by step with me through that January night of 1924, and tell you exactly what happened.

House surgeons go to bed late as a rule, and I was no exception. It would be about one o'clock when I was going to bed, that I was summoned to the 'phone. It was a doctor to ask for the immediate admission of a girl suffering from peritonitis.

" Could we take her in ? "

" Yes, we could take her in."

I gave orders for the theatre to be prepared, acquainted the night sister, notified my Chief, and returned to my room to await events. It did not seem worth while going to bed. I heard the ambulance drive up to the front door. I heard the shuffling noises of the stretcher being carried in, and in due course was summoned to examine the patient herself.

Most of you know what the wards of a hospital are like at night time—the green shaded light—the heavy breathing of sleeping patients—the nurse tiptoeing up the ward. There are screens around the newcomer's bed. I can see her lying there, her dark auburn hair lying damp on the pillow, her cheeks sunken and pale with the cold sweat of the severely ill on her brow. Her face has a strangely ethereal look about it, something like that picture of the girl in the " Soul's Awakening ". Yet her hands on the coverlet are the hands of a mill girl, rough and coarse.

My word, she is ill. She is barely conscious, just a flicker of a pulse. A rapid examination proves that the diagnosis is correct. She is obviously in a very serious condition. There is a dangerous perforation which we have simply got to find if we are to save her life.

I tiptoed down the ward with the sister.

" Well, you see for yourself how bad she is. If she comes off the operating table alive, she'll be lucky."

I go out to the hall to meet my Chief and tell him briefly about the case. However, he is an excellent surgeon, and he specialises in abdominal work.

As we wash up, the trolley is wheeled in and the anæsthetist takes his place on the little white revolving stool at the patient's head. My job is to assist the surgeon with the operation, and I am secretly thankful that I am not giving the anæsthetic.

We take our places on opposite sides of the operating table, and the surgeon commences the operation. I don't propose to recite its various steps, but I do want to say that we found our diagnosis to be completely correct. Soon we were looking for the actual perforation.

Strange, there's no sign of it. The theatre sister leaves her instruments and glances towards the wound. I look at the clock, 3.15. We go on with our desperate search against time. We know what we are looking for. There's a scraping noise as the anæsthetist rises from his stool to stretch himself.

No sound breaks the deadly stillness but the ticking of the clock. I cast a quick look at the time, 3.55. How extraordinarily quickly the time has flown. My Chief tries every possible trick known to him and to surgery. No luck. The minutes pass. The anæsthetist gives a cough. The surgeon glances at him.

" How is she ? "

" Well she's alive, but I can't keep her going much longer."

We bend to our task. It's like looking for a needle in a haystack. My mouth gets very dry when I suddenly realise that we are fighting for this girl's life, and that the next few minutes will probably decide whether she is going to live or die. Her life is in our hands, and we've simply got to find it. What the surgeon is thinking, I don't know. He goes on looking and feeling ; looking and feeling. Steadily, systematically.

I glance at the clock, 4.15. A voice breaks the stillness of the theatre. It is the anæsthetist.

" I'm afraid you'll have to stop now. She's nearly away."

I experience the wild clutchings of panic, but the surgeon makes no sign.

Against all usage, he starts again and quietly and systematically goes over the whole area once more. Four eyes are searching. The anæsthetist—a Scotsman—makes a noise with his stool, and in his soft Scots voice says quietly,

" I'm afraid you'll have to finish now."

Rapidly the surgeon closes the wound, and as she is bandaged up and lifted off the operating table I suddenly realise that I am very tired.

I try to tell the surgeon what I feel about it. I murmur something about " bad luck ".

" Yes, it's unfortunate."

He's a man of few words, but obviously he feels it keenly. I go to bed feeling terribly tired.

In the morning I go along to the ward. I don't expect to find her alive. The day sister knows all about the case and is a most reliable person. Contrary to custom I decide to do the dressing myself. I don't think she is conscious, certainly she doesn't know who I am. The angel of death is hovering very near. I hardly expect she will be alive this evening.

Evening comes and again I tiptoe to her bedside. Now she's conscious, and I think she knows who I am. I do her dressing on the morrow and on all the to-morrows while she is in hospital. For days the screens stay around her bed, denoting she is very ill. Gradually, ever so gradually, the thready pulse becomes stronger and more regular. She passes through all the stages of those who are desperately ill, seriously ill, and finally those " on the mend ".

Slowly, ever so slowly, the angel of death retreats from her bed, until one day he's gone altogether and she starts to convalesce. We become great friends. Ultimately, the day comes when she can get up and not long after that she is able to leave the hospital.

It is a forenoon when she leaves, and a group of her friends have come to escort her from the hospital and to carry her bag. I go along to the waiting-room to say " Good-bye " and find them all gathered there. I shake hands with her and wish her " Good luck."

" You're a bit of a miracle, you know ; by rights you ought to be dead."

There is a whispering among the girls. One girl speaks up.

" It's more of a miracle than you think, sir. You see, we are all members of a group at our church, and the night that Mary had her operation we had a prayer meeting in relays all night, and you say it's a ' miracle ', but we say that all answered prayer is a ' miracle '."

I slowly walked back to my duties. I realised with a queer feeling that I had not seen that night, the apparent failure of an operation, but I had seen God in action at the request of a few mill girls.

Of course, I know that the perforation was closed by a flake of lymph or by some internal organ adhering to the wall of the stomach. The point is this. Was it mere chance, or did God answer the prayer of the girl's friends by so arranging things that the perforation was closed? Either you believe it or you don't.

One morning each week was devoted to the removal of tonsils and adenoids. There are two ways of removing tonsils. They can be dissected or they can be guillotined. In my day the latter and quicker course was adopted. Guillotining tonsils requires a certain amount of dexterity which is born of practice. The great danger in it is that part of the tonsil may be left in and may grow again, so that the unfortunate individual has to have them removed over again.

I knew the operation in theory all right, but everyone knows there is a vast difference between theory and practice. It was so in this case. I was anxious to try my hand. The patient was a little girl who had tonsils like the pre-war Sunday joint. When she was completely anæsthetised, I started. The first one came away in my guillotine as clean as a whistle. I had notions of myself as an ear, nose and throat surgeon who was making lots of money and had more work than he could cope with. I got the second one away also complete. Alas! Once again I learned that a little pride is a dangerous thing. I opened the blade of the guillotine too soon. The tonsil slipped out and before I could do anything about it, it had slipped down her throat and she had swallowed her own tonsil.

Of course no harm whatever would result to the child. It is a thing which might not happen again in a score of years. But the idea was somewhat repulsive, and if the child was sick from the anæsthetic and brought up a spare tonsil, it would need a certain amount of explaining even to the dullest-witted infant. Well, the child wasn't sick, but the case had a sequel. There was a probationer nurse in the theatre who had just commenced her training. The parents of the child were neighbours of hers, and the foolish girl told the parents that their child had swallowed her tonsil, and that the tonsil was still inside the child. I, of course, knew nothing about the matter and was somewhat startled when two indignant and aggressive parents demanded an explanation. I naturally admitted it was true, but my explanation that the child would not suffer in any way was received with a certain amount of scepticism and reserve. I pointed out to them that the child would digest her own tonsil in the same way as she would digest her Sunday dinner. But this simple explanation only seemed to make matters worse. Ultimately the indignant parents went away somewhat mollified, but still far from convinced that their child could be fed with impunity on its own tonsils.

Talking about tonsils reminds me of a story which I heard recently. A young ear, nose and throat specialist was taking out-patients at a certain hospital. He was a very young man, and not many years before his appointment he had been a house surgeon in the same department of the same hospital. One of the patients was a child who was brought in by her mother. The child opened her mouth and the surgeon examined her tonsils.

" These tonsils must be taken out as soon as possible."

" Oh, they've been taken out before."

" Well, all I can say is that it's a disgraceful job, and doesn't reflect any credit on the person who took them out."

" Oh, but you took them out, doctor, several years ago at this hospital."

To cover his confusion he made an excuse to go and look up the books. Sure enough, in his house surgeon days, he had had a shot at guillotining the tonsils and left quite a bit in each. The small part had grown again, and that was what he now had to contend with. He thought rapidly of what he would say to the mother. He was not only an ear, nose and throat surgeon ; he was an inventive genius.

" I see what has happened," he said ; " the male tonsils have been taken out, but the female tonsils have grown again."

In quite a different mood did I wait for the ambulance on another occasion. About seven o'clock that same evening a man had called at the out-patients' department and said he was not feeling very well. The out-patients' department had long since shut and all the nurses had gone, but my tender feeling overcame my judgment and I consented to see him. He was a young man about twenty. I remember that he had a very waisted overcoat with a velvet collar, and that he carried a silver-headed Malacca cane.

I examined him and found nothing amiss, so wrote him out a prescription for iron, arsenic and strychnine, which is a very common and effective tonic. The youth took his departure, and I thought no more of the matter.

About three o'clock in the morning I was summoned to the telephone. It was my friend of the previous evening. He told me that he had taken a dose of the medicine and felt very ill after it. I did some rapid thinking. Presumably I had made a mistake in the prescription and given him too much arsenic or too much strychnine. I told him that I would send the ambulance for him in a few minutes and would admit him straight away.

I remember pacing up and down the front corridor thinking of all the possibilities of my mistake. I saw the dock with myself in it on a charge of manslaughter. At the very least it would mean ruin and disgrace. All my hopes of a career were dashed to the ground. It was all U.P. These minutes were certainly some of the worst I ever endured in my life. Subconsciously I listened for the ambulance, and at last I heard it turn into the gravelled entrance to the hospital, and in a few strides I was at the door to meet it.

The ambulance drew up to the door, but before anyone had time to jump down from its front the door of the ambulance swung open and out stepped . . . my friend of the previous evening. Not only was he wearing the waisted coat, but the silver-headed Malacca cane and the velvet collar were all present and correct. He looked remarkably spry for a man who was desperately ill, in fact he looked altogether too spry. I asked him if he had the prescription on him which I had given him earlier in the evening. He produced it, and I studied it intently. It was perfectly correct. I took him into the dispensary.

"What made you think you were seriously ill?"

"Well, the taste. It was very bad."

A few enquiries satisfied me that there was nothing wrong with him but a too vivid imagination. I thought of myself pacing the corridor a few minutes ago. I was never nearer to committing murder than I was at that moment, and undoubtedly I would have pleaded provocation.

I put him in the men's surgical ward for the night, and thoughtfully went back to my interrupted sleep. Before my eyes closed I was clear as to my course of action. In the morning he was wheeled along to the operating theatre and on the way there I casually told him that he was on the trolley which was reserved for those who had died. By the time he got on the operating table he was a shaken man. I pressed a mask on his face in spite of his protestations that he was all right and that an operation was not necessary. I sprinkled chloroform copiously around the mask and assured him that the poison must be cut out. I made sure that he saw all the instruments laid out, and I inspected the knives for their sharpness. It was a badly shaken man who leapt off the operating table, and the last I saw of him was making a hurried exit from the hospital along the front corridor, complete with waisted overcoat, velvet collar and silver-headed cane.

It was curious the way one got attached to some patients and some got attached to oneself. I had a striking demonstration of this with Murdoch Campbell. Murdo—to give him the name by which he was known in the ward—normally lived in a lodging house in Auchterkirk and might be taken as typical of one of its *habitues*. I had occasion to attend Murdo daily, and I became quite attached to the old man. He was ultimately discharged from the hospital, and I myself departed to other spheres far from Auchterkirk. Murdo, however, was constant in his affection. Apparently he took a trip to Edinburgh and found the flat where my sister lived, up for sale. He made his way to the house agents and thence to my lawyers, from whom I had a letter asking whether they should give him my address. I replied in the affirmative and, to my surprise, had a letter from Murdo saying that he proposed to call upon me. This was several years after I had left the hospital. I was then married and living in London. I wrote him a note and told him that a visit was impossible, but wishing him well for old times' sake.

What was my astonishment one day in London when the maid told me that a Mr. Murdoch Campbell was waiting to see me. He had come to London by sea because it was cheaper, and told me that he had slept the previous night on the Embankment. He carried with him a present of a fruit knife which is still in my possession. He would take nothing from me, however. I gave him a good meal and the last sight of Murdo was hobbling up the road on his way back to Auchterkirk. I never heard of him since, and he must be dead long ago.

But the most dramatic thing which I remember as a house surgeon concerned me personally. It was towards the end of my time there, and I remember that it was a Saturday morning. A motor accident had been brought in, and a woman was gravely injured. So grave were her injuries that there was considerable doubt as to whether she would survive the operation which was necessary. On the previous Monday I had sent a prepaid cablegram to India proposing to the lady who is now my wife. I had had no reply, and I was a worried man. The Chief knew of my anxiety and with his usual half-jesting, half-sympathetic manner exhorted me to keep my heart up.

It was my duty to give the anæsthetic. I got about half-way through the operation when the patient gave every sign of expiring and stopped breathing. The surgeon stood aside, and I put my hands underneath the sheet and carried out artificial respiration by compressing her chest rhythmically. I had been working for a short time when the door opened and a nurse slipped in carrying a buff envelope. She handed it to me, and I was unable to resist the temptation of opening and reading it, which I did by holding it in one hand while I carried out artificial respiration with the other. The cable was not in the affirmative, and as the surgeon stood back I heard him murmur,

" Any luck, Nicoll ? "

The woman eventually started breathing, and the operation was finished with her in a better state than we could have hoped for. I regret to say that she ultimately died, but I must be unique in having a proposal answered in such dramatic circumstances.

I recall another dramatic happening in which I was concerned. It was a Sunday afternoon. A tremendous gale was raging, and a little boy was brought in to the out-patient department with a small cut on his head. It appeared that he had been walking along a street in Auchterkirk when a tile, dislodged by the gale, came hurtling down on to the boy's head, cutting it open. The cut was a small one. The edge of the slate had hit him and a couple of stitches soon put him right. There was no sign whatever that anything further than a cut scalp had to be dealt with. The little boy wanted to go home and have his tea. I was adamant, however, and insisted on his being kept in the hospital overnight, to be on the safe side.

That night I was doing my round. I stood by his bedside and looked down at his sleeping head on the pillow. His hands were on the coverlet, but what was that ? The right thumb was twitching backwards and forwards with monotonous regularity. I got quite excited and watched intently. There was no doubt about it. I went to the 'phone and spoke to my Chief. He promised to come down immediately. Together we stood and looked down at the sleeping boy. The thumb was still twitching.

We went to my sitting-room and proceeded to work out which part of the brain was being irritated. The boy was prepared for immediate operation and taken to the theatre. It was the first trephine I had seen. Curiously enough, a quarter of a century later, I had a similar operation myself and the same steps that were carried out on the first occasion recalled themselves to me.

It was what is known as a beautiful operation, and a piece of slate about the size of one's thumbnail was extracted from the boy's brain. The boy was discharged completely recovered within three weeks' time. It has always remained in my mind as an excellent example of a successful operation which by observation, deduction and brilliant execution, saved a life which otherwise would have been terminated by a purposeless and painful death.

As the work grew gradually more normal, my thoughts turned to the lighter side of life. I determined, as usual, to carry out an impersonation. The matron had gone away for the week-end, and I determined to use the occasion.

I was just putting the finishing touches to my appearance before my sitting-room mirror when, in the mirror, I saw the door slowly open and a local doctor came in. He came to the hospital frequently, ostensibly to see me, but really to visit one of the sisters. He had apparently rung my bell, but in the excitement of dressing I had not heard it, and he had come straight to my sitting-room. When he saw a bearded and total stranger he apologised and backed out, but I recalled him in my normal voice, having quite forgotten that I was disguised. He stared at me in amazement. Was I or was I not? I sat him down while he steadied his nerves with a cigarette and I explained to him the nefarious purpose on which I was bent. He entered fully into the spirit of the whole thing, and eagerly promised his co-operation.

I took my departure through the window and made my way round to the front door of the hospital, while he went upstairs to the sitting room which was his real objective. I arrived at the front door unobserved and rang the bell. The porter came to the door and I asked for the Matron. Only too well did I know that she was not in.

" Would the assistant Matron do ? " —

" She would."

The assistant Matron, who in normal times was the theatre sister, duly appeared. I explained I was Matron's father and that I had come to see over her hospital. The assistant Matron regretted that Matron was away for the weekend but offered to conduct me round the hospital. I accepted gladly and as we walked along the corridors I related stories of her childhood which I noticed that the assistant matron was treasuring up, probably with a view to retailing later on in the sisters' sitting room.

I was taken round every bed in the hospital. I spoke to many patients and nurses and was introduced to the sisters on duty. Not a soul recognised me.

As we went along the top corridor I paused outside the sisters' sitting room. I pretended to be deaf and not to hear the sister's protestations that it was private. I opened the door and walked in. It was evident that my visitor of a few minutes ago was making rapid progress. I backed out, stammering apologies. I completed my tour of the hospital and was shown out ; made my way round the side of the hospital and entered it once more through my sitting room window. As rapidly as possible I got into my normal clothes and removed the shrubbery from my face before going up to the sisters' sitting room. My friend did not give me away and I had the satisfaction of hearing my own simple tales retold from other lips.

The story was not finished however. Gradually it filtered through to the nurses that they had been hoaxed. They determined on revenge. One night I was summoned from a deep sleep to attend a badly burned patient who had just been brought in. She was very ill. There were screens around the bed and a mask over her face as she had been badly burned about the head. I can't remember exactly why I had not been notified prior to her arrival. Anyway, at the time the reason appeared perfectly satisfactory. I bent down to undo the mask. I remember there were a lot of yellow picric acid stains on it. As I bent down, the patient's right hand, which had been hanging over the side of the bed away from me, came into action. A large and dripping sponge connected with the side of my head. It was a staff nurse and the burn was a complete hoax.

Honour was satisfied on both sides.

Time raced rapidly away. Before I realised it, summer had arrived. It came to my last night in hospital. I was invited to a party in the nurses' home to commence at ten o'clock sharp. An hour later festivities were in full blast. The telephone rang.

" Is Dr. Nicoll there ? "

A man had just swallowed his false teeth.

Reluctantly I made my way over to the X-ray room. The patient's breath smelt strongly of alcohol. He told me—between hiccoughs—that the accident had occurred while he was eating a supper of fried fish and chips. One might perhaps have expected a fishbone in his throat but not a set of dentures. He assured me that it hurt quite considerably and that the teeth were sticking into him like the biggest fishbone one could possibly imagine.

He lay on the X-ray table while I make the sparks fly and the air was filled with the pungent odour of ozone. I retired to develop my films. The patient by this time was asleep on the X-ray table. I examined all the plates under the strongest light I possessed. None of them showed any evidence of a foreign body in the throat. I examined his throat by the light of a lamp and a head mirror. Far, far down his throat I saw a small white glistening object. With the help of a fine pair of forceps, I extracted . . . a fishbone. I glanced at the clock. It was 2.30 a.m.

CHAPTER VII

INDIA

AFTER my strenuous activities at Auchterkirk I took a holiday in Arran. At the top of Glen Sannox and in the gullies of Goatfell I lay in the heather and basked in the sun.

In spite of the negative response to my proposal of marriage which I had received in the operating theatre, I still persevered. Then one day, at the top of Glen Sannox, the great idea came to me. I would go to India in person. The idea was no sooner born than it was acted upon. I want to Glasgow the next day and booked a passage to Bombay by the cheapest method possible. Funds did not permit of another cable, so I had expressed myself clearly on paper. The letter went to Glasgow in my pocket and I had just time to write on the outside of the closed letter the name of the ship and the date of sailing before posting it in Sauchiehall Street. Soon after that, I sailed from Birkenhead.

The father of the attraction in India was an accountant in Liverpool, and with the object of asking his permission to marry his daughter, I called upon him. I had stayed at his house some time before, but he was an absent minded man and when I sent up my name and was duly announced, he thought I had come to have my accounts audited. I hadn't the courage to disabuse his mind or to mention the real object of my visit. I hummed and hawed and sat on the edge of my chair and twirled my hat in my hands. Eventually I found myself outside in the street with my mission still unfulfilled.

I made my way to the boat and for many days lay in my bunk and wished for death. When I came to life, off the coast of Portugal, the sun was shining and the gulls screaming overhead.

When we got to Port Said a letter was awaiting me. It was not what the most ardent optimist would call a forthcoming letter, it strongly advised me to go home and not make a fool of the maiden by chasing her halfway round the world. I sat and debated the matter with myself that night as I sat on deck under a tropical sky. I felt the call of the East. I had paid my fare to Bombay. I toyed with the idea that I might see the East and not visit the elusive Pimpernel of my dreams. Alas? I toyed with the idea too long and I found the ship had started and so decided the matter for me.

When I got to Bombay it seemed to me a pity to be in India and not to do that for which I had come. I directed my gharri wallah to take me to the station. I had better say here that I naturally had no experience of weddings abroad and thought that a topper and a morning coat were at least as essential as the ring. Little did I know that toppers and morning coats were not worn in the out-of-the-way State where she lived. But Providence intervened. It appeared that I had considerable excess luggage for the railway journey, so I decided to leave part of it in the luggage office. Unfortunately, the morning coat and topper were left behind by mistake.

Eventually, after a journey of several days and nights, I was decanted on to the platform at the foot of the Himalayas. They rose like a solid wall a few miles away. A wall rising out of the plain and lifting its head to the clouds. A motor road had been made through the mountains, a road of hairpin bends and precipitous drops. It was the time of the riots with the Akalis who wore white turbans by which their anti-British feeling might be known. The driver of the car wore a white turban and my heart quaked at the driver and the road.

We stopped for lunch at a place called a Dak bungalow; a sort of roadhouse of the East where everyone had to sign their names. I scanned the register. My heart missed a beat and then started racing. Her name was in the book. I felt like Dick Barton when he gets a sign that he is on the right road—only there wasn't a Dick Barton in those days.

We arrived at a township perched in the hills. A man I knew was waiting for me there and as there were the two alternatives of walking or of riding a Tibetan pony, he had arranged for the latter. I have said that I am six feet two. I don't know how many hands the pony was—it was so small that probably it would have been measured in thumbs. Anyway, the beast threw me off so consistently that even the local heathen squatting in the dust could scarce forbear to smile. In the end, I gave the pony a miss and set out on foot. The way led over a pass of 8,000 feet and it was twenty miles to my destination. I wrote a brief note telling her to expect me in the late evening. As we clambered down to the mud-coloured city a familiar sound met my ears. It was a pipe band identical with the pipes of home, yet we were in a native State midway between Kashmir and Tibet.

One of the very few white people in the State was an elderly doctor, at whose house I put up. He was the head of the Mission Hospital where the lady worked. She herself came round to the doctor's house to pay me a flying visit about ten o'clock. It was obviously too late to commence tactical operations at that hour. Evidently in the East they started the day early, so I arranged to meet her at 6.30 next morning.

I met her as arranged and the outcome exceeded my highest expectations. By seven o'clock we were engaged, and by eight o'clock she had promised to marry me as soon as she could be released from her job. There was much cabling and writing of letters. In the end I repaid the Mission committee all the expenses for which they were out of pocket, and we arranged to be married in six weeks' time.

The banns were called by an Indian clergyman in Urdu and had I not heard my name pronounced in English I would not have known what was being done. We were married in the little Mission Church on the hillside. The old doctor gave my wife away. Her colleague was the bridesmaid. My best man—of whom more anon —was the elderly gentleman with whom I had walked down the mountainside. A clergyman came two hundred and fifty miles to marry us and quite a party of my wife's friends came up from the plains.

My marriage is memorable for more reasons than one. I got up about five o'clock in the morning, as we were to be married at ten o'clock. I spent the intervening hours pacing round and round the veranda which surrounded the upper part of the doctor's house. As zero hour approached, the best man stationed himself outside on the roadway, from which vantage point he could see both the church and the house from which the bride was leaving in a dandy—a sort of wooden perambulator without wheels which four men were to carry. The best man was to give me the signal when she had left the house. He called up to me and the two of us marched side by side to the church. The way to the church was lined with Indian Scouts and behind them stood the serried ranks of the heathen. Probably not one person there had heard of a Roman holiday, but nevertheless they were having one now, and I was only too well aware that I was the sacrifice. They burst into thin huzzahs. The Scouts waved flags and the crowd made noises indicating that they were pleased. It made me feel proud of my race. I stuck out my chest and strode along. Alas! When we reached the church door we found that we were much too soon, not a soul had arrived, and the departure of the ladies had been a false alarm. There was nothing to do but to return along the lane of Scouts. Both they and the crowd were now strangely silent. I returned to my eyrie in the doctor's house and resumed my pacing.

Once more I heard the signal. This time it was correct, but this time the Scouts and the crowd were silent. They had done their stuff. As we entered the church I gave the best man the ring and he deposited it carefully in his waistcoat pocket. The church was filled with friends of the bride and with scions of the heathen nobility. I stood there before the whole congregation and I am quite sure that I never was so nervous in my life. I would have been disagreeably surprised had I known that in the next minute I would be considerably more nervous. When the clergyman approached the part of the service to do with the ring, I caught a glimpse of the best man going through, not only his waistcoat pockets, but all his pockets. His next step was to turn them outside in and shake them before the whole congregation. Finally, a small hole was discovered in the lower right hand pocket of his waistcoat and the ring traced to its final resting place in the lining round at the back. By various contortions, the ring was worked round to the front. It was then eased upwards and ultimately was extracted through the original hole. While these operations were being carried on the clergyman, who was anxiously watching the proceedings, went slower and slower to give the best man time to retrieve it. He timed it splendidly so that the words sychronised with the ring's appearance.

The rest of the ceremony proceeded normally. We were husband and wife and during a quarter of a century of married life I have never had cause to regret it.

In due course my wife and I welcomed our guests at a wedding breakfast in her house. We noticed that scarcely any food was eaten. At last we sat down to have something ourselves. Everything certainly tasted peculiar. An excitable bearer of my wife's had filled all the salt cellars with bicarbonate of soda! Our adventures were not done yet, however.

The best man had a great reputation as a photographer. It had been arranged that he was to take the wedding photographs. But first, it was right and fitting that our relatives at home should be notified of our marriage. I gave the best man a twenty rupee note and asked him to go across to the post office and send off a suitably worded cable. The post office was only a short distance away and he agreed to go at once. He was away a long time—a very long time—so long, in fact, that I thought he might never come back. When he did, he arrived breathless. It appeared that he had gone to the post office, but that the Postmaster had been unable to change a twenty rupee note and had advised him that the only place to get it changed was at the State Treasury. When he arrived there, the Treasurer was at his country house and out of town. Undaunted, he set out for the country house but, by a merciful Providence, met the Treasurer on the road, and then the entire proceedings had to be carried out in reverse. On his arrival he reminded me of a king of the Old Testament who is aptly described as " faint yet pursuing ".

The Rajah had kindly lent me a horse and a syce for the occasion, My wife was carried in a dandy by her four bearers. A syce is a sort of horse engineer who sees that the horse is in good running repair. Incidentally, my chief endeavour was to keep the horse in low gear all the time. When we got to the top of the pass, the path winds for miles along a narrow ledge with a sheer precipice below and a sheer precipice above. I felt very naked as I sat astride my horse and peered into the depths below. I decided that the time for action had come. Calling the syce alongside I ordered him to take hold of the horse's tail. It gave me a great feeling of security to have him—literally—at my back.

We waited at one of the wider parts of the path for a Hindu wedding to pass us. The little Hindu bride pulled aside her curtains and the two ladies looked at each other with the eyes of connoisseurs. It was late when we arrived at our destination, Kajear, possibly one of the most beautiful spots in the world, with its deodar trees, its lake and its curious floating island. The Rajah had lent us his bungalow beside the lake and everything was made ready for us.

By easy stages we went down to the plains and saw many cities there. We went to Jummu in Kashmir. We saw the Taj Mahal by moonlight. Ultimately we caught the P. & O. liner *Karapara* at Bombay. We were bound for the port of Beira in Portuguese East Africa.

I chiefly remember that voyage for my peregrinations up and down the deck with a potentate from Zanzibar. He was, of course, an Arab and wore the long robes of an Arab, but wherever we went there was a little Negro boy carrying a brass tray with coffee and two cups. It was thick, treacly stuff, not a bit like the brew which is served after lunch.

I remember my wife saying to me that she had a queer feeling about a man who sat next to her at table. I talked to the man and found that he was the public executioner for the East African Colonies and that he was on his way to carry out a job of work. That was one of the earliest lessons I had that a woman is endowed with a sense of intuition which is lacking in us males. It is the same with a woman's reasoning powers. She often doesn't know how she gets there, but the answer is often beyond what a man can arrive at by mere logic.

CHAPTER VIII

AFRICA

WE arrived at Blantyre in Nyasaland. We were three months there and I remember it chiefly as a time of waiting. The rains made the journey to Lomweland, which was our destination, impossible at that time of the year. We were allotted the loneliest bungalow in the Mission, which at that time happened to be empty. We were warned that not infrequently it was liable to be broken into by natives and the contents burgled.

Undeterred, we slept with the long french windows of our bedroom open. The house was single storeyed and consisted of four rooms opening off each other. One night in the black darkness before dawn, I was awakened by my wife. She whispered that she had been roused by the sound of footsteps on the rush matting of the bedroom floor. The footsteps had come from the direction of the window and disappeared in the direction of the door leading to the next room. I sat up and listened. I listened for what seemed to me a long time. I was just in the act of lying down, and of reassuring my wife in the patronising tone of voice which husbands in similar circumstances are apt to assume, when there came a resounding crash from the far end of the house.

The crash called for investigation and action. I arose and put on my shoes, for a man without his feet shod feels a poor fellow. I lit a candle. I knew I had a revolver somewhere. I found it, with difficulty, wrapped in an old shirt. Unfortunately, it was innocent of ammunition so I determined to fall back on strategy. I seem to have a blind spot in my reasoning faculties when I am in such a situation. I reasoned that when the native saw the revolver he would throw up the sponge and speedily submit. My wife was determined to seek death or glory and armed herself with a walking stick. The little procession set forth. I went in front with the candle in one hand and the revolver in the other. My wife brought up the rear of the procession with the walking stick. The candle only threw a small circle of light around us, beyond that all was shadowy and dark.

The next room was devoid of furniture—for courtesy's sake we called it the hall. We crossed the blackness of the hall and were just about to enter the dinning-room beyond, when we froze in our tracks. A large and smelly animal rushed out of the dining room door, across the hall and out through our bedroom window. It was a hyena and we found that it had knocked over the milk jug and that was the noise which we had heard. My wife was in fits of laughter. I myself felt that the moment was not one for merriment, so asked her what she was laughing at.

"At you," she said.

"Me?"

"Yes, do you know what you were doing the whole time?"

"Yes, I was bluffing the burglar."

"No you weren't. You were pressing the trigger so hard that the barrel was going round and round, and every tick it made proved that there were no bullets in it."

The natives of Africa have a great liking for highly smelling fish. Rotten fish are the *piece de resistance* of native food. They are the black man's caviare throughout the length and breadth of Africa. It was no uncommon sight for a native with a pole on his shoulders, from which were suspended these highly smelling fish, to pass our house of a morning. It was rather like the Breton onion men at home. Only onions are to rotten fish what spicy breezes are to a gas attack. Highland chiefs are said to prefer their game high and the higher the chief the higher the game. The same rule applies to Africa apparently.

The head of the mission and myself did not always see eye to eye. The differences between us have faded with the years, and anyway he has long been called to that far bourne from whence no traveller returns. However, at the time, rightly or wrongly, I thought I had a grievance against him and determined to have honours even before I left Blantyre.

I determined to use my old weapon of impersonation. A broad brimmed hat, a double-breasted linen suit and some dye for my hair were about all the disguise I had on. Armed with these and a pair of rimless eyeglasses and pads for my cheeks to alter their contour, I set forth. When I arrived at his house, he was dictating a letter on the veranda. I introduced myself as Wilbur P. Wright from Cleveland, Ohio. I spoke with a strong American accent as I sketched out what we proposed to do. I led him to understand that I represented an American denomination that he had probably never heard of—the Sacramental Gospellers. I told him that we proposed buying some land on the other side of the road from the Mission and intended starting a Mission there. I told him a lot more. I told him that we Americans believed anything could be done with the almighty dollar and that the Sacramental Gospellers were prepared to pour out their last nickel. I wound up by telling him that we specialised in proselytising from other Missions and we believed in letting them do the spadework first. I watched his blood pressure getting higher and higher. He strode up and down in agitation. He murmured something about " moral standards ". I countered by replying that the Sacramental Gospellers hadn't got any. When his blood pressure was near boiling point I removed my eye-glasses and winked at the typist. It appeared that I was trying to put into effect the lack of moral standards which the Sacramental Gospellers stood for. As the head of the Mission was now beyond human speech, I decided to call it a day and spoke in my natural voice. When I had fully revealed who I really was, he took it remarkably well. To this day I am not sure whether it was due to relief brought about by the fact that Wilbur P. Wright and the Sacramental Gospellers would certainly not appear, or whether it was mere admiration for my histrionic abilities, but he insisted that I call on the other missionaries and carry out a similar deception. Yes, he took it very well, for it was a knock-out blow and I had rubbed salt into the wound which I had made.

One day we noticed natives about the place who were very different from those we were accustomed to see around Blantyre. Their only clothing was a loincloth made from the inner bark of a tree. They had the appearance of wild men from another world. It was a sign that our final journey was about to begin.

These men carried a long pole, beneath which was slung a hammock. This was called a " machila ", and I soon found that getting into a " machila " was a skilled business. Until one has learned the art one went in at one side, only to make a spectacular and unexpected appearance at the other. Two men carried the front of the pole and two the back. They neither walked nor ran. They shuffled, and they shuffled remarkably quickly. The four men sang as they carried, taking their time from the leader. When they had done their turn they were relieved by another four. That is the normal method of travel in primitive Africa.

Day by day we proceeded on our way. Sometimes we walked ;

sometimes we were carried. The rest of the boys walked in single file, one behind the other, each with a load upon his head. Our way lay by the foot of Mount Mlange, a tremendously high plateau —not unlike that described in " King Solomon's Mines ". There a remarkable coincidence occurred. When I was at Watson's I had been school champion at the annual games, and there, at the back of the back of beyond, I met the man who had been runner-up on that day. He was wearing a tie of the old school and for auld lang syne's sake insisted on taking it off and tying it round my machila pole.

It was a wonderful tribute to British administration that the moment we left Nyasaland we left a land of gardens and smiling contented natives. As soon as we had crossed the border we entered a land of desolation. We scarcely passed a village for many days. Forced labour and ill-treatment had played their part, the natives had fled to British territory.

One day the boy scout path on which we had travelled for so many days developed into a road, and we knew that we were near our destination. Our bungalow was the first one in the Mission. It had four rooms. The padre and his wife resided in one half, we occupied the other. The roof was of thatch and the bungalow was built of brick. It was a good bungalow. It was my idea of what a bungalow ought to look like.

It had one great drawback, however. Some previous owner had nailed a sheet on to the crossbeams of our bedroom and white-washed it to represent a ceiling. Our sitting-room and the padre's rooms were innocent of any such covering. In the thatch lived a colony of rats and a colony of snakes. They weren't small snakes, they were as long as one's arm and we understood that their bite was fatal. Every now and again one or the other member of the colonies would fall to the ground from the thatch up above. In fact the padre's wife, when she was sitting by her own fireside one night, got a squealing rat literally down the back of her neck. Every night, about fifteen minutes after the lights had been put out in our bedroom, the same series of events took place. First, across the sagging sheet above our bed would come the patter of a rat, followed closely by the slithering motion of a snake. Then would follow a sort of free fight when the rat would scream and the final sound was the rat being swallowed by the snake. After which we usually went to sleep and the snake presumably did likewise.

To go back to that first day, however. When night time came I descended on the hospital to do a night round as I had been accustomed to do at home. What was my astonishment to find not a single bed with a patient in it. The very ill ones—and they seemed few in number—were lying *underneath* the beds. The natives weren't used to beds and distrusted them at sight. The beds had been sent out all the way from Scotland at considerable expense, but not a native would sleep in them.

All the rest of the patients were huddled round the fire having their supper. Their supper was a black mass crawling up the mantelpiece. I walked over to investigate. It was a mass of black hairy caterpillars. Every now and again a native would absentmindedly detach one from the mass and singe off its bristles in the fire before popping it into his mouth.

The Elomwe—which, incidentally, means dogs—were a very backward race. Something of their state of development may be gathered from the fact that rats and mice were staple articles of diet and were consumed raw, being held by the tail in the fire until their fur was burnt off.

No female nurses were on the staff of the hospital. Only men —known as boys—a boy might be middle-aged, but he never grew beyond the stage of being a boy. These boys had a natural aptitude for hospital work. They gave all my anæsthetics, and in spite of the most extensive operations I never saw a death under an anæsthetic. As a matter of fact the African native seems to take an anæsthetic extremely well.

I was the only white doctor in an area exceeding that of France and Italy combined. It may be thought that in consequence I was considerably overworked. I wasn't, however. My biggest competitors were the witch doctors of the natives. It was just when I had to leave that I was gaining the confidence of the natives, and the numbers attending the hospital were growing very considerably. I remember, for instance, a man coming to me with a tubercular elbow early in my stay there, and as these things inevitably take a long time to get right, I lost him to my professional rival the witch doctor.

One curious phenomenon I couldn't help noting. I never saw a case of cancer all the time I was working there. Nor did I see a case of a gastric ulcer, nor duodenal ulcer, nor an acute appendicitis. When I worked among semi-civilised natives, who copied the ways of the white man whenever possible, these diseases were not common, but they did occur. It seemed to me that the only factor which they had in common with us was food and, it would seem, that preserved or adulterated food is one of the main factors in causing these conditions. I have no statistics on the subject. I am merely stating the facts as I saw them.

The mentality of these people is not high, though perhaps we are apt to judge them by the standards of civilisation. For example, I remember speaking to a raw native in a room of my house. I went out and shut the door after me. Many hours later I chanced to go back and found the boy still in my room. I had forgotten him, but all he had to do to get out was to turn the handle and open the door, but he had no knowledge of handles and remained an involuntary prisoner.

I also remember some yards of cotton cloth being awarded as first prize for the sprint at the school sports. The following day a native who chanced to be passing came to me and offered to run for cloth. Apparently he thought that all he had to do was to run and he would get the much-coveted cloth.

It was a wonderful country we were in. Far off, on the horizon, like the jagged edge of a saw, were strange-shaped mountains. Probably unexplored, certainly unnamed. The Mission itself was surrounded by irregular hills covered with trees, trees, trees, endless trees stretching to the horizon on every side and the green cultivated patch of the Mission ground in the centre.

It was curious to see the children coming to school and invariably carrying two things with them, a spear and a small bird-cage containing a captured bird. The use of the spear for defensive purposes was obvious in a country where one might meet a lion on the road to school. The bird-cage, however, was purely fanciful and was a symptom of the devotion to pets which is a characteristic of the African native.

As it was near the equator it got dark all the year round about five-thirty. There were only a few minutes of twilight and then it was completely dark except for the light of the moon.

I doubt if I did much real missionary work of an evangelistic nature. I am quite sure that the most efficient missionary work done among the natives was done by the natives themselves. I have grave doubts as to whether our standard of morality can find a common level to arouse the spiritual life of the natives. For example, how can a raw native leading his simple, uncomplicated life have anything in common with one who lives in a

THE SPAN OF TIME

house with totally different standards of living from what he has ?
The thing to realise is that these natives are just children, and as
children they require discipline, love and repeated teaching. So
the native has to be told simple facts repeatedly.

I remember coming one day to a native village which no white
man had previously visited. As the chief squatted by the embers
of his fire I told him the simple gospel story about the life and death
of Christ. He heard me in silence, and when I had done an
understanding gleam came into his eyes and he said, " That's a
good story, bwana. I like it, but the unfortunate thing is that by
to-morrow I'll have forgotten all about it. You'll have to come
back and tell me the story often if I am to remember it."

That is the problem of missions in Africa in a nutshell. So
often missions are criticised for metaphorically putting natives
into trousers and making them, at least outwardly, civilised. But
spiritual development and ethical development go hand in hand,
and at least, in my limited experience, the development of spirit
is always put first.

Looking back on it, I think that the efforts of a gifted and conse-
crated African are worth all the efforts of white missionaries put
together. We had such a man on our staff. This man spoke no
less than eight different languages and did practically all the
translating for the Mission. He was a very humble man. Several
times I have asked him to my own house to a meal, for he was a
man whom one would have delighted to have as a guest in one's
home, but I could never persuade him. He was an African and
I was a white man. He was far too sensitive to give me his real
reason, however. His father was a typical native, squatting on
his haunches beside a wood fire. The Christian word " grace "
is often spoken about, but seldom seen. One of the best examples
I have ever known is this man, who was an African, a Christian
and a gentleman.

Wild animals one was aware of chiefly at night, but one rarely
came across them during the day. It happened that one day
the Padre and I set out with a gun apiece and a pocketful of cartridges with the intention of shooting guinea fowl for the pot.
Not finding any, and as dusk was about to fall, we turned homewards. As we were walking along through the jungle I turned
to him and said :

" How many cartridges have you got left ? "

" One," he replied, " in my gun."

"So have I," I said. "It's to be hoped that we don't meet anything large on the way home."

We had a small white terrier with us called "Sugar", and "Sugar" had gone off to investigate something on our left. I followed him in that direction, for what reason I know not. Maybe a slight movement had caught my eye, maybe it was just impulse. Anyway, I soon made up on the dog, who sprang back and cowered between my feet, shaking all over. I looked to see what had frightened him, and there, only a few yards ahead, was a full-grown leopard lying alongside a fallen tree trunk. The beast was so near that I could look straight into his eyes. They were green and stared at me unwinkingly. I must admit that I was very frightened, as I expected it to spring at any moment. Actually it was almost certainly after the dog, and probably would not have harmed me unless I had attacked it.

I presented the gun at it and stepped slowly backwards. I had not gone two or three paces when I fell over something. It was the dog, who had run away from the first leopard and had almost fallen into the arms of its mate, who was lying by a fallen branch just behind me. The dog had rushed back to seek my protection and had shrunk into my heels. I picked myself up and luckily the gun did not go off. As I looked round and saw that my retreat was cut off I literally felt the hairs on the back of my scalp becoming vertical. Slowly I swung the gun from one leopard to the other. Whichever sprang first would get the contents of the gun in his head. I couldn't hope to kill it with a shotgun, but I might blind it. Slowly, ever so slowly, and making no sudden movement to frighten the beasts, I stepped between them and slowly backed to the shelter of a tree. My hand was shaking so much that I had to rest the gun against its trunk to keep it reasonably straight. Nothing happened. I rejoined the padre and we arrived home together in the dark. What had seemed to me an eternity of hours had only occupied a very few minutes. The dog "Sugar" was caught several weeks later by a leopard while he was asleep on the veranda. Dogs have a short life in Africa.

I had one other inglorious adventure with an animal of a different species. One day the Padre and I had gone out on his motorcycle, which, incidentally, the natives called a "tiki-tiki". I was seated in the side-car with a rifle over my shoulders. The padre on the cycle was unarmed. As we rounded a bend in the path we were astonished to see a lioness sitting in our way a few yards ahead. The lioness looked very rampant and was slowly swinging her tail from side to side in an aggressive spirit, which suggested that something had disturbed her. My first impulse was to stop the motor-cycle and to have a shot with the rifle. Not so the padre ; he drove the bicycle straight at the lioness and blew the horn loudly. The lioness gave a disdainful look over her shoulder and stalked into the forest. It probably thought that the danger to life and limb was greater from the motor-cycle than from a rifle aimed by my hand.

The Padre—like all men from Glasgow—was a born engineer. Both he and I had motor-cycles and side-cars with which we used to tootle along the paths wherever they were broad enough to take them. These motor-cycles had literally been sent up from Nyasaland in a bag, and Big Andrew—the Padre—had put them together in Lomweland.

One day he asked my wife and me to accompany his wife and himself to a new church which he was opening. It was in a well-populated district where no mission work had been carried on previously. We said we would be delighted to go, and one Sunday morning two motor-cycles and side-cars set out from the Mission. We got as far as the Moloque river, which was almost to our destination, and there the motor-cycles had to stop.

On the opposite side of the river were ranged the tribe which Big Andrew proposed to work amongst. Prominent among them was the chief—Muchema—arrayed in a khaki Balmoral bonnet and a loincloth. The rest had no clothes whatever, only the inner bark of a tree acting as a loincloth for them. There was literally not a yard of cloth among the many hundreds of natives present. We crossed the river by a fallen tree trunk and made our way up to the new church. I found myself next the chief as we walked.

My wife was surrounded by hundreds of women who, with true feminine curiosity, investigated a white petticoat which she happened to be wearing. The women uttered loud expressions of surprise and ooh's and wulus were universal, the gist of their remarks being that such a beautiful garment should certainly be exposed to public view.

As I say, I found myself walking beside the chief. We had not gone very far when he turned to me and said :

" Where's the snake ? "

Now, I had better explain that I owned an imitation snake. It was very realistic, and when one held it by the middle its tail

and body wagged. When I wanted to get a crowd together all
I had to do was to hold the snake aloft. I first found its potency
in Blantyre when I took it out of my pocket. Unfortunately, a
group of natives were lifting a piano nearby. When they saw the
snake they dropped the piano and ran for their lives. The piano
was never the same again. And now, in this out-of-the-way corner,
"Where's the snake?" The fame of my snake had travelled far.
I told him that the snake was probably in the foot of my side-car
on the other side of the river. He was very anxious to see it, so
I explained carefully to a small boy who was by my side that no
harm could possibly come to him by carrying it, and directed him
to go back across the river and fetch the snake from my side-car.
I regret to say the matter passed from my mind entirely and I
proceeded up the hill with Muchema.

When we got to the church it was packed. Outside it was
swelteringly hot, but inside it was pleasantly cool. The church
was made entirely of bamboo and had not a nail in its structure.
A very long aisle led up the middle and for coolness there were
gaps left in the side walls which served also as exits. The pews
were roughly-shaped trees resting on forked branches thrust into
the ground. One end of the church was raised as a platform and
contained a Communion table, a pulpit and a lectern. On the
platform were seated Muchema the chief, the Padre and his wife,
ourselves and the local Portuguese official. These, along with a
handful of native Christian boys, made up the platform party.

The congregation, as I have said, was large. From the platform
it looked a seething mass of black humanity—men and women
with young children lifting up their voices in the international
language of the young, and being pacified by their mothers in the
method common to all mankind. Through the doorways, clustered
scores of black piccaninnies, and stretching beyond them were
masses of humanity who had been unable to obtain a seat.

Andrew opened the proceedings with a hymn. The hymn was
that well-known children's hymn, " Jesus loves me, this I know ".
As Andrew and I were no choristers the singing resolved itself into
a duet by our respective wives, with the native Christians forming
a low undertone to the singing of the ladies. There are three
verses in the hymn, which had been translated into the Lomwe
language along with the refrain. The first verse, as I have said,
was a duet between the two ladies. At the second verse it became
obvious that the congregation had become aware that they were

expected to take part, for a low humming noise without words or tune was produced by the people present. The ladies came to the end of the second verse, but the humming increased in volume and made no pause whatever between the verses. By the time the third verse was reached the humming had risen to a shrill crescendo. Every soul in the building was shouting at the top of his voice. What they were saying I know not, but I can well remember a large number whistling shrilly, as evidently they thought they could make more noise by that means. The duet continued bravely, but their efforts were as nothing against that deafening background. The hymn drew to an end, but the noise continued, and eventually it was brought to a close by Andrew holding up his hand and announcing that he was going to speak to the great Mulungu—in other words to say a prayer.

Now, Andrew was a minister of the Auld Kirk, and, as is right and proper, prayed with his eyes shut. He did not, therefore, see what I saw. In the middle of the prayer, at the far end of the church, appeared the boy carrying the snake. He bore it aloft, carrying it as far as possible from his body. Slowly he made his way up the aisle and approached the platform. The congregation watched the snake fascinated, and then with one accord made for the doors. They moved silently but rapidly. Andrew must have sensed something wrong, for when he opened his eyes a most extraordinary sight met his gaze. The boy stood directly in front of him, holding the snake at arm's length. The congregation to a man—or rather to a woman—had vanished to the four winds of heaven. He had started his prayer with a crowded congregation, now not a soul was in the building except the few individuals on the platform. The chief soon got them together again, the snake was put away and Andrew started once more, this time with a greater measure of success.

I found leprosy was endemic in the place. Practically every village had one or two lepers, but, curiously enough, the other villagers were not frightened of them. There was no attempt at isolation or segregation. The treatment is long and costly. Invariably the natives ceased to attend for injection and the only way to ensure continuity of treatment was to carry it out in prison. As the Portuguese were always willing to arrest a person and the sentence was invariably indefinite detention, I found that prison sometimes had its uses as well as its abuses.

The language was another difficulty. Actually I was much

better at speaking the native language than my previous experience with French dared lead me to expect. It had its difficulties, however. In the native lingo a lot of the words sound very much alike. Sometimes I got into trouble.

I had a great desire to shoot an eland, and I had let it be known that if that animal appeared in the grounds I was to be notified immediately. One day I was down at what was known as the shop—a place where some trifles could be bought—when a native appeared breathlessly and told me that an eland was in the fields nearby. I hurriedly got a rifle and made for the place without a moment's delay. I bade the native remain in attendance while I crawled on my stomach across a bare field towards a tree he pointed out as where the eland was. The hour was that approaching lunch-time when the sun was at its hottest. I lay on my stomach and grilled. When eventually I got to the tree stump the excited native pointed to a further tree on the horizon where he assured me that it now was. Eventually I reached the place he indicated, only to find that it had once again moved. And so we progressed until I could stand it no more. Hunger and thirst and heat had done their worst and I was beaten. I had never glimpsed anything like an eland.

" There it is," said the native at my heels.

I looked and saw—a crow. The native words for a crow and an eland are almost identical to our ears, though to a native they sound vastly different. Anyhow, a crow I had been looking for and to a crow I was led.

When my wife was expecting her first baby we made the startling discovery that if it were a boy it would be liable for service in the Portuguese army—at least so we thought. Such a contingency was not to be contemplated, and ultimately it was decided that she should go home. She could either go back to Nyasaland and home from there or make for Quilimaine and get a boat there for Beira. Either way presented serious difficulties. The journey to Nyasaland meant a long trek in the machila with its inevitable sickness for her. She felt she could not face it. At that time a German lady from Quilimaine was staying with the Padre and his wife, who had moved into a larger house. It was arranged that the Padre should take the German lady, who was elderly and stout, in the side-car, while my wife would sit on the back of the motor-cycle. I myself was down with malaria at the time, and so took no further part in the proceedings. What actually happened I learned long afterwards.

The little party of three set off at dawn. The earthen roads were passable, but the shrubbery on them had grown knee high. Every bridge was down and the Padre, who was over six feet in height and of the build of Joe Louis, carried the ladies bodily across the rivers. Boys had been sent on ahead with the bedding and had been told to meet the party at a certain village, where they expected to be by nightfall. The travellers expected to pass the last Portuguese boma about 10 a.m., and as we had always been offered a meal there, they naturally assumed that a similar thing would happen on this occasion. Their later meal they took with them in the shape of a cooked chicken. This is what actually happened.

They duly got to the Portuguese boma and found that the meal was finished, and, unfortunately, they were not offered any refreshment. The trio drove on. When it came to their mealtime they found that the intense heat had made the chicken go bad, so that meal was unfortunately lost.

There was no sign of their carriers at the appointed place, and that night they found a deserted hut in the forest and wearily lay down on the floor. Hunger drove them to eat some green bananas which they found growing near the door, but the bananas only gave them severe pains instead of satisfying their appetites. Next morning, aching and hungry, they drove on again, and about 10 a.m. met their carriers, whom they found had mistaken the village. They had a good meal and drove on. In the latter part of the day, while they still had eighty miles to go, Andrew's back tyre blew out. They had no spare, but Andrew was a man of resource. With his knife he cut off the bark from a tree and tied it round the rim of the wheel so that a solid tyre was formed, and with that they pressed on. My wife was still on the back of the motor-cycle and the stout lady was in the side-car. In the evening they came to the house of a Portuguese and borrowed machilas from him.

They travelled all night to catch the train at five o'clock in the morning. They got there in time only to find that the train had left an hour before to suit the convenience of a Portuguese who was travelling by it. The train to Quilimaine only ran twice weekly and there was nothing to do but wait four days for the next.

The journey to Quilimaine is only fifty miles long but the Portuguese have been careful not to make any kind of a road from the railhead so that a traveller is compelled to use the railway. The railway must surely be unique among the railways of the world. It is divided into three sections by two rivers but—the sections of the railway have each a different gauge. There are bridges to cross the rivers and the bridges have been deposited at the appropriate places but owing to the inertia of the tropics they have remained there for many years. Maybe a passing native sees what he thinks will be useful to him and goes off with it. Maybe a bolt gets lost. Ultimately, the bridge is like a meccano without anything to hold it together, and so the old, old method is used of taking all the passengers across the river in a boat which is taken to the opposite bank by means of a native in the bows pulling on a rope stretched across the river. The bridges lie derelict.

The fact that the railway is only fifty miles long and the trains take all day to do the journey is a mere incident. On the slightest gradient the passengers can get out and walk, as they often do.

To return to the odyssey of my wife. The Padre had to leave them there and return to the Mission. The two ladies stayed with a Portuguese family near the railhead for the necessary days until the second train of the week was due. They then travelled down to Quilimaine and my wife stayed with the German lady there for three weeks until a boat which was going to Beira came in to the harbour. When she boarded it, she found that she was the only female on board. There wasn't even a female cat to accompany her. The journey to Beira was a stormy one all the way. When they got there they found a German ship in the roadstead. Her actual time on the sea was forty-nine days. Her baby was born at the beginning of June.

One more incident I have to relate. It happened when the ship was a day out from Lisbon in the Bay of Biscay. A storm was raging when there came a tremendous crash. The mother of a child in the cabin next to her got an attack of hysterics and the little child was left unattended in the cabin. Everyone thought the ship was going to the bottom. When my wife rushed down to the cabin to bring the child up to safety she found the cabin and the corridor knee deep in water. When she had duly delivered the child to her mother, it was found that a great wave had torn away part of the railing round the deck and flung it with tremendous force against the port holes, smashing them and allowing the sea water to pour into the cabins and lower corridors. No permanent damage was done and the voyage proceeded to its termination. Apart from the fact that she had a severe attack of ptomaine poisoning during the voyage, it was otherwise uneventful.

Every night I could hear the throb of the tom toms beating. Sometimes they were strangely quiet and were merely tapping out messages while on other nights they had a rapid dancing rhythm and beat faster and faster until the forest seemed to be alive with the sound. I used to listen to the tom toms as I went up and down on my late rounds of the hospital. One night the air was vibrant with them. I have neither liking nor ear for jazz but the rhythm of the tune seemed to pulsate through the night air and the jazz of the dance bands at home seemed but a pale reflection of what I was hearing.

I asked Alexander, my head hospital boy, what the tom toms were for.

" It's the miripelli," he said.

"Well, whatever it is, I'm going, and you are going to take me ! "

" Oh no, bwana, it is dangerous. The white man mustn't go to the miripelli."

I could see Alexander was seriously perturbed and didn't want to go. But whether it was his skin or mine that he was afraid for, I was unable to determine. Well, my wife was away, and as I walked up to the house from the hospital the tom toms sounded more alluring than threatening.

I turned back to the hospital.

" Come on, Alexander, we're going to the miripelli."

It was a very reluctant Alexander who ultimately came with me and we were got up like a couple of brigands when we set out. Alexander led the way with a lantern in one hand and a spear in the other. Round his belt was slung an axe, a knife not unlike a kukri, and various lethal instruments. I contented myself with a shotgun and a revolver. A walking stick was not so much for defensive purposes as to assist me on my way. Thus armed we set forth.

I have no idea whatever where we went. I don't even know which direction we took, for the path seemed to bend back on itself and then twist and turn in all directions. I know that sometimes we were going through swamps, for our feet would go squelch, squelch in the water, but generally it was steady going through the jungle with the lantern flickering on the tree trunks as we passed. It was a curious thing, but sometimes the sound of the tom toms would be loud and sharp and at other times faint and far away. I suppose it was due to the direction of the air currents or possibly to the contour of the land. We had been walking for what seemed to me hours, but was probably much shorter, when the most extraordinary sight met my eyes.

In the middle of a clearing was a huge bonfire. It was made of tree trunks lying horizontally on the ground and piled on top of one another till they reached some six feet in height. Round the fire were prancing several hundred natives arrayed in the strangest attire one could imagine. Their faces were painted white or red and most of them had horns from some animal or other sticking out of the side of their head. They had little gourds filled with pebbles tied to the back of their legs and thighs, and pieces of tin, probably salvaged from my ash buckets or my colleagues', slung across their backs. Round their waists was a thick grey grass, not unlike the skirt of a ballet dancer. A man was squatting on his haunches beating out a tattoo on a tom tom with his fingers. All the natives were gyrating in a wide circle round the bonfire, stamping with their feet and posturing in a sort of devil dance. Every now and again the whole circle of natives would stop and waggle their tails, when all the grasses would shake and the shudder would seemingly go right down their legs so that the pebbles in the little gourds would rattle and the pieces of tin on their backs would knock together.

When the natives saw me standing on the edge of the forest, they all stopped immediately. Then I did one of the few wise things I have ever done in my life. I laid down my firearms and went over to them with my hands in my pockets. I am not a particularly brave man but I had no sensation of fear whatsoever. I think I was too interested to be afraid.

I walked over to them and said,

" I have heard of the miripelli and I have always wanted to see it. We in our country have our dances and you have yours. As long as they are carried out in the right spirit, it's quite all right."

I noticed some large gourds full of native beer standing around. I also noticed some women in the offing. Nobody made a move and the silence grew marked, in fact it became ominous. Then I hit on the one thing which I thought would save the situation. I pushed the man away from the tom tom and started playing it myself. I soon found that carrying the fingers loosely and playing with the knuckles were the secrets of success. When the natives saw me playing the tom tom, or rather trying to play it, they started grinning. When they laugh they don't so much laugh with their bodies as we do, they grin with their mouths more, so that they show lots of teeth. An African's grin can be a really infectious thing.

Well, they started laughing and I knew I had won. Soon the dance started again with its posturing and stamping. Soon the whole circle were swaying round the fire one behind the other. I stayed with them a long time, most of the night I think. I became quite an expert at the tom tom by the time I had done. The native beer remained untouched and the native women disappeared. In the wee sma' hoors I bade them good-night and, walking to the edge of the forest, found Alexander patiently waiting to lead me home.

I think that night's performance was the high spot of my missionary career and I consider that it must be unique for a white man to have played the tom tom at the dance of the miripelli.

The following story was written for publication some time ago. For various reasons it never saw the light of day and as it contains the story of how I came to leave the Mission, I reproduce it now, without any acknowledgements or permission. It relates a strange experience which I had.

"It was that cool hour which succeeds the dawn, when everything is dripping with dew and the very air seems to sparkle with vitality. As was my custom, I was sitting on the veranda reading some technical work for an hour before commencing my day's work at the Mission hospital. At that moment I was deep in an article of the *British Medical Journal* and quite oblivious to my surroundings.

Dimly, with one half of my mind, I had subconsciously registered the fact that M'purukuma, our houseboy, was sweeping up the leaves which had blown on the verandah during the night. M'purukuma, I may mention, was covered with literally a veneer of civilisation, the veneer being represented by an old shirt and a pair of khaki shorts. Our regular houseboy having had to go home to Nyasaland, my wife was trying to train this raw product of the native Elomwe into the useful, non-smelly houseboy of civilisation.

"Bwana ti okwa." The white man is dead.

He made the statement as if it were some domestic fact of household importance. He continued to sweep the leaves. It must have been a few seconds before the statement dawned on my consciousness.

"Eh?" I said, and then as I came to a full realisation of what he was saying, I roused myself and said "Which Bwana?"

" Bwana a Garue," he replied—the white man at Garue Boma.

" Really," I replied, now thoroughly aroused to attention and intensely interested. " When did he die ? "

He indicated with his out-stretched hand.

" When the moon was there." Somewhere about two o'clock.

" Which night ? "

" This night, Bwana. The white man was very ill—he had been in great pain for some days. The pain got worse about midnight. He called for his machila and ordered his machila-men to carry him to you, Bwana. The ulendo started, but he had not gone a mile or two when a fresh spasm of pain compelled him to turn back. They carried him to his house and laid him upon the bed. He was in great pain. After a time he drank something out of a bottle— something dark and sticky—soon afterwards the pain seemed to grow easier, and then he died."

M'purukuma told me this story soon after daylight—some four hours after Senhor de Lingua committed suicide. There was no attempt at embellishment. There was just a plain statement of fact. I asked him how he knew.

" Kahi," he replied, which any man who has lived between the Congo and the Zambesi, knows to mean " I don't know," and if he has lived there for several years longer, he will know that it has the additional meaning of " I won't tell." Kahi can mean nothing or it can mean a lot. In this particular case it meant a bucketful. Evidently the bush telegraph, in the shape of tree-tapping or tom toms, had carried the news—complete with details—some seventy miles. That was the way I got to know of the death of Senhor de Lingua. I little thought that I was to be the next to lie on that deer-skin bed in the room with the high wooden Arab doors and the smell of death.

* * * *

I was worried about the thatch on our bungalow. One spark not immediately extinguished and it was goodbye to everything we possessed. In consequence I had a festoon of piccaninnies on the roof, each one with a jug of water and hugely enjoying themselves. A bush fire was no novelty but this one was more than a novelty— it was nearly a tragedy.

I distinctly remember the roar—like an express train—and the heat, as the natives burned ahead of the advancing fire. There must have been scores of natives—all very willing, all very excited. Gradually the fire was got under. Little tongues of flame licked the burnt grass, flickered, then died out. I rushed from group to group, encouraging, scolding. I suddenly realised that I was desperately tired.

Something caused me to look over my shoulder. A file of Portuguese sepoys were drawn up behind me. (How quietly these natives move.) The sergeant saluted and handed me a letter. My heart sank, for this conscience doth make cowards of us all. Immediately my mind flashed to the shooting I had done for which I had no licence. The letter was addressed to me personally. My Portuguese was none of the best, but I soon disentangled what it was all about. The writer was a Frenchman in the employ of the government of Portuguese East Africa. I gathered that he had much pain in the stomach and was very, very sick. His sepoys (pronounced sepeys) had a machila to carry me, food for the journey and, in fact, everything to expedite my progress. A postscript to the letter, which already stressed the urgency of his need, bade me, in the flowery Portuguese phrases, come quickly—very quickly, maybe in the hope that it would spur my energies.

My vision of the inside of a Portuguese prison faded and I thoughtfully went indoors to my wife. It was late afternoon when the message arrived and by the time the southern cross was gleaming I was on the road. Lying in the machila listening to the sounds of the hidden life around me, completely made me forget my tiredness.

After supper, I strode along with the sepoys and we got into the foothills of the Namuli mountain, an unclimbed peak of Himalayan proportions which dominated that part of the country. It so happened that I had never been that way before. In our ulendo, as it wound in and out the little native paths among the trees, the foremost and the hindmost men carried lanterns, and in that bobbing flicker of light I felt the air grow colder and colder as we mounted and the shadow of the trees grow fainter and fainter.

The harsh bark of a fox, the trumpeting of an eland—toot tootle ou toot—followed by the cry of the mate—too toot—and at not infrequent intervals the throaty cry of the leopard and the grunt of lion. It was one of those nights to hold in one's memory—a night when one felt untiring and filled with a strange elation.

However, this is not the record of a journey, suffice it to say that the next day I was deadly tired. When the sun came up I was weary and dispirited. I slept the hot sun round and continued the journey in darkness, trying to recapture the magic of that first night. I learned that lesson which we all have learned, that only once can the mood of the gods be captured and in mid-morning of the fourth day I strode into the Garue boma, where only one white man lived —a hot sun-baked group of white buildings lying in a hollow, surrounded by fields of mele corn and bananas. That night we had half waded, half squelched through miles of treeless swamp and the sight of an orderly civilisation with the restful green of the foliage, was good to the eye.

I came to a hut of wattle and daub, wooden windows and tall Arab doors to the roof. A man was lying on the bed inside, a bed made of strips of deer hide nailed to a wooden frame. Cahetic, hollow-cheeked, the tan of the tropics weakened to a sickly yellow, he was effusively grateful for my coming. I must spend a week with him as his guest. His competent houseboy would attend to all my wants. A white-gowned Mohammedan servant appeared to announce that a meal was ready. I waved him away and made my professional examination. It was as I feared, an inoperable cancer of the stomach. Thank goodness I had brought some opium with me for this very purpose.

I went into dinner very thoughtfully. Abstractedly I picked up a roll of bread with a hard crust—like our Vienna rolls—and broke it in two. The roll must have been baked many weeks ago, for a green worm the size and shape of a caterpillar reared itself from the centre of the broken half and commenced to make visible signs that it was alive. I am a man of few words and calm demeanour but I conceived a loathing for that Mohammedan houseboy and the cook and all that wretched crew who were taking advantage of a sick master. I ate a popeia and some oranges and smoked a cigarette while I debated in my own mind what course to pursue.

He was eagerly awaiting my return. His confidence in the " Senhor Doctor " was touching to see. One thing was certain, I was not prepared to eat anything cooked in that house. It was a case of stay and be starved or tramp home and eat. I decided on the latter alternative and pointed out to the Senhor, with a certain degree of truth, that it was impossible for me to leave my patients for an hour longer than was necessary. I regret to say, in all honesty, that the gymnastics of the green worm made my decision sound more imperative than it otherwise would have been. I explained to him that it was essential for him to travel back with me and undergo treatment. Apparently he had not considered such a course but required but little persuasion to give the necessary orders and shortly after noon we were on our way back to Alto Moloque.

The patient stood the journey wonderfully well and he stayed with us several weeks in our bungalow as our guest. During this time, under the influence of sedatives and the correct food, he improved enormously and was getting about the veranda and pottering around the house.

But he was continually worrying to get back to work, and if not to work, to the supervision of his boma. The trouble was this, so far as I could make out. Some years previously he had had a child by a native woman. I think the woman had died, anyway the half-caste child was brought up by him, and when she was old enough she was sent to a convent school at Delagoa Bay. Apparently it was a good school, for the fees were substantial, and the father, having no other source of income except from that of his government post, argued, quite correctly, that if he were absent from his post for any length of time and the authorities were to get to know of it, he might find himself superseded and the child forced to resume the semi-native way of living of the ordinary Portuguese half-caste. I understood his dilemma and though the resumption must, in the nature of things, be very temporary, I felt that that was the best course to pursue. I gave him opium to relieve his pain and such advice about his illness as one could. I promised to go and see him in the near future and made him undertake to let me know if he became suddenly worse.

He returned, and the sequel I have mentioned in the first part of the story.

*　　　*　　　*　　　*

But the end was not yet. Some three months later I was suddenly struck by that devastating, killing scourge known as blackwater fever. For weeks I hung between life and death. It is one of the kinder gifts of the Almighty that the memory does not hold a remembrance of the pain and the fever and the weakness of a bad illness. I must have been very ill but I remember singularly little about it. Strange how trivial things stick in one's mind. I remember lying in the intense heat of a tropical afternoon with the pillows burning into my back.

Gradually the fever left me. The terrible drain of blood from the kidneys ceased. I lay as weak as a babe and as one who was bereft of its mother. The weeks passed but instead of gaining ground I was slowly losing it. Ultimately, big Andrew—the parson —and I, along with the one of two other white people present, went into conference—as the barristers say—and spoke what was in our hearts. Briefly it was this, and we were all agreed upon it.

Either I must stay here and die, or take the risk and make for Nyasaland. Eight days journey by machila, eight days of jolting, swaying and machila sickness, but at the end of it 'beauty, home and England'. I had already made up my mind. A ulendo was made up, but for some curious reason, chiefly, I think, connected with the paucity of villages for food supply, it was decided not to make direct for the Nyasaland border, but to make a big semi-circular route by Garue Boma. No one, apparently, had been that route before. It was a question of seeing all the ills and choosing the route which offered the fewest. Little did we think it was to take us sixteen days.

We started at dawn. The first day we made fair progress, but stops were longer than we bargained for. That first night I slept very little. The next morning at dawn it was forward again. By ten o'clock in the forenoon I was unable to continue. The natives made a sort of hollowed-out haystack for me and pushed my machila into its shady depths. I stayed there till the late afternoon, when we ventured forth again. I forget how many days it took to reach Garue Boma, but each day the journeys got less and less and the mid-day stops grew longer and longer.

One morning we came to the swamps just as the sun was changing from something pleasant to the scorching heat of a furnace door. The swamp was unending. Splosh, splosh, went the feet of the machila men. The reeds were just the right height to irritate my head and my bare knees. When a man is about to faint, he generally is aware of a vacuum where his tummy ought to be and a feeling of intense sickness. I felt both, and soon unconsciousness mercifully supervened. The cavalcade stopped. Brandy, the white man's panacea, was administered. Through mists of intense headache and nausea I struggled back to life again.

I know that I whispered two words to whoever was bending over me—" Garue Boma "—and then I must have passed out again, for the next thing I knew was that the machila was approaching the boma and there was a lot of heavy breathing and grunting from the carriers, as from men who have made a supreme effort to get to their destination. There was some delay while the doors were opened. The tall wooden Arab doors which I remembered so well. Inside it was dimly dark and the temperature was chilly after the blazing heat outside.

The head boy gave an order and the machila was lowered to the level of a bed made of strips of deer-hide nailed to a wooden frame . . . and no human soul had been on that bed since a man had drunk dark, sticky medicine from a bottle—and died. I knew I would never get off that bed alive. The room smelt of death. Fear lent me strength. I protested. I fought. I struggled. Bewildered, the men carried me out to the warmth and the sunshine of the tiny veranda and placed the machila on the ground. More brandy, but strange to say, from that moment I started to get better.

We stayed at Garue Boma three days and then I resumed our journey to Nyasaland. What a journey! I have more memories of slowly cooking inside a haystack than I have of progress in the machila. I remember the onset of the rains, like turning on the big tap in the bathroom. I remember somebody trying to cook dollops of flour and water on the lid of a biscuit tin. I remember starvation, but I was not hungry. I remember two men setting off for Nyasaland and help. The good God gave us it all, food and help, and after many days, cool sheets in the hospital at Blantyre. Funny thing, but Garue Boma nearly cost me my life. I believe it saved it. The dynamic impulse of fear is a very potent medicine."

To complete the story, it only remains for me to add that when I had sufficiently recovered I took the train to Beira and thence to Capetown. The journey occupied many days and nights. As the train passed through Southern Rhodesia I felt dreadfully ill. Unfortunately, I had no one to look after me. At Salisbury I was carried off the train semi-conscious and taken to the hospital there. I went to stay with a doctor in Salisbury for several weeks. When I had recovered my strength I resumed my journey to Capetown and England. I landed at Southampton in the middle of the general strike. Luckily, my bother-in-law was waiting with a car to meet me. I had been just under a year in Lomweland.

CHAPTER IX

MY FIRST PRACTICE

WHEN I came home from abroad I first of all determined to have a long holiday in order to get reasonably fit. I was faced with the prospect of providing for my wife and my child, who had been born shortly after I arrived in this country. My eldest sister, who had kept house for us during most of my adult life, died after a brief illness, and her passing severed one more link with Scotland. I made up my mind to go to London, where my two remaining sisters were married and settled, and to seek my living there, where so many of my compatriots seemed to prosper exceedingly well.

I studied the " Practices for Sale " in the back pages of the *British Medical Journal* and found one which I thought would suit me admirably. It was a practice in London, not far from where my sister lived, and the price purchase was about what I could afford to pay. Unfortunately, I had to buy the house along with the practice, and as it was a leasehold house and not very convenient for living purposes, it was not altogether all one could wish for.

As regards General Practice, I was as green as grass, having never done even a locum in my life. I found I was to buy my experience very dearly. I duly bought the practice in London. It was scarcely what I wished, as, in spite of the legal phraseology of the agreement whereby my introduction was safeguarded, I was not introduced to any private patients whatsoever, for the simple reason that there were none. The practice chiefly consisted of panel patients and a club to which the patients paid a small sum every year and twopence for a bottle of medicine. The patients supplied their own bottles, and naturally a great diversity of bottles was forthcoming. Likewise, as the bargaining instinct was strong in the women who composed the bulk of the club, the size of the bottles sometimes reached mammoth proportions. I never liked the club and always thought that the annual cheque which I got from its secretary was well-earned money.

It will thus be obvious that the practice which I had bought was socially a poor one. The district in which it was situated had once upon a time been flourishing and there were still some better-class families in the neighbourhood, but most of the houses had fallen upon evil days and were let off in flats or even in single rooms. A great many of the inhabitants were " had-beens ", or rather " had never-beens ".

I determined on some radical alterations. Formerly the surgery was in the basement of the house where I lived and the cheerless waiting-room was filled with masses of women, chiefly in shawls, clutching a bottle in one hand and twopence in the other. Now, I abolished the basement altogether and had my consulting-room, as I called it, in the main part of the house along with a newly-decorated waiting-room containing a pile of *Punches* and *Tatlers*, none of which was under a year old.

The practice started to improve immediately, not only in numbers, but in the social standing of its personnel. Quite a few of those who lived in houses occupied by one family came to me.

Curiously enough, I found that the patients were attracted by simple, homely things. For example, it was the custom for our infant daughter to be put out in her pram during the morning consulting hour. I noticed that the people who came to the house went up to her in passing, and she gooed and gurgled to them all. If, however, any person failed to have a word with her in passing, she lifted up her voice and howled until the passer-by came back and made appropriate soothing noises. As most of the patients were women, they grew in time to appreciate this small act, and it became quite a recognised custom for the patients to pay their tribute to the doctor's daughter.

Gradually we slipped into the social groove of our acquaintances and friends. I found social life in England to be more mellow and more tolerant than that in which I had been brought up. In my heart of hearts I think I felt that the Scots folk among whom I had spent so much of my life were made of sterner stuff and were more real. At the same time I felt a trifle *gauche* in English society. I have spoken to other Scotsmen with a similar upbringing to mine, and they, too, have admitted this. The English are a peculiar people. A great number of those whom I met boasted about having Scots blood in their veins. Down south the Scot is admired for his integrity and imperturbability. Luckily the best of our race seems to have migrated south, for there is a class of perfervid Scot who brings many a blush to the cheek of their fellows. These loquacious and noisy individuals out-Scot the Scot, and they are terribly keen to assure the southerner that they come from north of the border. I think it is probable that these people to whom I refer have some inferiority complex hidden away. Gradually I lost my provincialism and came to see that the Scot has a lot to learn from the Englishman and vice versa.

But I soon found I was woefully ignorant of many domestic facts which are not taught in medical textbooks. For example, a lady came to see me one day. Her own complaint was one which was comparatively easily put right, but she mentioned in passing that she was worried about her little boy.

It appeared that his feet had been growing at an abnormal rate. He was four years old and took size ten in shoes. What could I do about it? Well, the fact of the matter was I could do nothing about it, but I determined not to let such an interesting case pass unnoted. I determined to report all the details to the *British Medical Journal*, along with photographs of the child's feet and of the child himself. I saw myself the centre of a lengthy correspondence on the subject, and possibly on the first step to fame. I determined not to let the opportunity slip.

The mother was obviously pleased at the interest which I was taking in her young son, and when I asked her if she would bring him along that evening for a (free) consultation, she readily assented. By the evening I had all my preparations made. The camera was in position and my notebook lay open on my desk.

At six o'clock sharp the bell rang and the mother and her young son were shown in. My mouth must have fallen open in my disappointment, for in walked a perfectly normal little boy in every way. I'd expected to see a pair of enormous feet coming round the door, followed by a small boy on top of them.

This was the actual conversation which took place between the mother and myself.

" I thought you said your boy took size ten in shoes."

" So he does."

" Well, I take size nine and a half and his feet are only a fraction as big as mine."

" But I meant tens in children's sizes, of course."

I did feel a fool, for I had never been taught that there was such a thing as children's sizes. As I say, I learned some things only by bitter experience.

I was very young at the time. In fact, I was only twenty-six, and, like most young beginners, was very unwilling to admit when I didn't know a thing. In later years I would simply say that I didn't know, and, if it was necessary, I would take steps to find out. At that time, however, I thought it most unbecoming to admit that I didn't know anything at all, a process which led me into considerable difficulties sometimes.

One day a foreign lady came in to see me. I don't remember what exactly was wrong with her. Anyway, she had something the matter with her stomach and she needed a diet sheet. I duly wrote out a diet sheet for her and she read it over carefully to see that everything was clear.

One of the items on it was scrambled eggs. She said she thoroughly understood it all except the scrambled eggs. What were scrambled eggs? I thought everyone knew what scrambled eggs were, and I described them to her as nice, irregular yellow masses, usually eaten with toast, and told her that we English often had them for breakfast.

"Yes," she said, "but how do you cook them?"

Now, I regret to say that I knew nothing about cooking, and had not at that time the faintest idea how to scramble eggs. I was unwilling to admit, however, that I didn't know. I hummed and hawed. At last I had to say something, and with great deliberation I spoke.

"Well, you see, you take an egg and you break it carefully into a pan of boiling water and stir it well. The water *must* be boiling. Then you leave it for ten minutes and keep the water on the boil. At the end of that time you will have—scrambled eggs."

She thanked me and took her departure.

Next week she came back again to report progress. I asked her how she was.

"Better," she replied. "My inside, it is much better. I digest everything on the diet sheet—except the scrambled egg."

"Didn't it come out a nice yellow mass?" I asked.

"No," she said. And she was a most expressive lady with her hands. "It came out a small mass of indiarubber, just like the inside of a golf ball—so," and she stretched an imaginary ball of elastic between her fingers for about half a yard.

I have never again tried to tell a person how to cook.

Shortly after I bought the practice I was informed that the elections for the local council were to be held. Partly because my practice was not very large and partly because I thought that being a town councillor might help me to expand it, I decided to stand.

Unfortunately, I had never taken any interest in politics, either municipal or national, but luckily my reputation was secure, as I learned that all the candidates stood as Independents.

I drew up a marvellous manifesto of which the principal ingredients were " efficiency and economy ". I felt that I deserved to get in on that slogan alone. I put two bills in the windows of local shop-keepers who had recently become patients of mine. Another " efficiency and economy " placard I stuck on the waiting-room wall with underneath an exhortation to my patients to vote for their doctor. It was a marvellous advertisement, as I took down all the other pictures and the patients were therefore compelled to look at my exhortation as long as they were in the waiting-room, which was sometimes quite a considerable time.

To my astonishment, I came out at the top of the poll. My panel had voted for me to a man. I had done less advertising than anyone else and was now a town councillor.

I found that being a councillor was most imposing. We sat round a horseshoe table and felt very important. Most of the other councillors were in the grandfather class and had been so for many years. It had previously been a sort of club for elderly gentlemen, and though they were very polite to me, I had no illusions that I was to them any other than an interloper and altogether an exceedingly young man.

I am not sure whether it is a tribute to them or to me that, by the end of my term of office, these same councillors had become my firm friends and the bulk of them called me in when they required medical attention.

I recall one incident which nearly landed me in for lots of trouble. One day, during a pause from our labours, I was doodling with my pencil. The subject of impersonation had been before the council.

" Oh," said the councillor next to me, " nobody could take me in. I'd spot him in a minute and that would be an end of it."

I stopped doodling and looked up. Unfortunately, I didn't

know the man very well. In fact all I knew about him was that he was a builder and was engaged in putting up a new housing estate at the moment. Nevertheless, I felt my impersonationist pride was at stake.

" I'll tell you what," I said. " I'll undertake to speak to you for half an hour at some time or other during the coming week. If you recognise me I'll pay a pound to the local hospital, but if I'm not recognised and get away with it, you will pay a pound to the same institution."

" Done," he replied, " I'll take that on with pleasure."

The meeting drifted away to other topics, but I kept turning the matter over and over in my mind, and the more I turned it over the less I liked it. To begin with, I had no point of contact with him at all. I didn't know him socially, and so far as I knew we had nothing in common. I could go up and ask him for a match, but that wouldn't take half an hour. I could even try to sell him a vacuum cleaner, but I did not regard my chances of passing half an hour in that capacity as very rosy. The more I thought about it the more difficult appeared the outlook.

At supper that night I had an inspiration. It's not often I get inspiration from the maidservants, but suddenly I remembered that our domestic had a brother in the Salvation Army. He was about my size and was a sergeant. If I could borrow his uniform the difficulty was half solved. Like the sportsman he was and is, he lent me the uniform.

The next step was to secure a female confederate. A friend of my wife's nobly rose to the occasion and the scene was set. My first object was to ring up the councillor on the morning of a day well within the appointed time and in an altered voice arranged with him to see over one of his houses that afternoon.

We set off in my car. My wife's friend did not attempt to put on any disguise as the prospective seller was unknown to her, but she did flaunt an engagement ring. I myself wore the uniform of a Salvation Army sergeant. We drove to the housing estate and left the car in a nearby road. Then we made our way to the rendezvous. The councillor was waiting for us. I won't go into details, but it is sufficient to say that we spent more than half an hour seeing over the house and discussing the drains and the hundred and one things which a couple about to be married have to take into consideration. We even discussed whether the space under the stairs would take a pram. We ultimately left the builder with the promise that we would talk the matter over and let him know our decision in the course of an hour.

We walked to the car and drove home, where I rang him up in my natural voice and requested him to give a pound to the local hospital. The councillor paid up like a man in spite of his natural chagrin at failing to sell one of his houses. We ultimately became firm friends and he bore me no ill-will whatever.

Generally the work of the practice was hard and exacting, and it was mainly those cases which presented some unusual feature of interest which recall themselves to my memory. The cases of the daily round and the common task got forgotten in the flood of routine which each day brought. Steadily day by day my practice grew larger, more and more patients kept coming.

My work always came first, but occasionally I slipped up. It was a glorious summer day and I had been playing tennis right up to the last minute. I did a thing I had never done before. I did not leave time to change my clothes and took my consulting hour in tennis flannels. None of the patients seemed to mind and all went well until near the end.

A young lady was shown into my room whom I had never seen before. She sat down and consulted me about the most delicate matters. Suddenly her voice trembled and then stopped altogether. Her eyes became dilated and her face grew pale. In fact she showed all the symptoms of being acutely afraid of something. Her apprehension was soon explained when she said to me in a panic-stricken voice :

" You are the doctor, aren't you ? "

I was about four months in practice before I bought a car, as I had made up my mind that I would not buy what I could not afford. I rode a bicycle before that. I was as proud as punch the day a dealer drove up to my door with a second-hand Citroen which I had bought. Since then I have had many more expensive and up-to-date cars, but I don't think any has given me such pride as that early Citroen. I can well remember the agent impressing on me the speed at which it could go, but as I had never driven a car in my life I wasn't terribly impressed. He must have been a surprised man when I leant forward and tapped him confidentially on the knee.

" Tell me," I asked him, " how slow can it go ? "

He scratched his head.

" Slow," he said. " Why, I reckon she'll go as slow as you like."

" That will suit me fine," I replied.

The dealer from whom I had bought it drove me once along the road where I lived and back again, and I was left at the kerbside of my own front door gazing at the dashboard with feelings of trepidation and apprehension. I had not had the courage to confess that I had never driven a car in my life before. Luckily it was the days before tests, and I was not altogether devoid of mechanical sense as I had owned several motor-cycles. I persevered in low gear until I felt reasonably confident.

My confidence reached its maximum about 7 p.m. At that hour I determined to drive over to Streatham, where my sister lived, and show her my purchase. With the aid of a protecting Providence and an excellent horn, I made steady progress in low gear and got there safely.

On the way home my troubles began. To begin with, as it was lighting-up time I put on my lights. Unfortunately, I put on my headlights by mistake. In a few seconds I seemed to have most of London sounding their horns frantically while looks and gesticulations were showered on me from all sides.

In my anxiety to do something I stopped the engine right in the middle of Streatham High Road, in fact just opposite St. Leonard's Church. The headlights were still on, and, unfortunately, I couldn't start the engine. A policeman came across to me with measured and purposeful tread. I didn't know what to do, so I sat still. He was a decent fellow. When he saw that I knew nothing about it he cranked the engine up himself and turned off my headlights. I had just time to learn that he came from Wick when further conversation was made impossible by the sound of a thousand horns—at least that's what it sounded like. I slowly made my way homewards in low gear and ignored the looks and noises made by indignant motorists as they passed me.

At this time I had a case of poisoning which caused me a good deal of worry. I had reason to suspect that someone I was attending was being given poison. I was in a quandary as to what to do. I still think I did the best thing possible. I consulted an elderly doctor whom I knew and whose opinion I valued and laid all the facts before him. He thought a minute when I had finished speaking.

" Are you sure of your facts ? " he said.

" As sure as one can be in the circumstances," I replied.

" Then drop a hint of what you suspect to the person whom you think is administering the poison. They will probably stop if they know you are after them."

I took his advice and the patient started to recover from that day. I never had any further reason to suspect that my patient was being poisoned.

As I have said, my car was not of current vintage. It went excellently, but it did not need a connoisseur in cars to see that it was somewhat long in the tooth.

I had one very wealthy patient. I remember glancing out of my window on her first arrival and seeing the chauffeur hold open the door of a Rolls Royce as his mistress stepped out. My first impression was that she had come to the wrong house, but the chauffeur was correct. She had come to visit me.

In due course it was necessary for one of her family to have an operation. At the preliminary consultation, it may have been my imagination or it may have been that I was overcome by the magnificence of the surgeon's trappings, anyway, I was conscious of being made to feel a very inferior being and I determined that I should not be placed in such a situation again.

The day arrived. The surgeon was to perform the operation ; the anæsthetist was to do his job and I was allotted the minor and humble rôle of assisting the great man at the operation. I made some excuse and borrowed the family's Rolls Royce and their chauffeur for the occasion. The operation went according to plan and afterwards the three of us had tea together in a room of the nursing home where it had taken place.

Afterwards we took our departure together. The anæsthetist got into a two-seater. The surgeon entered what looked like a Buick, and I entered the Rolls by the door which was held open for me by the chauffeur—resplendent in shining gaiters and peaked cap. As the car moved silently off I saw the surgeon glance at my car, and I thought I detected a certain respect in his eye. I think that at heart all men are children, but all the same it gave me a certain amount of childish and very human satisfaction.

It was my fate to have trouble in backing my Citroen. Going forward I never had any trouble, but to my consternation one day I backed into one of those perambulator affairs where a multitude of milk bottles take the place of the baby. It had long handles and I think it was a double decker. Anyway, I hit it full toss and though the road did not flow with milk and honey, it literally flowed with milk. It is extraordinary how much milk those perambulators hold.

On another occasion I backed the car and foolishly did so without looking where I was going. I heard the sound of a multitude of broken glass and discovered to my horror that I had backed right into an area of red lamps which had been put on the ground by some roadmen who had been excavating the neighbouring road. There seemed to me acres of red lamps but their number was reduced considerably when I had extracted my car from them.

Then there was the woman who had nervous dyspepsia. Every now and again she would come and consult me about her stomach. She was a very nervous, worrying kind of person and her temperament was the sole cause of her digestive trouble. I didn't see her again for some considerable time until one day I met her face to face on the same pavement. I had always had the most amiable relations with the woman but this time I thought she was a trifle distant. I enquired how she was.

" I've had gall stones," she said, but added pointedly, " thank goodness they are better now and I've got rid of them."

Now whatever she had it was not gall stones. I asked her how she had got rid of them.

" By massage," she said. " I went to a healer to whom I had been recommended. The healer felt the gall stones and he massaged them out of my system. It cost twenty guineas." She added as an afterthought, " and I reckon they were cheap at the price."

I regretfully thought of the many consultations she had had with me and of the small fees I had charged her. I also remembered that gall bladders are not palpable even by the most skilful fingers and that they certainly could not be massaged out of the system. Either my medical training was complete nonsense or this patient had been the victim of some charlatan who had rooked her to the tune of twenty guineas.

My face must have registered my disbelief for she said,

" Would you like to see them ? We are just outside my house and if you can spare a minute I've got them all. There are crowds of them and I've never had any trouble since I got rid of them. Marvellous, isn't it ! "

I went in with her to the house to see the gall stones. Sure enough, there they were. Polished smoothly on the sides where they had rubbed against each other. Brown in colour. Just the colour of gall stones. In fact, they *were* gall stones.

I felt beaten, puzzled and mystified. Everything that I stood for in my medical training had been proved utterly untrustworthy I asked the woman again about their discovery and removal.

"Well," she said, " I had several times to be massaged and then one day the healer gave me a big bottle of medicine to drink and told me to take a dose of castor oil and that the next day I would get rid of my gall stones. I did, and there they are."

I went on my way not knowing whether I was standing on my head or my feet. But it so happened that the story had a sequel shortly afterwards.

About a week after the meeting which I have described, I had occasion to take another patient up town to see a famous London specialist. While sitting in his room afterwards I took the opportunity of telling him about this remarkable case. He heard me through to the end and then he laughed heartily. He rose and crossed the room to a big oak bookcase with many drawers and leaded panels of dark glass. He pulled out a small drawer.

" What are these ? " he asked.

" Gall stones," I replied.

" And these ? "

" Gall stones," I answered.

In both drawers they were laid out in rows on a background of cotton wool like brown diamonds that had forgotten how to glisten. He shut the drawer with a snap.

" Right in one case and wrong in the other," he said. " I removed one lot surgically myself so I know definitely what they are."

" Well, they look exactly the same," I objected.

" Yes, they look exactly the same, but I've had them analysed. You know that every gall stone contains stuff called cholesterin ? "

" Yes."

" Well, there's no cholesterin in these others. If you take a big drink of that particular medicine and follow it with an ounce of castor oil, the next day you will pass these gall stones that are not gall stones. Unless you have them analysed you can't tell the difference. Your healer fellow knew of the trick. I've heard of him before. I believe he charges twenty guineas. Clever fellow. He deserves every penny of it."

I went home debating the matter in my mind. Was it, or was it not worth while to have dyspepsia permanently cured for twenty guineas ? Admittedly the healer was a " wrong 'un ", yet, he had cured the patient for all time. Never again did that patient suffer from that particular trouble. He had done what I couldn't do—permanently cured her. I never told her of my discovery or that her gall stones were not gall stones. To this day she believes that my knowledge of stomach troubles is elementary. I have never disabused her mind and I am still not sure about the ethics of the healer.

To a lay person, the most outstanding feature of a doctor's life is the night calls. Over a lifetime of General Practice, I find these cases generally go in a series. Weeks may elapse when one's rest is undisturbed and then one night call is shortly followed by another. The most common, naturally enough, are baby cases. The second most common cause of night calls is in my experience, curiously enough, bleeding teeth. Most dental men are responsible for their own sanguinary results, but, as is only natural, a certain number of patients go on oozing a small amount of blood from the cavities of their extractions. During the night the patient feels faint ; the relatives get alarmed and the doctor is summoned.

Though many confinements happen at night there are a large number which take place during the day. Such a one happened in the day of which I speak. Late one summer's afternoon I was called to a house where I had not been previously. The patient turned out to be a girl and it did not take me more than a minute to find out that she was going to have a baby and have it almost immediately. The girl was unmarried and had remained all day at work in the factory where she was employed until her pain had compelled her to go to her lodgings. I decided that help was both urgent and imperative. I took the landlady into my confidence.

" No child of sin shall be born under my roof," she said.

I explained that I only wanted some water and other absolutely essential articles. She was adamant in her refusal to help in any way whatsoever and repeated her article of faith about the child. It grieved me sorely to think of that girl staying at her work entirely alone and enduring the pain all day with not a soul to confide in. In terse and pithy phraseology I told the landlady exactly what I thought of her. I decided that something must be done and done right speedily. The baby must certainly be born somewhere and there was every indication that it would be born under that roof whether the landlady liked it or not.

I hurriedly ran to a nearby telephone kiosk and phoned the matron of a nursing home I knew and told her to expect a case immediately.

I hastened back to the patient's room to tell her what I had arranged. Hurriedly I put an overcoat round her shoulders to cover her nightdress and half carrying, half supporting her we made our way together out to my car. She sat in the back seat while I drove. Never have I driven so fast in my life. We turned corners literally on two wheels. By the time we were halfway there the girl was shrieking at the top of her voice and had discarded the overcoat in her distress. Unfortunately, it was a fine summer's evening with crowded streets. I considered stopping at the house of a colleague and then discarded the idea when I pictured his face and, even more vividly, the face of his wife. Hurriedly I tore past his house and just as we got to the nursing home the baby was born. Unfortunately the baby died, but I think the mother felt she had at least one friend on earth in whom she could confide.

Most of my confinements were normal humdrum affairs, but I vividly recall one which took place in a private house. It must be remembered that some women at that particular time scream loudly. It was the patient's first child and the confinement was proceeding normally. Every time the woman had a pain she let out a cry. The husband, who was an educated man, a solicitor I think, was pacing up and down the landing outside the bedroom. Whenever the woman cried out, which was at every pain, the husband would open the bedroom door, stick his head inside and say " For God's sake save her, doctor ". As time progressed and the same performance was repeated each time, I came to dread the opening of the door and ultimately only the most dire threat made him leave the house until the child was born.

Of rather a different nature were the actor and his wife. One night—or rather morning—I was summoned to attend a woman suffering from severe pain. I was not given any particulars. I was merely asked to come at once. When I got to the house it was at that black hour which precedes the dawn. The rain was coming down in torrents. It did not take long to determine that the wife was going to have a baby, and almost at once. She claimed to be innocent of the fact that she was having a baby and no preparations whatever had been made for its arrival. Summarily I despatched the husband in search of a nurse, and set about making such preparations as were possible. Apparently the couple had only furnished two rooms of the house, both of which were innocent of fires. I peeped into the other rooms but found them chill and unfurnished. My first objective was to light a fire so that I might boil some water.

The coal shed was at the top of the garden, and I well remember feeling my way in the darkness with the rain still coming down in torrents all around me. The husband returned home alone when daylight was well advanced. Apparently he had been unable to obtain the services of a nurse at that hour. In the meantime the child had been born, and I have the keenest recollection of wrapping the child in its mother's garments and carrying the newly born babe round the house while I got the water for its bath and proceeded to carry out all those duties which are usually assigned to a nurse.

Shortly after this event took place the couple left for pastures new without paying the modest sum that I had charged them. The case, however, was not yet finished. Some years afterwards a man walked into my consulting room and said :

" My name is so and so, do you remember me ? "

" No," I replied, " to the best of my knowledge I have never seen you before."

He then told me that he was the man in question and that he had joined the Oxford Group. He had come to pay me my fee after all those years. My regard for the Oxford Group has ever since been considerable.

I was sometimes consulted by a colleague who was consistently uncertain of his diagnosis. I remember that late one evening he was called in by a wealthy family to attend one of their servants who had suddenly been taken ill. The mistress was waiting to catch the doctor on his emergence from the sick room.

" What is wrong, doctor ? "

" Well, I think she's dead but I'm not quite sure. To be on the safe side I think one of you should sit up with her all night," he replied.

One day on a Sunday evening about ten o'clock I was summoned to a very poor house to see a child suffering from influenza. The child was ill, but not what I would call very ill. I attended to the little girl and told the mother that I would call back on Tuesday morning. Privately, I thought that ten o'clock on a Sunday night was hardly the time to send for a doctor to see a child suffering from influenza, but I bit back the words and resolutely said nothing.

On Tuesday morning I went to see the child and what was my surprise to see another doctor's car standing at the door. Being in a hurry, I did what many doctors in a similar position would have done. I knocked at the door with one hand and turned the handle with the other. The front door led directly into the living room where the sick child was lying. To my astonishment another doctor was bending over the patient.

" Hullo," I said, " what are you doing here ? "

He looked at me with an unrepentant gleam in his eye.

" Well, for that matter, what are you doing here ? "

We both turned to the woman who was standing in the background looking very embarrassed.

" Well," she said, " on Sunday morning I sent for Dr. X. He said the little girl had influenza. On Sunday night she seemed much worse so I thought it couldn't be influenza and I sent for Dr. Bell Nicoll to see if it really was influenza."

I was naturally somewhat angry with the woman and said to her, " Well, that will cost you twelve and sixpence. Seven and sixpence for Sunday night and five shillings for to-day."

The woman gladly paid me the twelve and sixpence and the other doctor and I took our departure together. As we crossed the pavement to our respective cars he turned to me.

" Well, I'm blowed," he said.

" Why ? " I asked.

" Well, you go in there and do nothing—in fact even less than nothing as you merely stood and watched me do all the work, and yet you come out with twelve and sixpence in your pocket. Whereas I've looked after these people for years and I've never been paid a penny."

Fees were always a difficulty. I have all my life rather undercharged people. That is one of the main reasons why I employed a book-keeper from my earliest days. She not only sent out the accounts regularly but saved me from either not charging them at all or charging them a ridiculously low fee. I have never found that doctors' fees as a rule remain unpaid. In the course of a quarter of a century of General Practice of all types, my bad debts have never exceeded two per cent. Maybe I have been lucky, but I think it is chiefly due to sending out my accounts regularly and charging fees which were well within the ability of the people to pay.

Sometimes it was not possible for all the items to appear in the books. A man came into my surgery one day. He was a rough looking man and I knew him to be a poacher of some sort. Apparently the cottage where he lived was close beside the local golf course and he visited his garden once a day to collect golf balls in much the same way as a person who has hens visits the hen house daily to collect the eggs. He wanted to come to an arrangement whereby he paid for my professional skill in eggs and rabbits or golf balls. I accepted the arrangement but I am afraid that I got the worst of the bargain.

He was not alone in wanting to pay me in kind. The most curious case I ever had was a man who was a novelist—or said he was. He suggested paying me out of the proceeds of a book which was not written yet—and I was to supply the local colour. I did not accept his suggestion.

Another bit of barter turned to my advantage however. The local carrier wanted his ears syringed and I wanted a fairly heavy parcel delivered at a certain house. I duly performed my share of the bargain and so did he. I met him walking a few days later.

" Hullo," I said, " where's the van ? "

He looked slightly sheepish as he replied, " Well, you see, I had to come off the van as the noise sounded so loud."

I laughed and asked him if he had ever heard of cotton wool.

" Never thought of it," he said.

I noticed that the van was running again next day and he was sitting in his usual place at the steering wheel.

Usually however my work dealt more with tragedy then comedy. I can remember a man in the fifties coming into my consulting room. He told me his symptoms and a brief examination revealed the fact that he had an inoperable cancer. Should a doctor tell ? Luckily the decision was taken out of my hands for he himself guessed what was the matter and asked me point blank if there was any hope. I shook my head, but added this rider, which is a factor which many medical men forget.

" You know," I said, " we doctors are sometimes wrong and he is an unwise man who says there is no hope." The man kept on with his work as long as he was able for the sake of his wife and the children dependent upon him.

One of the most heartrending moments a doctor has to face is when a patient looks at him with dumb pleading in his eyes and ultimately rises from his chair and goes out realising that all his work and planning and perseverance are in vain ; that in a few weeks or months he must go out into that solitary loneliness of death. This particular man had a lingering and painful end. Day by day his cheeks grew more hollow and gaunt. Day by day his pain grew more persistent and his weakness more marked. It was strange to sit beside him and to realise that shortly he would solve the great mystery. I have never got used to the utter loneliness of death.

But to return to the question of practices. A neighbour of mine, now deceased, who was famous among his colleagues for his avariciousness, had a very large practice. An Irishman of my acquaintance while talking of him one day said, " You know, Dr. X has never seen a patient in his life."

" Never seen a patient in his life ? " I replied in astonishment.

" No," replied the Irish doctor, " he's only seen five shillings on the chair in front of him ! "

This Irishman had a subtle sense of humour. He was always at loggerheads with the local coroner. The vendetta had gone on for years, with the coroner generally winning by virtue of his position. One day, however, the Irishman got the best of it. It so happened that someone was taken ill in the street just outside the Irish doctor's house. The sick person was brought into the waiting room to await the doctor's return as he was out on his visits. Before his return, the patient died. Now it was one of the laws of the Medes and Persians that a body must not be moved until authority had been given by the coroner, and his officials had examined the position of the corpse. However, in the case of the death occurring where the body is likely to interfere with traffic such as a death on a public highway, the body may be moved to the side of the road.

The Irishman rang up the coroner and reported the death, as was his duty.

" I want the body removed at once from the waiting room," said the Irishman.

" Not until my men have seen it and I have given permission," said the coroner. " You'll have to use another waiting room for to-night."

" But the surgery is just going to begin," said the Irishman.

" Well, my men won't get there for another twenty minutes. You'll have to use another room to-night."

" I most certainly won't," said the Irishman.

" Will there be women and children coming to your surgery ? " asked the coroner.

" Of course," was the reply.

" You would never let a thing like that happen," said the coroner. " Think of the fright they would get when they went into the waiting room and found a corpse in the room."

There was a long pause, then, " I'll tell you what I'll do," said the Irishman. " I'll meet you half way. I'll put a sheet over it."

Permission to move the body was given forthwith and it was duly removed. The Irishman felt that he had won a tactical victory.

I gave a lot of anæsthetics in this practice. It is a common misunderstanding that people talk a lot when they are going under an anæsthetic. As a matter of fact, I have rarely known an anæsthetised person to say anything. They are much more likely to do something or to say something when they are coming out of the anæsthetic.

I remember giving a dental gas to one man who was a stranger to me. As he was coming round, he kept putting one hand up with the fingers outstretched. As soon as I had put it down, the other one would immediately rise similarly. I turned to the dental surgeon who was extracting the teeth.

" What an extraordinary thing. I wonder why he does that ? " He laughed.

" Don't you recognise him ? He's the traffic policeman at the nearby crossroads."

Some patients tell only a part of the truth. These are mainly women. Many of their sex specialise in half-truths.

Men as a rule are more truthful. One day a rough-looking man came to consult me. I had never seen him before, and, as was my custom, I asked him what his occupation was. He was silent for a minute, then at last he spoke.

" I suppose one always ought to speak the truth to a doctor."

" Always," I replied.

" Well, I suppose I'd better tell you the truth."

" Better," I prompted.

" Well, I do a spot of burgling now and again," he replied. " I'm not exactly a professional yet. But I ain't no amateur—no, I ain't no amateur."

One day quite suddenly I determined to sell the practice. That forenooon I went up town and gave particulars to the agency who act in these affairs. I sold the practice for £500 more than I gave for it, and so became a capitalist.

Some weeks previously I had started a branch practice in a different district. The branch practice mainly consisted of a room, a plate and a chair. The chair sat on the landing outside my consulting-room door and was only occupied when two patients happened to come at the same time. I only remember it being occupied once. Luckily, those waiting never amounted to more than one.

The site was an excellent one. I determined to buy a house

as near a big road junction as possible and start from scratch. My next practice was to be my own creation entirely.

Some days before the removal was due to take place a patient came in to see me. In the course of conversation it appeared that he was starting in the neighbourhood as a furniture remover. With the idea of encouraging beginners, I asked him if he would like to take on the job of removing me. I took him round and showed him what furniture we had. He thought he could manage it all right.

I told him that it would need at least four men, as some of the furniture was very heavy. Absent-mindedly he nodded his head.

The day of our removal arrived, and with it my new-found acquaintance. What was my astonishment and consternation to see a van at our front door not unlike those used by some gypsies in their travels around the countryside. It was covered by some shiny black material stretched over two narrow hoops. The whole outfit could not possibly hold our piano apart from any other furniture. The four men resolved themselves into a man and a boy, who presented themselves at our door.

To make matters worse, the furniture of the incoming doctor started to arrive just after breakfast. I have never seen my wife so upset as she was on that occasion. Her oratory rose to great heights. Curiously enough, it was not how we were going to get transported to our future destination that worried her most. It was " What will the neighbours think ? "

In the end I slunk away and paid the man to take his van and boy out of my sight. I then set out to find a furniture remover who would move my worldly goods that day—if possible that hour. The first firm I tried happened to have the day free, so I returned in triumph with two enormous vans and four white-aproned scene-shifters. We were out of the house by tea-time, and thus came to an end my first and dearly-cherished practice.

CHAPTER X

MY SECOND PRACTICE

I BOUGHT a house on the main road. Unfortunately, it was not on the corner as I would have wished, but at that time there was no house actually available on the corner itself. The house which I bought was really ideally situated, as it was on the fringe of a new housing estate, and no other doctor had settled in the vicinity to compete with me. I was certainly going to start from scratch now.

I was free from debt, but, alas! without a practice. However, I found that a successful practice is like a snowball. It gathers momentum as it proceeds. When I first settled there my practice, as I say, was nil. But gradually one and another began to call me in, and in a few years I had one of the most extensive practices in the district. Within two years a large house actually on the corner became vacant and for sale, and I bought it, greatly to the benefit of the practice and to our own comfort.

In the early days my energies were devoted to furnishing our new house. A section of wall on the staircase of our new house had always struck me as being particularly bare, and I had it in mind to cover the area with a large picture or possibly a couple of pictures. One day I was passing along a nearby road when I saw a long line of cars drawn up to the curb and a red flag proclaiming that an auction sale was in progress. I stopped the car and went in. The front room, where the auction was being held, was crammed to suffocation, but I was able from my post at the doorway to see over the heads of the assembled people. Curiously enough, at the moment of my arrival the auctioneer was selling pictures. From my position I was unable to see the pictures, but I heard his description of them, and it appeared that they were masterpieces of a high order. They were large pictures with deep gilt frames. I bought two of them for twelve and sixpence. Strangely enough, I don't think I had any opposition. In due course they were carried through to a back room and set against the wall by an assistant, and I went through to inspect my purchases. As I entered the room an arty-looking man with a long beard and long hair was standing in front of the pictures. I heard him say to himself, " Remarkable, perfectly remarkable."

Naturally I thought I had purchased an old master, so I said politely to the owner of the beard, " Would you mind telling me what it is that you find remarkable about these pictures ? "

" Do you really want to know ? " he asked.

" Yes, I should like to know very much."

" Well," he replied, " they are the worst pictures I have ever seen in my life."

I took them home, but my wife refused to put them up. They reposed in the attic for many a day until somebody accidentally put a foot through them.

Most of the work was a dull routine of everyday sickness, but from time to time a case would arise which peeked my curiosity or whetted my sense of the dramatic. Such a one was this.

I had decided to take the morning off to see the Boat Race, and was coming down the steps of the house where I lived when a small boy accosted me with a note addressed in my name. The contents were peculiar. It was a leaf obviously torn from a note-book and merely said " My wife is committing suicide. Please come at once." It was the tense which impressed me—the present tense. I have seen many patients who have committed suicide ; many who threatened to do so at some future date ; but none in the very act. Anyhow, why did the unfortunate husband not stop her ? I was intrigued.

I grabbed a bag and ran. My car was away being cleaned and the address on the scrap of paper was not far away. As I say, I ran. The small boy panted along in my wake. He obviously had read the note and literally hoped to be in at the death.

The husband was waiting for me at the top of the steps leading up to the front door. He seemed perturbed—as he had every reason to be—but along with his perturbation was a look of per-plexity, and he kept glancing back into the dark recesses of the hall. He seized my arm.

" Do you hear it ? " he cried, and from the darkness of upstairs came a noise like nothing earthly. It was the sound of the hymn " Nearer my God to Thee " being sung over and over again. Every now and then it would die away to a watery gurgle and then would start afresh with renewed vigour.

" What on all the earth is she doing ? " I asked.

" She is committing suicide," he replied, and he dragged me inside the darkened hall. Together we dashed up the staircase in the direction of the bathroom from whence the voice was coming. The bathroom door was of the old-fashioned variety, with two glazed glass panels running half the length of the door. Some peeping Tom had scratched away some of the glaze so that by applying one's eye to the glass it was possible to see into the room.

The first thing I saw was clouds of steam rising.

" Why, you silly ass, she's having a hot bath," I said.

" I know," he replied, " but she's committing suicide in it."

The door was locked and I knocked peremptorily on it and ordered her to come out. She took not the slightest notice of what I said, but continued with " Nearer my God to Thee." Every now and again she would put her mouth under the water and the hymn would die away to a bubbling diminuendo. She was obviously out of her mind.

I determined to break down the door. My experience in breaking down doors was limited to seeing men on the pictures put their shoulders to it and seeing the door quickly burst open and the intruder rush in to save the heroine at the last moment. I tried that. Nothing happened. I could, of course, have broken the glass panel and put my hand in and unlocked the door. I mentally sized up the cost of a broken panel against a broken lock, and came to the conclusion that the latter could probably be put right by the man at my side. I ultimately put the flat of my sole against the lock and gave one or two good jabs. The flimsy old lock gave and the door burst open.

I indicated to the husband that it was up to him to go in and get his wife out. He went in, and then ensued the most one-sided conversation I have ever listened to. She absolutely ignored him and continued the refrain of " Nearer my God to Thee ". The farce was ended by his coming to the door of the bathroom and saying to me, " She won't come."

" Pull the plug," I bellowed.

He did so, and together we carried the woman to her bed. I hurried down to a telephone kiosk at the end of the road and requested them to get her into hospital as soon as possible. It was some time before I got through to the right department, and altogether I was delayed in the phone-box for some time.

When I returned to the house there was no sign of the husband.

I found him lying unconscious on the same bed to which we had carried his wife. He was suffering from a stab wound in the chest and an insane woman was laughing as she carried the knife in her hand. She allowed it to be taken from her and I was just in time to do something towards saving the husband's life. He bore the mark of that morning to the grave, however. In due course the ambulance arrived at the door and in due course it left—carrying two patients instead of one.

As I have said, most of the cases were orthodox, but occasionally one ran across someone who did not fit in to any recognised category. Such was Miss Boyle. At least let's call her Miss Boyle, for though she is long since dead I would not wish to hurt her memory in any way.

I remember that it was a summer's evening when I first saw her. She sat down in my consulting-room, took off her gloves, laid down her umbrella, and asked me if I would be her doctor. Apparently her previous doctor had died or retired. She was a very large woman, the stoutest, I think, I have ever seen. In fact, when it came to removing her to a nursing home when ultimately she had a stroke, members of the local fire brigade were called in, in addition to those usually employed. She sat down and settled herself for a chat, as women sometimes are inclined to do. Then she told me this extraordinary story.

She was a woman of limited income, she said, and she liked to consult her doctor once a week. In fact, not to put too fine a point upon it, she went to her doctor instead of going to the pictures. She told me that she always paid her doctor three and sixpence and liked to do her own prescribing. If she felt like a little digitalis or strychnine to-day she just told her doctor and he made it up for her. She had never been examined in her life and refused to begin now, though I guessed that her blood pressure was up to the ceiling. I thought over the matter and hummed and hawed. I told her that I didn't like it. Then she said to me, " Then if you won't have me as a patient, I shall just go to someone who will."

I thought of this simple-minded woman falling into the hands of some unscrupulous shark who might not only bleed her white but put the fear of death into her in the doing, and my heart relented. Things were slack at the time, and I said I would take her on. Every week she came to see me and was the first in the waiting-room. If I got rid of the woman under fifteen minutes I considered I was being speedy. She always left three and sixpence on the edge of my desk as she went out. I considered the possibility of having a small push-bell and of ringing it at the end of her allotted time, when I would ask her, "Will you have another three and sixpence worth or not ? "

Let me be truthful and say that she never got any digitalis or strychnine from me, but something entirely innocuous.

The following winter things began to get really busy, but Miss Boyle was always the first in the waiting-room, and her presence became more of a debit than an asset. Things came to a head one day when I was not well myself and had a locum in the house doing duty for me. He came up to my bedroom before the consulting hour one evening with a very dejected air.

"Miss Boyle is here and the waiting-room is full. What am I to do ? "

My wife was present and rose to the occasion immediately. She slipped out of the back door, went round to the front and rang the bell urgently and distraughtly. In loud tones she demanded to see the doctor.

"Can you come at once, doctor ? There's been an accident."

Hurriedly Miss Boyle gathered together her gloves, her umbrella and her library book, and making suitable sympathetic noises, took her departure. Shortly after that she had a stroke and died. She was one of the few people who have left me a small legacy in their will. Such is the reward of virtue. I will refrain from adding, "I always thought she was a bit odd—now I know it."

From these days dates my interest in professional soccer. I was offered and accepted the medical officership of one of the English League teams. It was the easiest job I have ever done, and, I think, the most remunerative. So far as I recollect, I was paid fifty pounds a year and my duties were to be present at the match on Saturday afternoons. I had a seat in the directors' box, an excellent tea at half-time and a spare ticket for any friend who cared to accompany me. In all the years of my association with that club I never remember being called upon to do anything on the ground. The trainer with the little black bag seemed to do all that was necessary, and if it was a case for hospital he was whisked off in the ambulance within a matter of minutes. My duties, I may say, were of the lightest. In addition I got tickets for the cup ties in which the team happened to be playing. I have ever since retained a warm affection and interest in English League football and in that club in particular.

Shortly after I started to practise there a disaster fell upon me. I developed a stone in my kidney which gave me the most excruciating attacks of pain at frequent intervals. For six months the condition lasted, and about twice a week I had an attack of renal colic. Early in the morning I would be aware that an attack was coming on. I would rush round all my patients and try to get as many visits done as possible. By midday the pain had become unbearable and I would give myself an injection of morphia which made me sleep all the afternoon. Incidentally, I cannot imagine how anyone becomes a morphia addict ; I was invariably sick when I woke up about five o'clock. I would then go out and finish my visiting list and be back in time to take my evening surgery. This gives some idea of what a person has to put up with when his own future is dependent on himself. I seemed to be dogged by ill-health in that practice.

My memory had several blind spots in it. Usually it was excellent and served me well. Probably I relied on it too much. I don't recall ever having a note-book in these days. I could quote the name and address, the treatment and the illnesses of every patient in my practice for several years past. Let me give you an incident of the blind spot to which I have referred.

I had come in late for lunch so that I might finish my visiting list and leave the afternoon free for a game of golf which I had arranged to play. When I arrived in due course for my belated lunch I found a patient waiting for me. He was a man I had never seen before, and as there did not seem to be anything urgent about his case I asked if he would mind waiting until I had finished my lunch. He readily agreed, and I sat down to my meal. In due course I finished what I was eating and then, having an hour to spare, I turned to the current copy of the *British Medical Journal*. As time went on I left the house for my golfing appointment, and it was only at the eighth green, when I was doing a long putt, that I remembered the patient in the waiting-room. Needless to say, I missed my putt, but, alas ! I also missed the patient, as when I reached home the maid servant told me that she had heard the front door click shortly after I took my departure. I must say these lapses from virtue were only occasional.

And again.

A patient of mine who lived in the neighbourhood was always

telling me about his son who was a clergyman in the West Indies. One summer's evening I was called to the house next door to where he lived. I drew up alongside the kerb and stepped out of my car across the pavement in a brown study. My visual eye saw, but my mind did not, two figures approach me on the pavement, the man from the house next door and another.

"Ah," I said as I held out my hand, "this must be your son from the West Indies."

What was my horror to look up and see a coal-black negro grinning at me.

About this time I began to specialise in nervous disorders, and was occasionally called in by my local fellow practitioners to such cases, but I was to find that I was not cut out for a specialist. I think specialists are born, not made. A doctor in the district asked me to see one of his patients at his (the doctor's) house. I arranged to go at a time suitable to the patient, myself and his own doctor. At the interview I listened patiently while he told me his story. I listened for half an hour without speaking. Proudly he told me that I was the twenty-third doctor he had seen in five years. I then examined him carefully. Nothing was the matter with him—absolutely nothing—he was a complete hypochondriac. I advised him that there was nothing wrong, and my parting words to him were, "Now you want to make a resolution the way some men promise to give up drink. You want to promise never to see a doctor for a year."

He promised and took his departure. As my friend the doctor showed me out through the hall to his front door he said as he put his hand on my shoulder :

"Nicoll, you're a good chap, but you're the worst consultant I have ever met in my life ; that was my best patient, and you've told him not to come near me for a year ! "

I could write a book about specialists. It would range from the immaculate poseur who holds out his hand in studied silence to the shock-headed nature healer who specialises in the "rude health" kind of stuff. Most consultations with specialists conform to type, but not this particular one. The specialist in question was a well-known surgeon from one of the big London hospitals. I had arranged to meet him at a certain hour at the patient's house. He made his examination of the patient who was an elderly woman, and after he had explained the condition to her and what could be done about it, we were shown downstairs by an elderly maid to what appeared to be the dining-room, as we wanted a further talk about the case. The house was one of those old Victorian houses with a sunk basement and nothing to relieve the flatness of its architecture.

The room which we were now in was on the street level, but it faced the back, and an idle glance out of the window showed the room to be one story up from the so-called garden. Actually a hen-run occupied the space just below the window—only, of course, it was one story down below—and a goodish way down at that. We had our little consultation and in due course rose to go. We went to the door. It was locked and the key was not on the inside. A peremptory knocking at the door brought the elderly maid. We demanded to be let out at once.

" It's that there lock has gone again," she exclaimed ; " there ain't no key to this door, but sometimes when it is slammed the lock falls and yer can't get out."

I inquired whether she could get in touch with the nearest locksmith in order that we would be let out.

" The only person who can let you out is my husband," she exclaimed, " and he won't be home until seven o'clock."

It was now about five-thirty in the afternoon. I thought of breaking down the door, but one glance at it showed how solid it was. They certainly built substantial doors in the previous generation. We crossed to the fireplace and sat down. The best part of an hour slipped away. I remembered I had a surgery at six-thirty and a good deal to do before that. The surgeon, on the other hand, had no consulting hour and was correspondingly unhurried.

I listened while the great man droned on about some obscure cases. I am afraid I was only listening with half an ear. In the middle of the conversation I crossed to the window and looked out. Alas ! I saw only the hen-run down below—so far down below in fact that if a man tried to jump it he would almost certainly break his leg and most probably his neck. But what was that ! Leading down to the ground, in fact into the very hen-house itself, ran a drain-pipe. A pipe that could be reached if a venturesome man stood on the window-sill and reached for it. My survey was the work of a moment. My decision was even quicker.

" I'm going," I called out to my colleague.

I went down that drain pipe hand over hand and soon I was standing among the hens, with that peculiar sour smell of hen-run penetrating my nostrils.

I looked up at the window from whence I had come. The great man was standing there in an obvious state of indecision. Should he, or should he not, follow me ? I can see him standing there now, the striped trousers and little black jacket of Harley Street—the dignity of a knighthood—and gripping a small leather attaché case containing his instruments.

We surveyed each other for a full minute. At last he said :
" Catch."

And down came the attaché case into my waiting arms. A minute later the great man was spreadeagled on the window-ledge. Down the drain-pipe he came, striped trousers, little black jacket, dignity and all. We foregathered among the fowls and made our way out through the hen-house door to the back of the house.

I don't know if it is permissible to talk about a humorous accident, but such a thing certainly came to my notice during that time. I was summoned urgently to the house of a lady whom I knew by sight. She opened the door herself and the colour of her face struck me as startling. A sickly pallor provided the background, but around her mouth was a large brownish stain which obviously was not meant to be there. When I got inside she told me that she had been poisoned accidentally. It appeared that she was in the habit of going to the cupboard and taking a swig from a black bottle without pouring it into a tumbler. She was alone in the house at the time and had taken this opportunity of going to the cupboard as usual. Apparently she poisoned herself by taking a swig from the wrong bottle. I smelt it very carefully and then tentatively poured some out and tasted a drop. It had neither the smell nor the taste of any alcohol known to me. It was a weak solution of permanganate of potash. The accident was purposeful, as it turned out that her husband, with a strong desire to teach her a lesson not to drink from bottles—black or otherwise—had filled the bottle with the solution, and this was the stain that I had seen around the lady's mouth. Apart from some simple remedies, the chief thing that she needed was reassurance. So far as I am aware, the lesson was effective.

Most of the cases I had to treat were medical cases. In the course of the years I did less and less surgery, though I would have liked to have done more. I felt that an operation was more suited to the facilities of a hospital than the consulting room of a doctor. I used, however, to do a number of sebaceous cysts—commonly called wens. Many people have them, chiefly about their head, and sometimes the condition is multiple.   Luckily it does not lead to anything, and their removal is a permanent cure.   I remember a woman coming to me with twenty-eight of these cysts on her head. She looked like a human brussels sprout.   I removed them in four lots.

Sometimes it is said that the standard of medicine in General Practice is not very high.   I doubt this myself, but let me give one reason for it.   The General Practitioner is almost forced to come down to the level of the patient and curiously enough the patient has not yet got beyond the stage of wanting his cures in a bottle. A bottle is the outward and visible sign of treatment.   Let me illustrate what I mean.

A man came to see me one day suffering from arthritis.   He had a particularly revolting mouthful of teeth which required immediate extraction.   I advised him that this was probably the cause of his arthritis and that their removal would probably cure his condition. I learned afterwards that he thought me a very poor doctor as I did not give him any medicine for his illness.   In fact, he went right down the road to my nearest rival, who, being an older and more experienced man that I was, gave him a bottle containing some harmless antidote.

I remember a man coming to me who was most indignant because a specialist in Harley Street whom he had consulted about his rheumatism had advised him to take a daily dose of salts.   He thought he was being defrauded.   However, like the man in the Old Testament who was told to wash in the River Jordan, he did as he was advised, and again like the man in the Old Testament—his disease left him—if not immediately then a short time after.

A doctor must constantly be on his guard against himself.   He must not allow himself to get into the mentality of a person who says to himself as soon as a patient tells his story—let's imagine he has rheumatism—" Ah, sodium salicylate, veganin or aspirin."

In imagination he is prescribing one or the other while the patient is speaking.   He has let himself get into what I call an " aspirin-minded condition."

In the course of years I have heard many humorous remarks— unconsciously humorous—by patients.   I could fill a book with the remarks which patients have made to me at one time or another, only I feel that the book would not be suitable for publication. They are, anyway, only enjoyed when another is there to share them. I have never had the slightest tendency even to smile when I have heard the most extraordinary statements made. I only treasure them up in my mind so that they may be retailed to my colleagues at the earliest opportunity.

An example of what I mean happened to a colleague one day. A very old lady—who was shy and timorous—consulted my friend. To put her at her ease he adopted his best bedside manner and soothing tones.

" Tell me," he asked, " what is it you are complaining of ? "

" Constipation," said the old lady hesitatingly.

" Ah dear, dear. Is it bad ? "

" Yes, doctor, it is very bad."

" And what do you take ? "

" I just take my knitting."

In another of my cases, where two elderly sisters lived together, I received a phone call from a retired Colonel who lived next door to them, saying that one of them had had a stroke and could I come at once, etc., etc. I went at once, but alas, I was too late. When I got there she was dead and the Colonel was vainly trying to restore her with such remedies as he had at his command. The house was stone built and not unlike my own. I knew the deceased very well, both socially and professionally. Her face was all drawn up on one side and she was scarcely recognisable. The Colonel and I carried the body up to her room, and then set about looking for the other sister. She was nowhere to be found. I was very anxious that she should not return to the house unwarned and find her sister dead on the bed. With this end in view I persuaded the Colonel to remain on watch outside the house and prevent her entry. As there was no more to be done I came home and had my tea. While I was in the middle of that meal my wife returned from her shopping expedition. I broke the sad news to her.

" You'll be sorry to hear that Miss X died this afternoon from a stroke."

" Miss X," she replied, " why I've just been on the bus with her and her sister as well, they are just going home at the moment."

Without a word I rushed from the tea table and into my car. I was just in time to see the two sisters go along the road arm in arm in the direction of their house. I did some rapid thinking. Speedily I realised that I had made a mistake and I guessed where the mistake lay. Dexterously I manœuvred the car alongside them and engaged them in conversation.

" Did you by chance have another sister staying with you ? "
I asked.

" Oh, yes, our sister comes to stay with us once a year from
Glasgow, and she is with us now."

Gently I broke the news to them and suggested that they get into
the car and I run them home. I had quite forgotten that my friend
the Colonel was standing on guard over the door, and when the
car door opened and the corpse stepped out, it was more than his
gravity could stand. He laughed and laughed until I thought he
would never stop. Hurriedly I explained to the bereaved sisters
that great grief affected the Colonel in such a manner and ushered
them into the house of death. The Colonel vanished. He is
normally the most sedate of men.

Many of the friends I made in these days remain my friends to the
present day. To these days I date the beginning of my friendship
with Teddy, who is now a well-known surgeon, and his wife Ida,
who has fought a grand and winning battle against ill health. I
cherish the friendship of these two very greatly. Then there is the
" Bishop ", looking very Episcopal even in those days. Also there
is Frank—at whose hospitable house I have spent many a late evening. These and a host of others are typical of friendships which
have existed for many years and which have their roots in that
second practice. Curiously enough, these I have mentioned lived
within a stone's throw of each other.

I found that building up a practice required all the application of
one's time. I used to be thrilled each time I was asked to call at a
new house or when a new patient came to consult me. I found that
the majority of patients were from new houses themselves and that
people were comparatively slow to change their doctor once a choice
had been made. To begin with I had got a lot of time on my hands,
but as the years passed I found my time more and more occupied.

At this time the Great War had been over for some fifteen years,
yet I remember coming across its traces even after such a long time
had elapsed. A patient came to me one day complaining of an
irritation at a certain spot somewhere in the middle of his abdomen.
I arranged to see him again later and this time I thought I detected
something hard under my fingers. In due course a jagged piece of
metal was extruded from his skin. He had been hit in the back by
some shrapnel in 1916 and a large piece had remained in his body
all these years, working slowly round to the front and ultimately
making itself felt in the way I have indicated.

On another occasion I was showing a patient out while another man was coming in to see me. The two patients passed each other in the hall, hesitated a moment, and then one spoke to the other.

" Are you so and so ? "

" Yes," replied the other, " are you so and so ? The last time I remember seeing you was on the first of July, 1916, before we went over the top together. I heard you were hit that day but I have never had a chance of seeing you since."

It was a far cry from the Battle of the Somme to my entrance hall.

Lastly I had a case of my old friend Jacksonian Epilepsy. The patient had been wounded in the Great War and a small piece of shrapnel had lodged on the surface of his brain. Like many patients he had what is called an aura, that is to say a warning that he was going to have an attack. He had had the warning the night before and experience told him that he might expect another attack during the course of the coming night. He lived in a house alone. What was he to do ? I thought over the case carefully and, though he was a stranger to me, yet this man suffered in a sense for me. I invited him to spend the night in my house. He turned out to be a most charming companion and I have always counted it a privilege to have him among my friends, though a stranger way to get to know a man can hardly be imagined. I suppose the Great War has left its traces on most men who were in it.

I was expected to be an authority on everything. There was a house which I had to go to each week. In the front lawn was a small fishpond with a few goldfish swimming about in it disconsolately. One day while waiting for the door to be opened I idly noticed that the goldfish were not swimming about with their usual abandon. At last the door was opened for me by my patient's married son.

" Oh," I said, " your goldfish are looking a bit sickly."

" Yes," he replied, " they are."

He was one of those simple souls who evidently expected a doctor to know about everything.

" What should I do for them ? " he asked.

Now if there is one thing I know nothing about it's goldfish, so I idly said, " Oh, I'd give them a dose of salts."

On my return the following week I noticed that there were no goldfish in the pond, and when the same man came to open the door to me, I said, " What has happened to your goldfish ? "

To my astonishment he replied, " You have killed them."

He had put an ounce of Epsom Salts in the water. No wonder the fish were dead.

I was called to many accidents but surely this was one of the strangest.

It was the hour between dinner and bedtime when the day's work is done and a man dons his slippers and relaxes with his feet on the mantelpiece. I heard a ring at the front door and my own name mentioned urgently several times. It appeared that an accident had taken place at a nearby house.

A husband had given his wife a present of an Airedale dog especially with a view to its acting as a guard during his absence. They had a little girl aged three and it so happened that on this particular evening the husband had gone out and the mother was at work in the kitchen. The dog therefore had been left in the same room as the little girl.

The people were not patients of mine, but I knew the little girl well by sight and had often waved to her cheerily in passing.

Apparently the dog had savagely attacked the little girl and it was her screams which had brought the mother from the kitchen. All this was told me as my companion and I hurried along to the house in a nearby road.

The door was opened by the mother herself, and to my horror and without one word, she opened her hand and disclosed a small white semi-circular object which on closer inspection turned out to be her little girl's ear. The child was still bewailing its loss.

The dog had apparently been shut up as there was no sign of its presence. I was not hopeful, but washed the ear and placed it in a solution of ordinary common salt and lukewarm water. The family doctor was summoned. He was an old man with failing sight and an unsteady hand. He asked me if I would do the operation while he gave the anæsthetic.

I tried to fit the ear in various positions—it was rather like fitting together two pieces of a jigsaw puzzle. Ultimately I found what I thought was the correct position and sewed the ear on securely to the tags of flesh remaining. The child's head was bandaged up, and when she had sufficiently recovered I took my departure.

Some time later the parents took the child up to see a plastic specialist. He said that he was unable to improve on the condition. The ear had stuck on and that in spite of the fact that it had been in the dog's mouth, on the dining room carpet and ultimately in the mother's hand. The sequel to the story was that I received a guinea for my night's work.

In the last year I had every minute packed with work. It was really more than I could cope with single handed. Not that it was my ambition to have a big practice. It never was. Let the public beware of the men who are continually attending to more people than they can comfortably deal with at a time, and more especially —he who boasts about his continued busyness.

I remember how appalled I was in the days before I went into General Practice, to hear a doctor say :

"Well, I must get along now. There will be at least sixty people waiting for me when I get back."

"How on all the earth are you going to examine them all?" I asked.

"I don't," he replied. "At least fifty per cent will have coughs, and it's really quite easy. I ask all those with coughs to come outside into the passage. Then I ask those with wet coughs to stand on one side and those with dry coughs on the other—each individual in the same group gets the same medicine. Simple."

I have often regretted since that I did not ask him how he dealt with his constipated patients and their opposite numbers. Did he line them up against the wall too? But I am quoting a very exceptional case. Most medical men have a very high standard of professional ability and cope with their crowded surgeries in a thorough and very efficient manner.

As I have said, I never had any desire for a large practice. When one has little to do one's patients get over-visited, and when one has too much to do they get under-visited. If one becomes too busy then a pile of British Medical Journals remain inside their wrappers. I found towards the end I was continually working against the clock —or rather with one eye on it. A thoroughly bad state to get into, so I decided to take a partner.

Looking back, I would say that probably I have kept more up-to-date by picking the brains of specialists than by systematic reading.

This practice virtually came to an end when I took a partner who moved into my house and I left the district. Thus finished five happy years of hard work and solid endeavour. I had achieved what I set out to do. I had had my dark moments when I seemed to be getting nowhere. Alas ! I was apt to forget that all the time the practice was going ahead. I think the patients were very sad at my going. I know I was.

CHAPTER XI

MY THIRD PRACTICE

I AM calling this my third practice, but I want to make it quite clear that throughout the entire time I was in my third practice I was in partnership with the doctor who now occupied my old house at the corner. It was therefore more a continuation of my second practice then an entirely new venture.

A goodish number of my patients had moved to the outskirts of the suburb wherein we lived to a district some four miles away. I decided to follow them.

The house we occupied was commodious and detached. Unfortunately unlike my previous one, it was not on the edge of a new housing estate and therefore I found progress somewhat slower than I had previously done.

I was distinctly going up in the social scale with my patients, and the district where I lived contained a wealthier class of people as a rule than those among whom I had worked previously. No longer did my work lie amongst rows of small houses, but my daily visits took me among large establishments, only a few of which had succumbed to the modern tendency of being divided into flats.

I soon saw that a branch practice would present greater possibilities than even my own house, and very soon I had got an excellent pitch and an excellent housekeeper installed in a suitable house. My expectation was fulfilled. Soon the branch practice was busier than my own house, and though I went over every day to my partner's house to see such patients as wished to see me, yet I found that I had to spend an increasing amount of time at my new surgery.

I found that working up a practice here was much the same as previously. It was a case of becoming known to a sufficient number of people. When one was first consulted professionally it was a matter of retaining their confidence in increasing measure.

I found that the best advertisement for increasing my practice was the patients themselves, and though progress was slower than formerly yet in the three years I was there I had got together quite a considerable practice.

I have found that wherever I have started a practice my medical colleagues have been most considerate and understanding, and though there were considerably more of them in this new area yet they invariably made me welcome and sometimes worked in close association.

An example of this close association was to be found in the case of a colleague who phoned me one evening to tell me he was very worried about a young woman whom he had seen that evening in his surgery. It appeared that he was doing the work of another practice while his friend was on holiday for a few days. The lady in question was not a patient of his own but of this other doctor and had come in for an injection which was due that same day. His colleague had left directions for the dosage which was very minute —almost infinitesimal in fact—it was one of so many thousands part of a drop, a dose requiring a special syringe to measure it. It appeared that my friend had read the noughts wrong and given her ten times the amount he ought to have done. The drug had been injected into her and the damage was already done. The poor fellow was obviously very upset and apparently thought he had killed the girl. I enquired if she lived locally. " Oh, yes," he replied, " I often see her cycling to her work in the mornings. I know her well by sight." And then a bright idea struck me. " Stand behind the curtain and see if she passes to-morrow morning. You will at least know if she is able to attend her work or not." It was a very relieved voice which phoned me up next morning. He had hidden behind the curtains and seen her pass on her bicycle. As I went back to my interrupted breakfast I could not help smiling at the idea of the maiden cycling to her work blissfully unconscious that her every movement was being carefully watched by the doctor of the previous evening.

This house seemed to have a hoodoo on it after we left. First there was a violent outbreak of typhoid in the neighbourhood. It was traced to the water supply. Our water tank was affected and one person in the house contracted the disease and died.

Not long after that the second world war broke out, and though the house itself was not damaged, several bombs fell in the immediate vicinity and destroyed the neighbouring houses. Had we stayed on there the practice would almost certainly have disappeared owing to the mass evacuation from the district.

An incident of the honesty inherent in most people came to my notice during these days. I had acquired some skill and reputation in connection with skin diseases.

A police inspector from the other side of London consulted me one day about some skin trouble which he had. It appeared that he had consulted a very large number of doctors and had been to various skin hospitals. In fact, he was like the woman in the Bible who had spent all that she had on doctors and was no better. I examined his skin. I could tell him for a certainty what was the matter, but alas I could only suggest such treatment as was advised in the text books for that condition. I advised him to carry out such and such a line of treatment and see if it worked. Frankly, my fellow feeling for my predecessors was very strong and I never expected to succeed where they had failed.

When it came to paying I suggested to the man that, as I was not a skin specialist in the accepted meaning of the term, he pay me the ordinary consulting fee of seven and sixpence, but if by any chance he found that the condition had cleared up within six weeks he send me a consulting fee of three guineas, less the seven and six which he had already paid me.

Some two months later I received a cheque for two pounds, fifteen and sixpence. I did not even know the Inspector's name or address. It would have been quite easy for him to be dishonest had he been so inclined.

About this time King George V died. I well remember the night of his decease. I was visiting a patient near my home and the news of the progress of his illness was coming over the wireless with monotonous regularity, "The King's life is moving peacefully towards its close". I stayed on to listen as long as I could in all decency, but ultimately I had to leave as the hour advanced. I remember the feeling of almost personal sorrow in our hearts. I remember feeling that an age was passing away and we would not see its like again.

One day I woke up in the pitch dark of a winter's morning to hear the scurry of many footsteps passing down our usually quiet road. I glanced at my watch. It was five o'clock in the morning. People were already passing down the road in their hundreds on their way to the funeral of the late King.

The previous night an elderly spinster who lived next door had asked if she might accompany my wife and myself to the funeral. The three of us set out in my car. As we got into the centre of London the crowds became thicker and thicker and near Buckingham Palace we had to wait a long time for the troops who were going to line the streets and were marching across the head of the road. We got a view point looking down the Mall. I have never seen so dense a crowd in my life. A man next to me took half an hour before he could take his handkerchief from his pocket to blow his nose. People fainted frequently, but they were unable to fall and they remained vertical but unconscious. They were handed over the heads of the crowd to the ambulance men in the rear.

I remember the skirl of the pipes playing " Over the sea to Skye." I remember the serried ranks of the bluejackets pulling the ropes of the gun-carriage. I remember the new King walking behind his dead father, and I remember the crowd of notables in the procession following.

To revert to the practice again, some of the cases I attended had their lighter sides. Such a one happened one day when I was least expecting it. A call came one morning when I was at breakfast asking me to go urgently to see an elderly lady who lived in a road nearby. The lady suffered from delusional insanity. Her delusions took two forms. One was harmless, the other not so harmless.

Generally she sat placidly enough on a wooden chair placed on a sort of elevated platform at the end of the room, with a walking-stick in her hand which was meant to represent a sceptre. She was under the delusion that she was the Empress of some place or other—Russia, I think. Sometimes, however, she would be under the delusion that she was Venus and would act accordingly. I may say in all sincerity that she was no beauty—even in the dimmest light—and that the Venus delusion was quite as grotesque as her Empress one.

The old lady lived mostly in a sunny room facing the road and on the first floor up. There was a small veranda outside her window with some pots of geraniums on it. I didn't bother to get out my car as she lived not far away. I went along at once. I can see the house yet, with the strip of lawn running down to the hedge.

It appeared that the nurse had left her on her throne with the walking-stick in her hand, as the Empress, clothed and in her right mind, or at least in her normal mind. The nurse had then gone downstairs to make the breakfast. The metamorphosis came on the patient very suddenly. When the nurse returned with the tray the room was empty. Or was it? Among the geranium plants on the balcony was a shrivelled pink figure. Her patient had entered upon the Venus stage of her delusions and had arranged her costume, or rather lack of costume, accordingly.

It was the work of a moment for the nurse to seize her by the wrist and force her back into the sitting-room. The old lady was not fit to resist the propelling power of the younger and more robust woman. She knew when she was beaten. As a last gesture of defiance, the old lady took out her upper dentures and with much the same careless abandon with which the gallant Douglas hurled the heart of Bruce against the advancing foe, threw her teeth into the garden below.

When I arrived she was clothed and seated as the Empress once more. The nurse, looking a trifle dishevelled, was rearranging the tray. I did not know why I had been sent for. I still don't know. I thought I would justify my existence, or rather my fee, by going down to the garden and retrieving the teeth. I opened the front door and immediately saw them near the corner of the strip of lawn beside the gate. I was just in time also to see a dog nosing around the gatepost.

It was a curious looking mongrel. One part appeared to be spaniel, the other showed all the characteristics of a dachshund, at least its chassis was extraordinarily low slung. Unfortunately, the dog saw the teeth at the same moment as myself. I could read that dog's mind like an open book. We made a simultaneous dive for the teeth. Partly owing to their proximity to the dog and partly because he was a quicker mover than me, the spaniel-cum-dachshund got there first. I regretted not having the car, but I was young and in excellent training.

When I emerged from the gate the dog was leading by about fifty yards and taking the slope with determination. When the lead had increased to two hundred yards I gave up, and the last I saw of the dog and the teeth was the dog taking a corner at speed with what looked like a bone in its mouth.

I came to know households from a different angle from the ordinary individual. In doing so I learned many things. I learned, for example, that more people than one would imagine lived up to the limit of their income, and that people whom, from the size of their house, one would have judged to be very well off, sometimes turned out to have very modest incomes. As one got to know the family better one learned that there is a common stratum in all families. The aspirations and hopes of parents turned out to be the same for all children. I found that almost all parents not only give their children the best possible education, but try to start them off in life at the point where they themselves had arrived. They were apt to forget that their children had to learn by bitter—sometimes very bitter—experience, and that the lessons of life are sometimes very harshly acquired.

It was a surprise to me to realise that the biggest class of unconscious malingerers was among children. I myself have the most vivid recollection of standing on the linoleum on my bedroom floor in my bare feet with a view to getting a cold if I had not prepared my school work for the following day.

It was a surprise to me also to realise that a normal child has little or no sense of fear, but that fear is very quickly caught from its elders.

When the head of the house was the patient, one naturally got to know the foundations of the family much more quickly than with other members of the household. I have always noticed that when a man has shed the black hat, pin-striped trousers and little black jacket of the city and assumed a horizontal position clothed in pyjamas, he takes on a totally different significance.

One other thing I have noticed is that very ill people cannot really make the effort to think. People are apt to look upon a severe illness as a time for mental relaxation. So it is, but the relaxation generally does not require any conscious effort.

In a sense every happening in a doctor's life is associated with the dramatic. This is more especially so if one defines drama as the sudden change from the normal to the abnormal. I remember three doctors—a general practitioner (myself), a surgeon and a physician—being stranded for a night in a cottage on a lonely stretch of the coast of Cornwall. To pass the time away we told the most dramatic incidents in our experience.

This is the surgeon's story. He was apparently on the staff of two hospitals, and on that particular day had amputated a man's leg at the hip for a rare tumour of the bone which he thought would make a suitable specimen for the museum of the other hospital. He asked the house surgeon to wrap the limb up in brown paper and put it in the back of his car. While on his way to the other hospital he called at a nursing home in the centre of London, and during the time he was inside seeing his patient the package was stolen from his car. He said that he got a tremendous amount of enjoyment picturing the thief's face when he came to open the parcel, not to mention how he disposed of his booty.

The physician's story was of the days when he was a house physician in hospital. Apparently he was attached to the ward where people are sent for three days to be under the observation of the physician in charge. His room was right below the Observation Ward, and one night he was just going to bed when he saw a pair of feet suspended outside his bedroom window. Only a pair of feet were to be seen. Gradually they got lower and lower, and ultimately a man appeared in view. He couldn't think who it was, but it turned out to be an escaping patient.

Although the story which I myself told has to do with a later practice and occurred many miles from London, I propose to relate it here.

I was having my breakfast one morning when a woman asked to see me urgently. The story she gave was that she and her husband and some friends had been playing cards on the previous Saturday night. By now it was Tuesday morning. The husband had gone down the road to get some cigarettes, but apparently he had been attacked on the way and had received injuries which produced a complete loss of memory. He had only returned home the previous night and had kept on repeating that he had been to the white house with the big man.

I promised to make it my first visit. When I got there I found their house to be the upper flat of a semi-detached villa. It appeared that the occupants of the lower flat were away on holiday at the time, so that it was unoccupied. A strip of lawn ran up to the door on each side of the pathway, and it was dotted with several poplar trees. A thick hedge separated the lawns from the road and in the middle of the hedge was a little wooden gate by which one entered.

When I got there the man was sitting bolt upright in bed with a strained and far-away expression in his eyes. To all my questions he would only reply that he had been to the white house, and when I inquired with whom he invariably replied, " With the big man." I could get no other information whatever from him. I could detect no sign of injury, and, apart from his mental symptoms, he did not seem to be seriously injured. When I made as if to go the wife asked me for a certificate, a not unusual happening in these days of insurances and sick clubs. But, strangely enough, she insisted that I state in my certificate that he had been attacked and wasn't responsible for his actions. I cannot say whether it was due to my natural Scottish caution or whether it was due to the fact that I don't like being dictated to by a lay person, but I declined. I would either write a certificate in my own way or not at all. As a result it was not at all.

I arranged to go back and see the man that night. When I arrived at the house in the late evening I asked the woman whether her husband had shown symptoms of violence during the day. She told me that at one time he had become very restless. In consequence I left an opium pill on the table for her to give to her husband should he need it in the night. The man was in the same condition, and again the woman asked for a certificate in the same way. Again I refused. By now I was thoroughly worried about the man and wanted the wife to have him removed to hospital or a nursing home as soon as possible. She indignantly refused. I visited the man the next morning, and again the same series of events took place. I only got " the white house and the big man " from the patient with the staring eyes who sat up in bed, but there was one other thing I noticed when I made a careful examination of the man.

It is a well-known fact that opium contracts the pupils, but the extraordinary fact was that this man's pupils were of normal size, although his wife told me she had had to give him the pill in the latter half of the night. By now I was thoroughly worried about the case, and told her that I could not be responsible for her husband any longer unless he was removed to some place where he could be under proper observation and treatment.

As I went out through the wooden gate in the hedge and crossed the pavement to my waiting car a man who appeared to have been hiding in the hedge beckoned me up the road. A second man from a similar position joined him. I was naturally taken aback.

" Who are you ? " I said, " and what do you want ? "

" We are from the C.I.D., and we will be glad of your help," they said, showing me their authorisation.

I naturally said that I would do what I could.

" Did you leave a pill on the table last night for the man to take ? "

" Yes, I did," I replied.

" Would it surprise you to know that as soon as you had gone the man got up from his bed and had a cigarette with his wife, and that the pill which you left was put in the fire ? "

" How on earth do you know that ? " I replied.

" One of us was up a tree watching," was the answer.

" What is it all about ? " I asked.

" This man collects the week's takings of some multiple shops, but he did not hand in the money last Saturday. The whole thing is a blind to get you to write a certificate which they thought you would stand by if the case ever came to trial."

Apparently they had selected one as the most likely doctor they could find to help them with their activities.

And that was the story I told on a wild night in a cottage on the Cornish coast.

I feel I must relate an incident which occurred to a colleague as it illustrates the more humorous and grotesque side of General Practice. It so happened that my colleague was called to attend a lady. He went back several times during the course of the day. Unfortunately, one of her staff went completely off her head during the same day, and, to complicate matters still further, a fierce and bloodthirsty dog took up its position under the mental patient's bed. It was essential that she be got away to hospital as speedily as possible, but whenever anyone came near the dog sprang out from under the bed with a snarl and a snapping of teeth. Towards evening the doctor decided that the situation was becoming intolerable. The son of the house had been a sportsman of renown and included in his activities the art of fencing and of cricketing. Luckily his kit was available. Armed with a fencer's mask over his face, cricketing gloves over his hands and thick padding over his body, the doctor crawled across the floor and bearded the dog in his den. A short but sharp struggle ensued, and the dog was ultimately removed by the scruff of his neck, while the patient was sent to hospital in the waiting ambulance.

In the course of years I had amassed a great deal of information which was not to be found in text-books—medical or otherwise. I had learned, for example, that the great majority of people who consult a doctor have no recognisable disease, and I think that my experience is probably that of most of my fellow practitioners. I learned, too, that those suffering from unbalanced mental conditions are much commoner than is generally supposed. These people as a rule make charming companions, but nevertheless they are distinctly volatile in temperâment, like mercury. They are generally up in the clouds or down in the depths. I learned that it was not wise to take the face value of a patient whilst he or she is speaking to their doctor. Almost certainly after the doctor has gone away these people will collapse like pricked balloons and plumb depths of solitary misery which are unknown to the normal person.

I learned, too, that those who suffer from functional unbalance, for example, those with rapidly-beating hearts but no heart disease, those who complain of pain which has no physical cause, or those who suffer from insomnia but never hear the chimes of clocks, are commonest of all. I discovered that patients—especially women patients—don't like to be told the truth, the whole truth and nothing but the truth. Pain is like wealth. It is a relative term.

I think I have mentioned previously that renal colic is one of the severest types of pain. I recall a case which arose under most extraordinary circumstances.

I was treating a patient at this time for renal colic and had occasion to ask him when he had had his first attack. He told me that it was during the Great War of 1914–1918. In that war he was attached to the Tank Corps. The night before the tanks were to make their first appearance on the Somme he spent in the open beside his tank. At daylight he was to go into action, and to his consternation he developed this appalling pain a few hours before. He had the prospect of spending the day in his tank, fighting a severe and unprecedented action in it or of going off sick. It was a situation which few would care to be in, as it was impossible to replace him in the tank. I asked him what he did. He said that he drank a full bottle of whisky and that he had no recollection whatever of the attack.

He must have done pretty well in it, however, for he was awarded the Military Cross for his exploits that day. He had not the least idea what he had done until he read the citation. I still think it was the best possible line of action he could have taken.

I found that I was not always right in my judgment, however. A woman came to see me one day complaining that she had been bitten on the ankle by a snake. There were some woods in the neighbourhood, and it appeared that she had been picking black-berries along with her little girl. She felt something sting her ankle, and was just in time to see a black object slide away quickly through the grass.

I examined the woman's ankle and found two adjacent spots on it which were so small that I did not think they could possibly be the result of a snake-bite. Though I had lived abroad, I had had no experience of snake-bites, although naturally I was cognisant with their symptoms and their treatment. I reassured the woman, but just to be on the safe side advised her to rest for a time on a couch in the waiting-room.

As the hour was approaching tea-time I left her in order to have my tea. About an hour later I looked in to see if she was fit to go home. To my astonishment and consternation I found her almost unconscious with the ankle swollen up to the size of a tree trunk and with all the symptoms of acute poisoning. It was now too late to open the wound and rub in crystals of permanganate of potash, the treatment recommended in the textbooks.

I walked the patient up and down as far as I was able and gave her copious draughts of brandy. Gradually she recovered and ultimately the leg subsided, but never again was I sceptical about the history which a patient gave.

One of the strangest incidents which occurred to me in those days was this. I was sitting down to my midday meal when the phone bell rang and I was asked to go to a case immediately. It turned out to be a father who had gone off his head suddenly and unexpectedly.

When I arrived at the house I found a group of relatives huddled together in a downstairs room and a white-faced policeman standing guard at the foot of the stairs. Upstairs the patient had been left to his own devices and was at present employed in drinking a bottle of whisky with great persistence and enthusiasm. Unfortunately, a thick pea-soup fog was descending over London and its environs, and I had only just managed to get there in time. I knew the patient and liked him, and, moreover, I was pretty sure he had a liking for me. In consequence I mounted the stairs with less trepidation than I otherwise would. The patient was consuming whisky in a tumbler with less and less water.

He greeted me enthusiastically, even boisterously, and nothing would satisfy him but that I would sit down and accompany him. I got rid of that whisky by every possible method, and I regret to say that when I ultimately rose to go there was a small sea of whisky on the floor around my chair. Unfortunately, the ambulance could not reach the house for three hours owing to the fog, and it took six able-bodied men to move him when he came to realise that he was being taken from his home. I shall always remember the effort it was to appear to consume whisky and yet to keep my head clear alone in the room with a lunatic.

One other story of these days about a mad person comes to my mind. The patient was a homicidal maniac and I had been requested by his family to take him from the place where he was staying to the hospital. On my invitation he jumped into the car readily enough, but when the car was going about 40 m.p.h. he suddenly opened the door and jumped out, landing on all fours. He picked himself up and proceeded to chase someone against whom he considered he had a grudge. Luckily the victim saw him coming and fled for his life to the safety of the nearest house.

I turned the car as quickly as possible and caught up on my patient as he ran along the road. I invited him again into the car and we resumed our interrupted journey. Unfortunately, he had opened the back door and was sitting directly behind me on the back seat. I don't think I have ever been so frightened in my life, and I watched his every movement in the little mirror above my head, expecting every moment to get the starting-handle or some such object down on my head. He made no move, however, and remained quite quiescent all the journey; but such an experience did not inspire me to further efforts in dealing single-handedly with lunatics.

I want to mention here a group of cases which one might term the psychical which also occurred at this time. They have no relation to any known law, but are worthy of recording.

I had booked a confinement which was due the following month. One day the young husband called to see me. He made the following extraordinary request. He said that he and his wife had always shared everything and at this coming time it did not seem right for his wife to suffer all the pain and he himself have none. Apparently they had talked it over and he had come to me to express the views of both of them.

He asked me if he might sit quietly in a corner of the room throughout her labour. He promised that he would not interfere or say a word—in fact he indicated to me just where he proposed to sit during the time. I pointed out to him that even though his wife was willing, neither the nurse nor I would agree to his suggestion, and that probably when the time came the woman herself would not wish it.

A day or two afterwards he was killed in an accident, and the following month a beautiful baby girl was born.

The labour did not go as one would have wished and a doctor who was staying with me at the time accompanied me to the house and acted as my assistant. Ultimately, as I have said, the woman was delivered of a baby daughter, and after the invariable cup of tea my " assistant " and I drove home in the dusk of a winter's evening. When we were seated in the car the other doctor turned to me and said :

" Did you notice anything odd about that confinement ? "

" No," I said. " Did you ? "

" Well," he replied, " there were only four people in the room, you and I and the nurse and the patient, but I persistently kept feeling there was a fifth person there, too—not counting the baby. I felt that this person was seated in a corner," and he described the place. " I felt it so strongly that I kept turning my head in that direction to see if there was anybody there. I wondered if you had the same feeling."

I had not told him anything about the husband, but the chair he referred to was the same as that which the husband had asked to occupy during the confinement.

Another incident is somewhat different and the only factor in common with it and the previous one is that neither conform to any known law, and both verge on the supernatural.

Both the people concerned were working. It was in the days before their children had been born and I suppose that an extra amount of cash was very welcome to the domestic budget.

The wife carried on with her work as a typist with some firm of publishers in the City, while the husband was employed at a nearby garage.

One morning, just as I was going out, the husband was brought up to me in a car. It appeared that in the course of his work he had slipped and sustained a compound fracture of his leg. I saw that it was a case for hospital and after doing what I could to make him comfortable, I climbed into the front seat beside the driver and directed him to drive to the nearest hospital.

I turn now to the doings of the wife. In the course of the forenoon she found herself unable to settle to do her job. It was so evident that her mind was not on her typing that her employer asked her what was the matter. She said that she felt something was wrong with her husband. Like a wise man he saw that she would not be fit for any satisfactory work until her mind was at rest and suggested to her that she go home and find out.

She took him at his word and caught a train down to the suburbs. When she arrived at her destination she went straight to the hospital, which incidentally lay in a different direction from that which she would normally have taken, and inquired if a Mr. so-and-so were there. She was told that her husband had been admitted less than an hour before.

During this time ill health continued to dog my footsteps. It was not chronic ill health but rather a succession of major catastrophies each of which had to be faced in turn and overcome. For example I woke up one morning with a severe pain in my face. Thinking it was an abscess in my teeth I paid a visit forthwith to my dentist who X-rayed them and assured me that the trouble was not there, so I made my way down to the hospital where I caught the ear, nose and throat specialist at the tail end of a clinic.

He examined me thoroughly and then shook his head ominously. " Both your sinuses are full of pus ", he informed me. " You must have them punctured and washed out as soon as possible."

I promised him that I would come in to-morrow and that I would keep the day clear for that purpose. He laughed a trifle grimly.

" You must have the operation as soon as possible to-day."

I pointed out to him that I had thirteen visits which I must do. Nevertheless I climbed on the operating table and under a local anæsthetic he did what was necessary. When I came off the operating table I felt somewhat sick. I sat for about an hour before getting into my car. It was impossible to get any help as late as that and the thirteen patients were duly visited by me. The last one of all was a patient in a large house, where the door was opened by a butler. I had just had a severe bleeding from the site of the operation, in the shrubbery beside the house, and was probably looking somewhat shaken as a consequence. Anyway, when he came to the door I remember asking for the cloak-room in order to clean myself up.

I think that day I felt considerably worse than many of the patients whom I visited. When I got home to a belated dinner I went to bed and phoned up a neighbouring doctor with the request that he would do any calls for me which came in. Luckily it was my free half-day. He assured me that he would do any visits for me but that meantime he had his own work to finish. I was just getting warm in bed when the telephone bell rang. It was the doctor's wife to say her husband had gone out. One of his patients—a personal friend—had suddenly passed away and could I come at once. There was nothing for it but to get up and dress myself and make my way to the address indicated. Next day I carried on just the same and was not off a day as a result of the operation. Such is the penalty of General Practice.

I think it fitting that I should relate here the biggest medical howler which, to my knowledge, I have ever made. There was an epidemic of influenza on at the time and I had had a tremendous number of night calls. Not that I had been up the whole night, but that every night over a long period had been broken into by some call or other. On the last night of all before I fell a victim myself I came in about one o'clock dead tired and lay down on the top of my bed, having only taken off my shoes. I pulled the quilt over me and at once fell into a heavy sleep from which I was awakened by the sound of the telephone ringing.

The instrument was beside my bed and in those days it consisted of two parts, one part applied to one's ear and the other into which one spoke. It can be imagined how drunk with sleep I was when I could not even remember in the darkness which end one spoke into. Eventually I got the apparatus right and a man's voice spoke to me. I recognised his voice. He proceeded to tell me what was the matter. He told me that his wife had an internal hæmmorrhage, though not a very serious one. At this point I think I must have gone to sleep again for a moment or two because when I woke up he was saying, " And what do you think I should do, doctor ? "

The previous conversation had departed entirely from my head and I had not the slightest recollection of what he had told me about his wife. However, I felt that I had to say something and what I did say was this.

" Tell her to gargle every hour and ring me in the morning at eight o'clock," and then I rang off with the telephone beside me in its various bits, which my wife with her usual forethought collected and put in position.

At eight o'clock the next morning the husband duly rang up. I still had no recollection of what was wrong with his wife, so when he rang up I asked him to refresh my memory. He told me about her trouble and what I had said in my reply.

" You told me to get her to gargle every hour ".

I explained the circumstances and luckily he was most sympathetic. The implicit confidence which is shown by some patients in the medical profession is sometimes shattering. I remember a patient —who had more money than sense—being advised by me to eat grapes as a part of his diet. Shortly afterwards his butler rang up to know whether I had meant black grapes or white grapes ! Such is the faith of some human beings.

This reminds me of a man who came to me one day and whom I advised to take some gentle exercise. He was a stout man and had not been in the habit of taking any exercise whatever. In fact, he was what one might term a bit of an old woman. Ultimately he agreed to undertake some swimming at the local baths. At the door he turned back.

" Doctor," he said, " I have never been without my body belt and I don't think it would be right for me to run the risk of contracting a cold. When I go to the baths I cannot go into the water in my body belt. What shall I do ? "

One day a lady came to see me. Tall, dignified and self possessed. She was wearing what I believe is known as a two-piece costume. She was a stranger to me and told me that she had just been appointed to an important post in the neighbourhood. Before starting work she thought it was wise to have the opinion of a doctor as to her fitness as she had a minor disability on which she wanted some advice. I examined her and found that she was suffering from advanced cancer. I remember doodling with my pencil on the desk. I felt in a terrible position. It was absolutely necessary that this woman should undergo immediately an extensive and dangerous operation, and on the other hand she was sitting there utterly unconscious of the fact. She had reached the summit of her ambition in this new appointment. I summoned up my courage and told her. There are various ways of wrapping a thing up however unpleasant, but no amount of wrapping could possibly disguise the unpleasantness of what I had to tell her. She took it like the brave woman and the Christian which I afterwards found her to be.

The operation was performed at the local hospital. For many weeks she lay between life and death and the angel of death hovered very near her bed. Gradually she began to recover until ultimately she made a complete recovery and was able to take up the threads of her life at the point where they had been left off. She took the job which had been kept open for her, and is now doing a great work in the sphere to which she had been called.

The vast majority of my patients were ordinary simple folk with nothing dramatic or unusual about them. They tend to become stunted in one's memory of the daily round, but one case comes to my mind. It was that of two elderly sisters who lived together.

I suppose their income was modest, though they lived in a fairly large house, for they had no resident maid. It happened that during the course of one of those epidemics of influenza which descend upon us from time to time in the winter both the sisters caught it, and it both cases it turned into pneumonia.

I remember sitting between the beds of the two wondering which would go first, and then I knew of a certainty that it was the artistic one—the one who would have found it most difficult to live alone. The two sisters were lying in the one room both gravely ill, and late one evening one passed from the struggles of her life into the quiet peace of death. I thought the other was about to follow, but to my surprise she recovered and now in that big house all alone she waits like a person in the waiting-room of a station for the train to come in which will carry her to her destination where her sister will be waiting for her on some far bourne.

Out of the many hundreds of visits I paid only the one or two had some abnormality attached to them which makes them stand out in my memory. Such a one was, to use the language of Sherlock Holmes, the episode of the narrow staircase.

It was a Monday in the month of January and my first visit of the day. They were new patients and the house was one of a long recently erected row on one of the new estates. The husband was the patient and he was in bed upstairs. I don't remember any children. In any case they were an elderly couple and whatever family they had would have left the home long since. The door was opened to me by an extremely stout, elderly woman. The staircase was steep and narrow and she motioned me to precede her up the stairs. Normally I would have followed her up the stairs but her wheezing and grunting made me think that she would prefer me to go first. I thought that she wanted to take her time because of her stoutness. As I went up the staircase struck me as being abnormally narrow, and we had got about two-thirds of the way up when I distinctly felt the jab from a pin in my back. I am calling it my back but in reality it was that portion of one's anatomy which butchers call the rump, which navigators call the stern, and which Presbyterians call the latter end. The pin could only have come from one place and only one hand could have guided it. Had I wandered into a madhouse inadvertently? The woman looked sane enough but one never knew. I proceeded up another step. Oh! I had got it again. A hard one this time—no possible doubt about it. Now I am not a man who suffers in silence.

Moreover I had quickly glanced round and thought I detected the woman withdrawing her hand.

I stood on the step of the stairs and looked round at the woman. I am not one to say nothing.

" Excuse me, but did you stick a pin in me just now ? " I said. The woman looked startled—as well she might.

" No," she said, " I didn't."

I apologised and mounted the next step. Oh ! A vicious jab this time—certainly deep enough to draw blood. I still said nothing, convinced that I had entered a madhouse. I climbed steadily on. Great Scott ! I got it again. There was no doubt about it this time. A pin—and a large pin at that—was sticking into me at every step. There was only one thing to be done. I asked for the privacy of a room in order that I might examine my clothing. I felt rather like the schoolboy who examines the seat of chastisement to see if there is any blood. Certainly it felt like it. In the privacy of the bathroom I undressed. It was not a pin as I expected. My wife had visited the Christmas sales and the ticket announcing that the price of the garment had been reduced from so-and-so to so-and-so was affixed by a three-pronged trident which had drawn blood, much blood. I considered that apology was due to the fat woman waiting on the landing outside, so I explained.

Similarly I can recall the case of the deaf tobacconist. He was elderly and he was deaf and he kept a little tobacconist shop into which it was my custom to drop occasionally when I found myself short of tobacco. He came to consult me about an intestinal trouble which is very prevalent, very persistent and practically painless, in other words, he suffered from constipation. Having made sure that there was no special cause for the condition I recommended that he take half a teaspoonful of liquid cascara in some water. He thanked me and took his departure. A few days later he turned up again to report that my suggestion had proved useless.

" Oh ! " I said light-heartedly, " take a full teaspoonful. I know it is twice the maximum dose but lots of people take that amount ".

" Eh ! " he said, cupping his ear.

I repeated what I had said. He seemed dubious and went away shaking his head. The next morning I was sent for to his address where a most irate man was awaiting me. It turned out that he had taken a full tablespoonful instead of a full teaspoonful.

CHAPTER XII

SCOTLAND

I SUPPOSE every Scotsman has periods of nostalgia for the land of his birth. For twelve years I had been chasing the elusive dollar along the hard pavements of London, and there came to me a longing for my feet to be on the heather once more and to see the distant peaks instead of rows of houses.

I recalled having gone to see an old doctor—a man of much experience and sagacity—and asking his opinion as to where I should settle next. He said a strange thing to me.

" Don't practice in Wales or Yorkshire, but a good Scotch accent is worth about £200 a year in the south of England ".

I can readily understand why not Wales, for a stranger there is a foreigner until the day he dies, but to this day I don't understand why he advised me not to settle in Yorkshire. Maybe he thought there were too many Scotsmen there already ; maybe he thought that the dourness of the Yorkshireman and the alleged thrift of the Scot would inevitably clash. I know not, but anyway, I accepted his suggestion and went to the south of England. Nature had equipped me with a good Scots accent at no cost to myself, and I was determined to try his suggestion of turning it into money in the south of England. So I set out for London.

I well remember how I had first left Scotland for London. I would then have been about eighteen years of age and had come down on the night train to King's Cross. Having been recommended to Lyon's Strand Corner House, I went thither for my breakfast. Unfortunately, though I believed that a fortune was to be made in London, yet at the same time I believed that the majority of its inhabitants were thieves and vagabonds. I, being a simple Scottish youth, was going to make doubly sure that the Londoners were not going to have me for their prey, so I took the precaution of tying round my waist the small amount of money which I had to spend. I remember the blush of shame which mantled my cheek when I had almost to undress in Lyon's Strand Corner House to pay the bill for my breakfast. I recall the amusement caused to the young ladies employed by Messrs. Lyons & Co.

Now, from time to time I found myself studying the advertisement columns of the *British Medical Journal*, with special reference to those which advertised practices for sale in Scotland. And then, out of the blue, came the very thing I was looking for. It was a case of where " every prospect pleases ". The income was adequate ; the house satisfactory, and the locality one of the most beautiful in the Highlands. But I think it was the etceteras which tempted me most. One was a free pass on the railways in the area of the practice. Another, as reward for some first-aid lectures to railway employees, was the promise of first class return tickets for myself and my wife to any station that I might choose in Great Britain. I saw myself having all the privileges of an M.P. without the responsibilities.

After investigation I decided to acept the offer, and in due course two huge pantechnicons containing our furniture set out from London on their way to the far north. My wife and I went up by car. The children were to follow when we were settled. It was early spring when we set out, or rather late winter, for the snow was still thick upon the ground. I remember the heavy snow clouds which lay over the sea at the mouth of the Firth of Forth, and I remember also the little daubs of melting snow which lay beneath the birch trees as we neared our destination.

These birch trees made a profound impression on me for reasons which are not usually associated with that tree. There was a wood of them just behind the house where we lodged for the first night of our stay, and I could see lights moving about among the trees in the gathering darkness. I naturally enquired what was happening. Apparently they were carried by moth hunters who had travelled up all the way from London for the sole purpose of securing a moth which was only to be found on the trunks of these trees. My respect for moth collectors has ever since been profound. Apparently they got what they wanted, for in due course they hied themselves back to London beaming geniality on every one.

The house where we lived was typically Scottish, stone built with three gables and definitely middle class. The village was long and straggling and our house lay near its end. All the woodwork in it, probably from the local pine trees, was stained a light brown. This colour gave it an air of lightness and airiness—and over all hung the smell of wood smoke which I shall always associate with that particular village. The consulting-room was very different from the up-to-date establishment over which I had presided in London. I was at a loss for a waiting-room until I found that the villagers were more at home talking to the maid in the kitchen than sheltering behind the anonymity of last week's *Punch*. The better classes were accommodated in the dining-room.

The dark forest came down almost to the back garden, and at night during the rutting season we could hear the roaring of the stags and the clash of their antlers as they fought. I doubt if there was another house between us and the nearest town over thirty miles away. In front of us stretched the mountains, probably the most wonderful panorama in Scotland, with its ever-changing light and shade. In the mornings the great huddle of mountains was often wrapped in a white mist out of which huge humps of hills projected. As the day advanced, the sun would disperse the cloud and the high peaks would be visible and the long ridge of the summit made sharp. Towards evening the mist would come down again, but this time the play of sunlight would bring out many colours. They would range from pink in the upper parts to a deep plum at the base, and always the mouth of the great glen would be etched in shadow. They were the highest mountain mass in Britain, but curiously enough they did not give one the impression of tremendous height so much as of utter massiveness. I came to know every peak of them, by personal experience as well as by sight.

Over all was the sound of running water. The gurgle of a multitude of streams was always in one's ears, and from the summit of the slight hill behind the house it was possible to count nearly a score of lochs.

Shortly after my arrival I decided that I would look the part of a Highlander. With that end in view I invested in a kilt of my mother's tartan and, what is more to the point, I wore it. During my sojourn in the Highlands I don't suppose there was a day on which I did not wear the garb of old Gaul. For the benefit of those who have only gazed from afar I would say a kilt is the coolest garment for summer wear and the warmest for winter. For some reason or other I had considerable difficulty in keeping mine at the right length, which is measured by a person kneeling so that the kilt just touches the floor. I wore an evening-dress jacket with small silver buttons, but never got beyond the one kilt which had to do duty for the two very different jackets—one for daily use and the other for evening dress. I did, however, have two different sporrans. A leather one by day and a beaver one by night, like the cloud by day and the pillar of fire by night. I have a very strong affection for that kilt as it once saved my life up north.

Not far from where I lived was a stretch of water which was a great place for pike, and some islands in the middle were the nesting-place of wild fowl, chiefly black-headed gulls. The eggs of these birds are considered rather a delicacy in spite of their somewhat fishy taste, and I set out with a keeper one day to collect some. We rowed out to where the prospects seemed good and from the boat I took a flying leap on to the island. Unfortunately, though the island looked solid, it was merely a floating collection of sedge, mud and roots. I was in my bare feet and wearing the kilt to which I have referred. To my horror, my feet went right through the floating island and were suspended in the water underneath. Luckily my kilt saved me. It ballooned out and held me up long enough for the keeper to lay some planks from the boat to the island, along which he crawled and pulled me out. Had I been wearing trousers I would probably have gone right through and lost my life. The memory of these few moments when my fate literally hung on a kilt gave to me a further affection for that garment which has only deepened with the years.

The bread and butter of our lives was supplied by the villagers and the isolated farms round about, but the jam came from the big hotels with which the place abounded. It was by one of these that my fame was spread abroad in the countryside. I remember the occasion as though it were yesterday.

It was a glorious summer evening. One of those days when the rain clouds have taken their departure and a brilliantly clear evening takes their place. I was rang up by one of the hotels, and was told that the patient had been unconscious for two hours. Would I come at once?

When I got there the courtyard of the hotel was crowded with people, mostly chauffeurs and servants of one variety or another. In the middle was a group of maidservants, all hanging over an unfortunate woman who lay on the ground covered with coats. A brief examination made it evident that her "unconsciousness" was a case of simple hysteria. No person who is not truly unconscious can bear having his or her eyeballs touched. Inevitably they screw up their eyelids, thereby giving the show away to whoever is examining them. I made a great show of calling for water, which was speedily brought to me and put beside the patient. The multitude stood around open-mouthed to see what would happen next. I felt rather like the miracle man in some play. Obviously they expected me to do something, and do it quickly. What the patient expected is not on record.

I knelt down beside her and breathed into her ear so that nobody else could hear the whispered words.

" If you don't get up by the time I count ten I am going to pour the entire contents of this jug down your neck."

I then started to count in a whisper—one, two, three, and so on. When I got to ten she slowly got to her feet and went indoors to " lie down ". The onlookers thought that a suitable miracle had been provided for them, and from that day my reputation as a worker of wonders was established.

I found General Practice in the Highlands a very different matter from General Practice in London. To begin with, there was the temperament of the Highlanders themselves. The Highlanders are a race apart ; in many respects they are somewhat like the Welsh or the Southern Irish, and there is a world of difference between the ordinary Lowland Scot and his brother from the mountains. Certain virtues the Highlander possesses to an unusual degree. They are patriotic to a fault, but their patriotism is strangely local and provincial. They pay allegiance above all to their race and their name, and for the sake of these they are prepared to pay a heavy price. I found them brave, generous, with an old-fashioned courtesy which was very attractive. On the other side there were pagan elements which lie just below the skin of most Highlanders. They were intensely superstitious— fairies, elves and pixies have a very real place in their mental make-up—and I am not sure that their undue respect for the Sabbath is not unconnected with this strain of superstition. I remember a young man coming to me with a forefinger which had been damaged by an axe. He rather took my breath away by saying, " This is a result of cutting sticks on a Sabbath Day," and, what is more, he believed it.

Like most people who live their lives in communities apart from their fellows they were apt to say things which were pleasing rather than unpleasant things which were true, and, like many people who live near to nature, many of them were guilty of the grosser sins of the flesh.

I have referred to their pride. It was quite a usual thing for a panel patient—or, more commonly still, a private patient—to leave a rabbit or two or three eggs at my house when requesting a visit. Such a thing would never be dreamt of down south.

In the Highlands it is the custom for a doctor to attend the funerals of his patients. In consequence I won't exactly say that I was never off the road, but at least I became an expert on that particular subject. The Highlander dearly loves a funeral. It provides him with a subtle pleasure—almost amounting to a pain —which nothing else can provide. It was the custom for the coffin to be brought outside the house and laid on two chairs in the open. The mourners standing around would take what shelter they could from the biting wind and the scurrying snow if it were winter time. It was unusual to have a hearse, partly because of expense and partly because of the distance. After the service at the front door the funeral cortege would set off. Four bearers carried the coffin on wooden poles, at the head went the nearest male relative, and at the feet the second nearest. After proceeding in this manner for about a hundred yards the front rank of those following in the funeral procession would step forward and relieve the bearers of their burden, and so on, each group of bearers being relieved by those behind them. I have gone down many a mile of lonely glen in this fashion. Our own lych-gates in England are a reminder of this custom. In the days when there were no hearses, shelter was provided at the gateway for the coffin and for the mourners as they rested after their long and arduous journey from the home of the deceased. In the Highlands another service was held at the graveside, after which the entire company departed to the house, there to partake of a bumper feast washed down with whisky.

How very different was the last occasion on which I attended the funeral of a patient in London. There I was arrayed in a topper and a morning coat. As the patient was a personal friend and there did not seem to be a superfluity of cars to take mourners to the graveside, I had offered the family the use of mine, which was gratefully accepted. In due course I collected the owners of three other top-hats and we took our place in the funeral procession. Unfortunately (this was in the days before petrol gauges), my car ran out of petrol and I was compelled to draw into the side. We had not stopped anywhere near a petrol pump, and so the only thing to do was to ask my companions to leave the car and walk to the cemetery. We left the car by the roadside and set out, arriving just in time to meet the rest of the party returning from the obsequies at the graveside.

The subject of funerals reminds me of a time long ago when I had another unfortunate experience. In Scotland walking funerals were almost universal. On the particular occasion of which I speak I was riding a motor-bicycle which was innocent of any brakes whatsoever. Unfortunately, I had a maiden riding pillion behind. I came over the brow of a hill, and, to my horror, came suddenly upon a funeral with the mourners walking behind the hearse and straggling over the entire width of the road like a flock of sheep. Before I could stop the cycle I went through them like a knife cutting cheese, and ultimately came to a stop some six inches from the rear of the hearse.

In many respects Scotland is a much more democratic country than England. Golf is one of the chief reasons for this. In England it is a rich man's game ; in Scotland practically every town and village has its public golf course where one can have an excellent game at the cost of a few pence. When I was a boy at home I was a member of a good club which only cost me five shillings a year. Of course, the reason is that land is so cheap up north and so expensive down south.

I had in consequence been brought up to play golf from my earliest years, and one of my first visits on my return to Scotland was to the local golf course. I had been informed that the village policeman was the best player in the district, and so one of my first objectives was to seek him out. I had reason to believe that the policeman lived in a cottage up a side road, but I was not sure. Two men were squatting at the end of the side road. I inquired of them where the local policeman and golf champion was to be found.

"He'll be meanin' Andra," said one, taking his pipe from his mouth and slowly spitting into space.

Andra it was, and I should add that Andra and I had many a happy game together.

Not long after my arrival I was having dinner one night with a well-known surgeon who was staying at one of the shooting lodges nearby. I took my departure fairly early as my host was going out stag-shooting on the hills next day. The following day, after lunch, a shooting brake driven by a ghillie drove up to my front door with the request that I would accompany him and Andra to the hills where there had been an accident. The three of us went as far as the road would take us and then took to the heather. About half-way up the mountainside we found him. It was my friend of the night before. He was quite dead, and there had been no accident as was proved subsequently. The strain of climbing had been too much for an already weakened heart. When we discovered him it was as though he was alive, sitting on the heather and facing right down the glen, with a wonderful sweep of open country at his feet. A strangely peaceful look was on his face. He was to be congratulated not only on his successful life, but also in the manner of his death. I shall never forget carrying him down the mountainside with my friend Andra and the ghillie helping, nor the ride home in the shooting-brake.

Every medical practitioner has his quota of accidents, but some of mine have happened in a most unusual way. When I came back from hospital one day I found a very small boy weeping because of a painful eye. It appeared that some boys had been playing in a room at the station and that this small urchin had kept on putting his eye to the keyhole and taking a bird's-eye view of the interior. Apparently the boys inside the room decided to keep him out and heated a poker just short of red hotness. The next time he put his eye to the keyhole they thrust the heated poker through the keyhole from the other side. The result was disastrous, as may be imagined. Luckily, my wife was at home and rendered first aid until my arrival. His eye was saved and it ultimately recovered completely, so that his sight was unaffected.

But one of the accidents with which I had most frequently to deal was removing pellets as the result of a shot-gun wound. Another was removing a hook from a fish cast—as often as not imbedded in the lip. I suppose it was only natural, as fishing and shooting were so much practised in that part of the country where I was. The pellets from the shot-gun were seldom serious provided the gun had been fired from a distance and the eyes had escaped. But it was a different story with the fishhooks. They could not be pulled back and had to be pushed forward in the direction of the curve. Commonly enough, they had to be cut down upon and removed in that way. Children are geniuses at pushing foreign bodies up their noses, down their ears and into the most extraordinary situations it is possible to imagine. The majority of coins and other small articles which children are alleged by their mothers to have swallowed turn out to be a false alarm. What happens is that the child is playing, probably in his cot, with something of that nature. The mother is busy and she glances up to see if the child is all right, then in a few minutes she misses the small object he has been playing with and jumps to the conclusion that the child has swallowed it. This is more probably the sequence of events if the child is complaining of a pain in the stomach at the time. The doctor is sent for forthwith, and he almost invariably arranges for an X-ray to be taken.

I remember when I was a medical student a child in the ward who had swallowed a clinical thermometer which some foolish person had put in his mouth and left. The thermometer had slipped down his throat and the child was subsequently admitted to hospital. The thermometer remained unbroken, and, strange to relate, in spite of all the kinks and loops in the length of the intestine, the thermometer was ultimately passed unbroken.

Every now and again during the summer—and during the winter also—there were accidents on the hills to which I was called. There were even more accidents on the main roads nearby, such as the incident on a Sunday afternoon when a well-known financier went over a cliff in his sports car and broke his back. I remember the difficulty we had in lifting him up the cliff to the ambulance. It is no joke moving a man with a broken back.

Being so far from a hospital compelled me to do more minor surgery on my own. I found what wonderful healing power the body possesses. If Nature is given half a chance she will heal completely. The main job of a doctor is merely to assist nature.

The great curse of the Highlands is—whisky. Probably the reason it is drunk so freely is because the weather is so cold. The bodily urge is for a warm drink. There is something in the peaty water of the streams which gives to Highland whisky its peculiar flavour and potency. Almost every glen has its distillery, and the lonely spiral of smoke still marks the place where the Highlander distils his whisky in secret far from the watchful eyes of Customs officials.

It is a common saying that mere speed is not in itself dangerous. The following incident happened to me during my stay in the Highlands. I was driving between fifty and sixty miles per hour. The road was straight and level. There was not a vehicle in sight, but I could see that the far end of the road bore sharply to the right round the end of a wood. I pressed the accelerator hard until it was flush with the floor-board, and as I approached the corner I gradually relaxed the pressure. Horror of horrors, the car did not respond in the least, but sped on at sixty miles per hour. The corner loomed ominously near, and it would be nothing short of a miracle if I could take it at that speed. I had the sense to switch off the petrol and apply the brakes gradually. As it was, I must have taken the corner at something approaching fifty miles an hour. The connecting cable to the accelerator had jammed, and no efforts of mine could dislodge it. My experience made me sceptical about there being no danger from pure speed !

One day in midsummer I was leaving one of the hotels after seeing a patient when I heard my name called behind me. I turned round to find a man as unsuitably dressed for the Highlands as anyone I have ever seen. From his patent leather boots to his starched collar and bow tie he looked altogether ill-clad for the heather. The slight figure struck no responsive chord in my memory.

" I am afraid you have the advantage of me," I said.

He told me who he was, but omitted to mention his title while doing so.

" Not *the* so and so ? " I exclaimed.

" Well, if you care to put it that way, it's very good of you," he replied. " The manager pointed you out to me when you were passing through the lounge."

So it was that I came to meet one whose name was a household word in Britain, and one whose fame as a surgeon and as an anatomist was known wherever medical students were to be found. After some general conversation I suggested that he might care to accompany me on my round. He readily assented, and we made our way out to my waiting car. Outside, his clothes seemed more incongruous than ever, as his city clothes were surmounted by the black homburg—much beloved of Stock Exchange men and others who have reason to frequent the inner sanctums of London. He must have guessed from my glance—or possibly he himself was conscious—that his clothes were not very suitable, for he added apologetically, " You see, I didn't mean to come here at all. I got wearied with the rush and bustle of London, so on the spur of the moment I went to King's Cross and took a ticket on the Highland Express as far as it would go. This place looked so attractive from the train that I got out here and went to the nearest hotel."

My round that morning lay past a church built at the end of a peninsular jutting out into a loch. It happened that many years ago, when the floor was being relaid owing to dry rot, a ghoulish congregation of skeletons had been found underneath the floorboards. They lay in two huge concentric rings, one inside the other, with their feet all pointing towards the centre. There was absolutely no history, or any record, of how these grim relics came to be there or in that position. The bones were all removed to a common grave in the churchyard, but evidently they were not buried very deep, for usually one or two bones were to be found protruding from the surface.

I happened to be telling that story to my new-found friend as we were passing near the church.

" Do you mind showing me the grave ? " he asked.

" Certainly," I replied.

So I stopped the car and we made our way over to where the bones were buried. A little scraping and pulling laid bare a considerable quantity of bones. And then I received one of the greatest anatomy lessons of my life. He took a bone—say a femur—and resurrected the entire person from it.

" This is the femur of a young man about eighteen, somewhere about five feet two inches in height, and very well developed muscularly," etc., etc.

It was fascinating to listen to him. He came to the conclusion that they had all died fairly suddenly. There was no sign of injury on any of the bones he examined, and both sexes and all ages were represented. He decided that the skeletons were the result of some plague which had fallen upon the community, though why the bodies had been laid in that position and in that situation it was impossible to say.

I remember that one of my patients whom I had to see that day was my own small son. Some time previously I had been called to an accident at some local sports. It appeared that in the sack race one boy had fallen heavily on his shoulder and broken his collar-bone. What was my astonishment on disentangling the sacking to see the features of my own son.

That day was the first of many on which the famous surgeon accompanied me on my round. One blazing hot afternoon I was called to a very lonely cottage which lay far from the track of human habitation. I asked him if he would care to accompany me. He readily assented, and soon the patent leather boots from Harley Street were accompanying the kilted doctor to the lonely clachan on the hillside. I explained to the patient that I had a medical friend with me, but did not say whom he was. It always struck me that the man would have been astonished had he known who it was who was attending him, for my friend from London insisted on all the facts being put at his disposal, and in making the examination and diagnosis himself. The man certainly had the best possible attention, and though the cottage spoke of the poverty of its owner, yet he had such skill as kings would have paid a ransom for.

I found the patients up here to be suffering from much the same diseases as they did down south. Sometimes I could help them, sometimes I couldn't. What I did find was something I was dimly aware of in my London days. It was this. Apart from a few drugs of outstanding merit, the chief factor in restoring a patient to health is the doctor himself. No one else knows the patient's background as he does. He is the patient's friend. The understanding of the medical practitioner is one of the most potent factors in the patient's recovery.

One of the commonest causes of my visits was P.U.O.—pyrexia of unknown origin—or, in other words, fever of unknown cause; everyone has had it. The doctor has examined the patient thoroughly, and in answer to inquiry possibly he has looked wise and murmured something about a summer chill—or maybe an autumn chill—depending on the season. But if he is a wise man he will admit his ignorance and tell them to "wait and see". Sometimes a doctor can tell where the infection is coming from, but sometimes he can't. It disappears as quickly as it has come and the cause is never discovered. It remains P.U.O.

I cannot tell of my days in Scotland without mentioning the ceilidhs (pronounced Cailey, to rhyme with daily), which were held in an old disused schoolroom in the nearby forest. The walls were all discoloured with mildew and a huge fire of birch logs blazed in the hearth. Not a word of English was spoken. The ceilidh was an effort to preserve the Gaelic language and to encourage it to be spoken. As many kilts were on view as possible and the laird was in the chair. Gaelic songs would be sung by a group of women, and then an old Highlander would get up and tell a long story quite without any self-consciousness. Incidentally, I remember one story was about a doctor who put a leech on a patient, but the patient, not feeling any better, thought that a ferret would be more effective, and the tale went on to tell of the effects of the treatment on the patient. A forester would come on and play the pipes. I am all in favour of listening to the pipes when they are played out of doors, but in a small building already packed and heated to saturation point it is no instrument to be played. Following him would come a boy with an accordion—the " box ", as it was called. I must give that boy full marks ; he certainly could play the " box ". Half-time arrived and with it cups of tea and oatcakes, along with a small quantity of cheese. Such is the ceilidh. They gave to those situated in outlying places an opportunity of foregathering with their neighbours and of encouraging the young to speak their native tongue, as well as to cultivate local talent.

I found that most of the local inhabitants could speak Gaelic, and usually did so in the privacy of their own homes, but that Gaelic as the everyday language was somewhat despised and looked down upon, so that only with reluctance could a person be persuaded to say that he or she spoke it. Most of the children said they could understand Gaelic, and, owing to the efforts which are now being made to popularise the language, an increasing number of children are able to speak it.

All around us were evidences of a byegone civilisation. Even across the road from where we lived stood a circle of stones, mute monuments to some old, forgotten time. The standing stones at Clava are the best preserved of their kind, and probably outshine Stonehenge in their completeness and state of preservation. Many of these stone circles were scattered around, and I thought, rightly or wrongly, that these signalised the burial-place of some bye-gone race. I proceeded to excavate one with a view to finding something of interest or of value in it. It chiefly consisted of a pile of stones covering some granite slabs which had been set on end and which evidently had led to the burial chamber of the deceased. I found nothing, but the local people did not approve at all. Evidently they thought I was desecrating the graves of the dead. They gave me black looks and looked upon my action as sacrilege.

I have said that General Practice is fundamentally the same whether it is carried on in London or in the Highlands—with the exception of the temperament of the patient and the environment of the doctor. Sore throats, leg ulcers and influenza were just the same whether they were in the north or in the south. Only the people were different. A lot of people, chiefly the elderly and the visitors, came to have their blood pressure taken each week. Now the sphygmonanometer, or instrument for taking blood pressure, is an excellent invention and it has great uses, especially in pregnancy. But it falls into the danger of becoming a curse instead of a blessing ; of becoming an instrument of terror instead of one of usefulness.

THE SPAN OF TIME

I think one of the unhappy moments of life is to see the anxiety on the faces of patients as they watch the mercury fluctuate and then settle at a point maybe five points higher than it had been previously. The five points difference doesn't matter in the slightest.

I remember attending a Highlander who was dying and who had been nursed by some elderly relative. He looked at me with the large and unwavering gaze of the dying.

" Tell me, doctor, is it dying that I am ? "

He said this in the thin sing-song voice of the very ill. I hesitated a minute and then I told him the truth. His eyes turned from me and I asked him if there was anything he would like me to do.

" Yes," he said, " I would like someone to pray with me in Gaelic."

I would have given anything to be able to accede to the man's request. But alas ! My Gaelic was of the most elementary.

Both the Highlander and the Highland woman have a due regard for the pearls of wisdom which fall from a doctor's lips. One unfortunate case comes to my mind. She was a woman who held doctors in veneration, and treasured up their commands as though they were the words of the oracle at Delphi. In this particular case I was called to see an elderly woman who had had more than her fair share of the rough and tumble of life. There was nothing definitely wrong with her, only the wear and tear of which I have spoken.

" Stay in bed till I come again, and I think you should be much better."

With these words I took my departure, and unfortunately the case departed from my mind also. Several weeks later—I think it was six to be exact—I suddenly remembered the woman and dropped in to see how she was getting on. To my astonishment she was still in bed, and had been waiting patiently for my return. The prolonged rest had done her no harm. Rather did it do her a considerable amount of good, but I would not recommend it in every case.

The Highlanders as a rule are great talkers, but apparently the Gaelic language does not lend itself to brevity. It was my duty to attend the local hospital once a week. We had there a man from the Islands who spoke no English, and we got a Gaelic-speaking nurse to translate for him. It was important to find out exactly how long he had had this trouble, so the nurse was instructed to discover this from him. For a long time they conversed together in

Gaelic. It seemed as though the conversation would never come to an end. At last the nurse turned to the waiting doctors.

" He says, a while."

I can't leave the Highlands without saying a word about the religion of the Highlander. Pre-eminent among his religious virtues is that of being an eminent Sabbatarian. In fact an English friend once described the religious Highlander to me somewhat unkindly as one who keeps the Sabbath Day and everything else he can. This, I think, is a gross libel on a generous race. He may have been unlucky in the particular people he met, but certainly it does not apply to the race as a whole.

Well over ninety per cent. of Scots who are Protestants, are Presbyterians, and the Episcopal Church up north has no great hold on the people. Strange to relate, as the Episcopal Church does not "conform" to the State Church, which is Presbyterian, they are therefore Non-conformists, which is rather shattering to the pride of an average English person. The Highlander is no more religious than his lowland brethren, by that I mean that he does not go to church more frequently.

The village school, as I have said, was in the forest, and the playground of the children was its undergrowth. One would imagine that living in the open air would be conducive to a long and healthy life. As a matter of fact, possibly through inter-breeding and hereditary taint, or it may have been the hermetically sealed cottages in which so many of them lived in later life, but the strain of tuberculosis was strongly in evidence among them.

During the summer our house was flooded with visitors from down south. I never knew I had so many friends. Unfortunately, this came at a time when the district was full of visitors and I myself was working from morning till night. The hotels were full during the summer and all the accommodation in the glen was taken. The season was short, and by early in September most of the visitors had disappeared. My own harvest thanksgiving coincided to a large extent with the agricultural one, and thereafter a long silence settled down on the countryside.

I had many opportunities and invitations to join in so-called sport with the local gentry, but my tastes did not run in that direction. I found pike fishing to be as much sport as salmon fishing, and the chasing of the prevalent Arctic hare to be as stimulating as shooting grouse in a battue.

It was part of my duties to visit the hospital in the nearest town once a week. This town was between thirty and forty miles away, and on my return journey during the winter it was a common sight to see snow-white hares playing on the roadway in the headlights of my car.

As winter came on the cold became more and more severe. The roads then were divided into two classes—white and black according to whether they were snow-covered or not—and the black roads became rarer and rarer.

I nearly lost my life through inexperience on one occasion. It happened in this way. A friend and I had to do some business in a place some sixteen miles away from my home. It was a wintry afternoon with one of these grey leaden skies. We each had taken our own car as I was anxious to visit a few houses on the way home. Soon several large snowflakes began to fall, and a powdering of white covered all around. There were two roads from our destination. One was fairly frequented while the other lay far from any habitation, and was higher and more exposed.

" I am going home by the quickest way," said my friend. And with that he sped along the road to home and security.

I had to take the lonelier and more exposed road. When I had gone about ten miles, and the light was beginning to fade, I ran into one of the worst blizzards it has ever been my lot to encounter. I could not see where the side of the road began or where the moor ended, and the driving wind speedily swept the snow into deep drifts through which it was difficult to force one's way. My car soon came to a stop, and I got out and began to dig. I had always been warned to carry a spade in the back of my car for this purpose, and now I was to find its real worth. When I had dug a sufficient passageway to let the car pass through I climbed back and started the engine again. To my horror the wheels would not grip, but just went round and round. In the gathering darkness I could detect no sign of habitation, and pictured myself frozen in the car with a search party finding me days later. I tried again. This time the wheels seemed to grip and I charged the snowdrift as fast as my engine would permit. I just got through, but it was a near thing, and when eventually I arrived at my nearest patient it was to find myself sweating in every pore although the day was an icy one.

I would like to tell many more adventures which I had during my year's residence in the Highlands. Of the time when I had to take a patient suffering from mental trouble down to Edinburgh, and of how she nearly ended my life by hitting me violently on the head with the heel of her shoe. It was only when we got on board the ferry at the Forth that the massive dose of morphia which I had given her began to take effect. Doubtless the other passengers on board the ship must have come to the conclusion that I was abducting the female for ulterior motives.

In the spring my wife and I went to Skye. I am one of those people who have the courage to say that I was disappointed in Skye, probably because of the marked absence of trees in the island. A countryside is to me clothed and made complete when it has a covering of woodland. The Cuillins are mostly scree and rock, and I fear that these far-famed mountains made little impression on me. To me the beauty of Skye lay in the clearness of the atmosphere and the extraordinary effect of light and shade on the surface of the water. It may be the sun shining through the water in the atmosphere which makes the colours seem so vivid.

I stayed in the Highlands through all the different seasons of the year—in the summer in the sweltering sunshine when the stags moved high on the mountainside—when a speck in the clear sky was a circling eagle ; the autumn when the stillness of the departed summer crept over the countryside—when the birch trees turned from green to gold in their foliage ; winter when the cold was intense, and the dance of the Northern Lights lit up the sky at night ; the spring when the black and white oyster catchers announced their coming shrilly and loudly as though to say, " We're here, we're here, we're here," and when the melting of the snow made the music of many waters in our ears.

I dearly loved the Highlanders and the Highlands, but they were no place for me. So I sent in my resignation and with a light heart I set out for England and the south once more. Scotland may be a good place to be born in and to die in, but it is no place in which to earn one's living.

CHAPTER XIII

A VILLAGE IN SURREY

A S I sped down south I had ample opportunity for considering the type of practice I would choose in future. One thing I was determined on—this was the final move. We were not getting any younger, and I could not expect my long-suffering wife to make any more changes. Moreover, I wanted roots—deep roots —which would take a long time to grow. I wanted to be one with the people among whom I was working. I wanted to win the regard of the community among whom I lived and not merely evanescent gratitude towards one who was here to-day and gone to-morrow.

I would have a country practice. I had had enough of village life up north to whet my appetite for more. I had had more than enough of streets and pavements and rows of houses all looking exactly the same. It must not be too far from London, for my only remaining relatives were there and I liked to see them as often as was possible. There must be good schools in the neighbourhood to educate the children, and lastly there must be a fairish section of jam in the shape of private patients, as well as the bread and butter of the panel.

These thoughts and a hundred others ran through my brain as I sped down the Great North Road. I spent the night in Durham, and by noon next day was in London. I determined not to decide in a hurry ; the right thing would come along if one waited long enough for it. Meantime, I could not be idle. I would do a locum while I waited.

After due consideration I came to the conclusion that an asylum job offered me all the facilities I was looking for. It was work that I was interested in, with every second day off at one o'clock, which gave me ample opportunity for viewing practices.

In due course I found the ideal post. The staff were congenial ; the Chief was an excellent fellow to work under and he gave me every facility for investigating the different practices which presented themselves.

I was in charge of some five hundred women, and was asked to carry on with the work which my predecessor had been doing. It was the early days of shock treatment, and they were experimenting at the hospital with various methods of inducing shock. The work I was given was to inject a drug which speedily rendered the patient unconscious, to wake up feeling much refreshed. Before I had the needle out of her vein the patient was unconscious and breathing deeply. She would have all the symptoms of a major attack of epilepsy. In due course the drug which I administered was given up as other and more up-to-date methods of administering shock treatment were discovered.

I soon found that a great deal of the administrative work was performed by the patients themselves, and it was some little time before I discovered who were actually patients and who were not. I had a foolish dislike of being mistaken for a patient, and took the precaution of ostentatiously flourishing a stethoscope in my pocket.

One night a group of doctors on the staff were sitting round the fire in the Common Room when a knock came on the door. It was a male nurse to report that number so-and-so had escaped.

" All right," said the senior man present, without removing his feet from the mantelpiece, " do the usual."

" Very good, sir," was the reply.

I sat in stunned silence, as I had thought that when a patient escaped the warders would man the battlements and possibly run up a flag to indicate that someone had escaped. I sat for some five minutes in silence and then could restrain myself no longer.

" Would you mind telling me what the usual is ? " I asked.

" Oh," he replied, good-naturedly, " they always go home. It's just a question of ringing up the nearest police station and sending a policeman along to fetch them back. They always come quietly."

So that was " the usual ". Truly we live and learn.

I investigated many practices in the environs of London, twenty-eight altogether, I think. The method one adopts is to notify one or more of the Medical Agencies of what one wants and they send particulars of the practices they have for disposal. I must say that some of the practices were such as to offer little in the way of what I had in mind. In fact, not to put too fine a point on it, it was amazing how some doctors had the courage to sell the goodwill of the few patients they had.

One day I received a telephone call from one of the Agencies telling me that a death vacancy had occurred in a practice in a

Surrey village. It seemed to be the type of practice in which I was interested. I thanked them and said I would go down to-morrow.

" Oh," they said, " we advise you to go to-day. This practice has not been advertised. There is bound to be considerable competition for it."

It was not my turn for a half day, but the Chief let me off—to my everlasting gratitude, and I went down to the village in Surrey to investigate. There was no doubt about which was the doctor's house. A long line of cars, like that at an auction sale, stood outside the door, and inside the house doctors and their wives moved about in every direction. The house reminded me of a hive of bees which one had knocked over accidentally. I remember one man standing on the staircase and jingling some coins in his pocket as he said to his wife in a loud voice, " Yes, my dear, I think I'll have it. The house isn't exactly what we want, but of course one can't have everything."

I was not impressed by the manners of my confreres. Their disparaging remarks were made in a loud voice, and often in the hearing of those who had lived in the house previously. I had already had particulars of the practice from the agents, and it only remained for me to clear up one or two points. I decided to have an independent opinion, and with that end in view I went over and had a cup of tea at a neighbouring Guest House. I soon got all the information I wanted and learned that the previous doctor had been a much respected man. Fortified by these recommendations I went back to the house and inquired the name of the lawyer who was acting for the estate. Having got that I crossed the hall to a small room where there was a telephone, waited until the room was empty, and then locked the door so that I could pursue my business undisturbed. I rang up the lawyer and asked to speak to him personally. Ultimately I tracked him down at a garden party in Hampshire, and when he came to the phone he was vastly amused to find that I only wanted the first refusal of the practice for twenty-four hours. He readily assented, and the following day I drove my sister down to see the house and view those aspects which a mere man is not supposed to understand. My wife was still up in the Highlands with the family. My sister agreed with me that both the house and practice were eminently suitable, and we went straight from there to the lawyer.

I remember the start I had when he named the price. I remember only having such time as it takes to smoke a cigarette in which to make up my mind in his waiting-room. I remember weighing the pros and cons of the matter. I took a decision which I have never had any cause to regret. I bought the practice and the house. My next endeavour was to move in as quickly as possible.

As I have said, I had no introduction to the practice. It was a death vacancy, and the previous doctor had died some six weeks before I arrived. A succession of locums had filled the vacancy in the interval. I naturally set about knowing as many people as possible in the neighbourhood. With that end in view I attended as many social functions as possible. I shudder to think how many sherry parties I attended. I literally sherry-partied myself into that practice. What is certain is that when my wife ultimately came down from the north she had over one hundred calls to return. She came to the point where she would pray for the occupants to be out, and many is the time she has returned to me and said, " You know, I quite forgot to leave any cards."

Some of these social events were not so easy as the sherry parties I have described. We were asked out to dinner frequently, and it was up to us to return the hospitality we received. I remember one man—an extremely wealthy person—who had asked us to dinner at his house where all the appointments were of the very best. My wife, for her part, determined to leave nothing to chance on the return visit and spread herself accordingly. An hour or two before our guests were due to arrive I remembered that he smoked nothing but the best cigars. What was I to do ? I never smoke cigars myself, and I had not a single one in the house to offer him. Then a brilliant idea struck me. I went to the inn opposite and asked the landlord there if he had any really good cigars. He assured me he had, half a crown each. I explained the situation to him and asked him if I might borrow the box until to-morrow and promised to pay for every one which was smoked. He laughingly agreed, and as a box of good cigars costs a considerable amount, it was balm to a Scotman's soul. My guest smoked two and congratulated me on my choice. Unless he reads these words, he will never know that they came from the inn opposite.

The practice had exactly those qualities which I had determined upon. The cottagers were my friends, and the well-to-do were my friends. There was practically not a house in the village into which I could not go and be made welcome.

The village itself is a real bit of old England. Nowadays it has some fifteen hundred inhabitants, but the old village with its winding main street is much the same as it was long ago. Everything about it is old. The half-timbered inn was built in the days of Queen Elizabeth; the church was built before the Battle of Hastings. and the upper storeys of the houses in the main street project over the roadway as they did in the days of long ago. The very inhabitants have their roots in the mists of antiquity. A list of householders for the year 1332 shows that at least four families have descendants resident in the village to-day. One curious thing that the records seem to indicate is that through all the centuries these families have occupied approximately the same position socially. This would appear to be very strong argument in the perrenial dispute of heredity versus environment.

The very names of the tradespeople suggest " Cranford ", for the village has its " Cranford " characters. We are a happy family—all the folk are kindly and there is a marked absence of malicious gossip which poisons so many villages such as ours.

Our house is roomy and comfortable and in the garden is an old cottage which in byegone ages was occupied by generations of weavers. In fact, the frame for the loom is still there, and the ingle nook, and the old gnarled beams which looked down on generations of weavers' children. The cottage is used as a surgery now. The kitchen with its open fireplace and wood-smoked beams is the consulting room, and the patients wait in the room where once the weaver spun his cloth. Upstairs is where the housekeeper lives. It is strange to think how generation after generation have been born, have lived and have died inside its walls. On a summer's day when the sun is shining on the roses round the doors and windows, it is a place of great beauty. By night, however, when it lies in shadow and the ghosts of its byegone inhabitants cluster under its roof, the villagers pass it quickly.

Having the surgery away from the house has certain advantages. One can always lock the door at the close of the consulting hour. Also there is not nearly so much opening of doors, and one does not live quite so much on top of one's work. Moreover I find that the mere fact of going outside to the surgery has a definite psychological effect on me—at nine o'clock I feel the day's work has started.

From the brief sketch I have given, it will be seen that our lives have fallen in pleasant places. The countryside around is picturesque—well-wooded and hilly (few Scotsmen will live in a flat district if they can help it) and almost from the edge of the village one can walk for ten miles without touching human habitation and all this within forty minutes by rail of the centre of London.

We had only been settled about a year or two when war came. It came to the village on a sunny day. Groups of evacuee mothers were seated about the common in careless abandon. They were openly and unashamedly attending to the needs of their infants. In our village these things were done in private and behind closed doors. Evidently our new villagers preferred to do these things on the communal system. However, the majority of the mothers preferred the attractions of the Old Kent Road to the dubious pleasures of the country and hied themselves citywards in a few days. The children remained behind and became so much a part of village life that it was only at the end of the war that we realised with a start that they were evacuees. We, ourselves, had a little boy for several months at the beginning of the war. He was very obviously from the City and one of my chief recollections is of him trying to shoot a rabbit with a home-made bow and arrow.

I remember one child, a most adorable-looking little boy, adorable until he opened his mouth—and then the language that issued from it was beyond description. Almost every family in the village had him at some time or other. Three months was generally the limit. One day, when he was not much beyond his toddling days, he clambered along the uneven pavement of the village street. Suddenly his toe caught and he fell down heavily. A gentleman who was coming along behind him lifted the child up and with an " oops a daisy " stood him on his feet.

" Oops a daisy be damned," said the child. " I'se hurted myself."

In the early days of the war the effect of bombing was quite unknown. I recall one summer's evening being sent to consult a nervous patient of mine. Her garden was situated on high ground and from it one could see at one's feet all the weald of Sussex, looking widespread and peaceful in the light of the summer's evening. She was alarmed at what she had heard about bombs. I took her up to the end of her garden and explained to her that the chances of a bomb falling near her with such a wide expanse to cover were infinitesimal. She seemed satisfied, but took the precaution of sleeping downstairs. I was awakened one night by a terrific bang. The first bomb which had fallen had dropped within three yards of her sleeping head. Luckily she wasn't badly hurt, as the wall of the house saved her.

I remember the first big air raid we ever had, some five hundred bombers which sounded like an underground train approaching a station. It was an August afternoon and the sun was blazing down. Everyone had been warned to remain indoors, but the villagers were outside to a man, gazing upwards. I was visiting a house on the common. As I came out the aged inhabitant of the village was leaning on his stick and gazing upwards. He was evidently disappointed at not seeing any brought down, for he said in his broad Surrey dialect, " There baint no sport."

The memories of these war years come crowding back on me. I recall one evening when the Luftwaffe was particularly active overhead. I happened to be out to dinner and the family with whom I was dining were among the aristocrats of England. Two male servants waited at table. Suddenly there was a crash outside the house as though the end of the world had come. It made my plate jump up on the table and me want to crawl underneath. No one took the slightest notice. The lady sitting next to me evidently felt compelled to keep the conversation running smoothly.

" Do you like bombing ? " she asked.

Did I like bombing !

Quite a number of bombs fell on or near our village, but the only casualty occurred outside the village on the heath where a soldier was walking with a girl. A bomb fell quite near the walking couple, and they both flung themselves to the ground. Unfortunately the soldier's tin hat was situated somewhere around his middle, and the zeal with which he sought to protect the maiden resulted in the tin hat fracturing several of the poor girl's ribs.

After France fell I sent my wife and children up to Scotland to be out of the way in case of invasion. A curious incident happened in connection with this. I did not want to be left penniless should we be invaded, so I went to the bank and drew £100 in one-pound notes. These I put inside a metal steriliser, which I buried behind the garage. As the months passed and no invasion materialised I bore the hundred pounds untouched to the bank, only to find, alas ! that there were but ninety-nine pounds. To this day I don't know where the missing pound could have got to, as the sum was checked by me on the day I got it and the bank verified that a hundred pounds had been given me.

One of the more pleasurable aspects of the war was the fact that it brought us Gretch. She came to us for ten days to see whether she and the family liked each other, and stayed for four and half years. During that time she and my wife ran the house between them. She had a curious experience. Prior to coming to us she lived in a village in Hampshire. It had been arranged that the church bells would be rung should the Germans land. Late one night, when she was alone in the house, she heard the church bells ringing. Apparently the rumour that the Germans had landed had started somewhere in the West of England, and from parish to parish right across the land the church bells were rung until eventually the false alarm reached that quiet village in Hampshire.

It would be appropriate here to relate how Greta—or Gretch, as the family came to call her—became known to us. At the beginning of the war I suffered from pneumonia and had an operation. From this I recuperated at the house of a friend in Hampshire. I kept hearing my hostess refer to a friend of hers called Greta, until one day I rather foolishly said, " I think I'll go and call on Greta and see what she is like. I might pretend to sell her a vacuum or something."

" Oh, no," said my hostess, " you'll do something much more than that. You'll go to Greta and ask her to join the Women's Purity League," an institution which, I may add, was entirely mythical.

I scorned the idea, as I had no intention of asking an utter stranger to join such a body. I would probably end up by mortally offending the lady. However, my wife joined forces with her, and together they made life miserable for me, with the result that one fine day we set out in her car for the house of Greta. We left the car some distance up the road, and I regret to have to say that when I got to the gate my courage failed me and I returned to the car crestfallen. The next day life continued to be made miserable for me, and back we went in the car again. I was entirely innocent of any disguise and had merely taken a visiting card from the hall table with the name Major Reid, Retired Indian Army, printed on it.

This time I summed up courage and knocked on the door. Greta came to the door herself and courteously invited me in, while I hesitatingly told my story. I pointed out to her that the place was full of troops who had nowhere to go, and that the Society in question, which incidentally had amalgamated with the Young Men's Morality League, proposed to obtain a hall and provide suitable recreation for the troops. The committee insisted that it was necessary for one to be a member oneself before one could take part in its activities.

I well remember the roars of laughter with which my proposal was greeted, but nevertheless she assented, and with the promise of further information I took my departure. The next day she was to come over to meet us and have tea. My hostess was going to fetch her in her car. On the way over Greta naturally told her friend the story of the man and the Purity League. My hostess, who had heard it all before from me, appeared to be tremendously impressed, and when she arrived home she said, " You must tell the story to Lucy."

With a certain amount of diffidence she did so. Ultimately I came into the room while they were all laughing at the story. Not a glimmer of recognition shone through her features. She was badgered to tell the story again for me. I listened with a perfectly solemn face. By this time she was getting a little tired of it, and I pointed out to her at the close that she had missed out the bit about the hall. I shall never forget her face. It went perfectly white.

" Are you that man ? " she exclaimed.

The exploit cost me the biggest box of chocolates to be found in the district.

I doubt whether that incident could be classified as " moral courage ". Probably the most famous example of that virtue is to be found in this story of the schoolmaster who was giving his class a talk on " moral courage ". A story which bears repetition in spite of its hoariness. The teacher wound up the lesson by saying " An example will explain what I mean. There were ten boys in a dormitory and nine of them jumped into bed while the tenth knelt down and said his prayers. That is an example of moral courage. Moreover, that boy might grow up to be a bishop some day." The following day he thought he would do a little revision, so he went back to the subject of yesterday. " Give me an example of moral courage," said he, pointing to a particularly inattentive youth and thinking of his example of yesterday. Slowly the boy got to his feet and tried to recollect the words of his teacher. " Please, sir, there were ten bishops, and they all slept in a dormitory and they all knelt down and said their prayers except one, who jumped into bed. He had moral courage."

During the time that my wife was in Scotland with the children one of my sisters, who was having a gruelling time in London,

came to live with me. At the same time a retired general was
residing in the house for a similar reason. One night, when
bombing was particularly bad, I could stand it no longer and
got up noiselessly to make my way downstairs. At the top of
the stairs, in the darkness, I touched something soft. It was my
sister. We breathed into each other's ear that the drawing-room
couch offered better prospects than our beds on this particular
night, and we made our way downstairs to the lounge. We had
been forestalled. The general was stretched on the couch at
full length, fast asleep.

The spirit to win was exemplified for me one night. It was towards the end of an evening's surgery and a man of the labouring
classes came in to see me. As a matter of fact he was a worker
in the nearby munitions factory.

" Grand news on the wireless to-night, sir," he said.

" What's that ? " I replied.

" They're taking men up to thirty-nine now as rear gunners
in aeroplanes. I am thirty-nine past. They made me have
exemption before in order to do munitions, but they can't refuse
me my release now. I am off to Reading to-morrow."

I asked him to let me know how he got on. Apparently he was
turned down because of deficiencies in his mathematics. With a
view to correcting this, after working hours he attended night
school in the Technical College in the neighbouring town at his
own expense. Such is the spirit that made us win the war.

My chief war work, apart from running my neighbour's practice
with a vast increase in the local population, lay in acting as medical
officer to a convalescent home which had been established in one
of the nearby large houses. It was my custom to go there every day
and see each patient on admission and discharge. Sometimes
I got into grave difficulties, as when I recommended a man to be
specially put on beer. I thought he looked considerably below
par. It occurred to me that the matron looked strangely dis-
approving, and I was right in my surmise. It turned out that the
man had arrived the day previously much the worse for drink
and that his present low condition was due to a hangover from the
day before.

It was in the autumn of 1940 that I developed the pneumonia
I have mentioned previously. It settled into an empyema—a
form of pleurisy where the fluid on the surface of one's lung turns
to pus. An operation was necessary for it. Ultimately I was

taken to hospital and operated on there. The operation was performed by a celebrated surgeon, and most of the staff crowded into the theatre to see the great man operate. Unfortunately, I, the victim, had to lie on the operating table while he carried out a running commentary on the operation. I may add that as I only had a local anæsthetic I could not help overhearing every word he said.

"We shall now sever the rib, gentlemen."

Crash would go my rib, followed by another crash a few seconds later. During part of the operation I felt as though I was about to collapse. I shut my eyes tight and stretched out my hand to grip that of a fair sister whom I thought would give me moral and physical support. In due course the operation was successfully finished, and only the next day did I find that I had been gripping the hand of a doctor standing near.

The Canadians were stationed around us. A wonderful race of men they were. Some of them were billeted in a large house belonging to some patients of mine. The family and the servants were allotted a part of the house to live in—the Canadians were in the other part. The head of the house had a bottle of wine taken by the butler from the cellar each evening. One night— what was the butler's astonishment on opening the cellar door— to find the cellar ankle deep in wine and broken bottles. There was no window to the place, only an air-hole slightly above the ground and too small for a man to enter. The mystery was solved by a Canadian who was found alcoholically asleep outside the ventilator with a bottle tucked underneath each arm. It turned out that he had extracted several with the aid of a fishing-rod and a torch. An investigation took place, but my patient declined to prosecute.

Slowly the war dragged on, and ultimately peace was celebrated in our village by bonfires and dancing, but what I shall never forget was the service of thanksgiving held on the green near the church, with the joint co-operation of the Free Church and the old Parish Church. A great company stood around, and from the nearby tree came the song of the blackbird proclaiming peace on earth instead of the rattle of the doodlebug.

I had a branch surgery in a neighbouring village, so a considerable proportion of its inhabitants were patients of mine. The branch surgery was a bungalow set some way back from the road, and usually only a handful of people visited it each day.

One day, however, I saw an astonishing sight. A queue of people stretched down the garden path and overflowed into the roadway. At their head stood a gentleman with an umbrella and white hair. I could hardly believe my eyes. It appeared that the servants from the big house in the vicinity had been sent down to join my panel *en masse* in charge of the butler. There were thirty-six of them. Needless to say, this was in the palmy days before the war.

I can claim that in these years I had become what I set out to be long ago—namely, the father of my people. Once upon a time they or their parents would have gone to ask advice from a clergyman. Nowadays they go to their doctor. Possibly they know their doctor better. He is the one of their acquaintances whom they think has more wisdom—and possibly more all-round knowledge of the world—than they themselves. A tremendous responsibility and a tremendous privilege rests upon the doctor. During the years that I have been in practice no less than three maidens have consulted me as to whether they ought to accept proposals of marriage which had been made to them. In each case I asked them the same question :

" Are you in love with him ? "

And each time I received the same answer : " What is love ? "

It has often amazed me how a doctor's reputation for cleverness is assessed by the public. To begin with, I think it is almost essential that he be eccentric in some form or other. Possibly if he insisted on wearing a cricket cap at all hours of the day and night he would get a reputation for cleverness surpassing the ordinary. It would appear that foreign blood is a great recommendation to cleverness.

I find that a woman's judgment differs from a man's. A woman thinks a doctor is clever if he agrees with what she subconsciously wants—a man, on the other hand, likes to be told some piece of knowledge which he has not known before.

In the practice which I now had the patients were divided roughly into two classes, the cottagers and the well-to-do. There was a comparative absence of the £300-a-year man of the clerky type—and still less of the type of woman who carries all her wealth on her back and who furnishes on the hire-purchase system.

I worked hard. I may say I worked very hard, but my labours were punctuated with regular holidays—generally in far-away places. It was our custom to make up our minds at the last minute that we were going on holiday, and as often as not we had covered a considerable distance before breakfast. I remember on one occasion when we were bound for Cornwall, and we had set off rather late the previous evening, so that we only got as far as the village in Somerset where my wife's mother lived. For some reason or other I could not sleep that night and went down to the kitchen very early in the morning to make myself a cup of tea. I found the children's nurse there on the same errand. My wife couldn't sleep either, so in consequence we found ourselves on the road by three o'clock that morning. I shall never forget the sight which met my eyes as we came over the Mendip Hills. Glastonbury Tor was standing up like an island surrounded by a sea of fog. It looked exactly as it must have looked long ago when it actually was an island, and there and then I told the children the story in Morte d'Arthur of how the dead king was rowed over to the island accompanied by the weeping queen. They have never forgotten it.

Occasionally I did not go very far afield. There was a small inn on the high ground of the heath where the peace and quiet of the country recreated my frayed nerves and overworked body. The landlady was goodness and understanding itself, so that she would put me up at any hour of the day or night.

A blind spot, of which I have already written, has persisted all my life. Sometimes it takes the form of speaking my thoughts without thinking previously, sometimes of failing to see the incongruity of what I have said. Let me illustrate what I mean from my social and medical work here.

I recall on one occasion my wife and I being asked by some friends to a dinner-party. There I was introduced to a lady and found myself sitting next to her at dinner. In the hurry of introductions I caught her name, but not whether she was Mrs. or Miss. I thought it was Miss and addressed her so. At the beginning of dinner I saw a wedding ring on her finger. Quickly I apologised for my error. She was very nice about it and graciously accepted my apology; in fact she added, " We were married before the war."

Now the lady in question did not look in the first bloom of her youth, nor yet in the second, so I tactlessly asked, " Which war ? "

Her kindness did not stop at my first apology, but extended to the halting excuse with which I hastened to cover up my blunder. There was really nothing left I could say, and after all those years

I do want to pay tribute to the sportsmanlike way in which she took it.

This failing is not confined to the medical profession. In fact only recently my attention was drawn to a church magazine in which the clergyman was acknowledging a gift for the organ fund from some wealthy lady in his congregation. The words he used in the parish magazine were not too happily chosen : " The organist will now be able to change his combinations without removing his feet."

As the person concerned has been dead a considerable time, there is no harm in my telling this story. One Sunday morning I was called to a large house—a very large house—some five or six miles away, where some patients of mine lived. This time the patient was someone who had come down from London for the week-end. Unfortunately, I did not catch his name. As I say, it was a large house, and on my arrival I was handed on from servant to servant until I ultimately arrived at the patient himself. He turned out to be an elderly man and luckily there was nothing serious the matter with him. After I had examined him and told him what to do, the following conversation took place between us :

" Before you go, doctor, I would like to settle up with you. Tell me how much I owe you."

I took a good look at the patient and decided to exercise my charity. He was not only old, but he needed what is known as a brush-up. In fact his clothes struck me as being distinctly thread-bare. I rapidly thought and had almost decided to charge him nothing when I recalled that it was a Sunday morning and I had come five or six miles to see him. So I said, " I am going to charge you half a guinea, but if you can't pay that it doesn't matter. Pay me what you are able and I shall be quite content."

" Oh," he replied, " I'll pay you half a guinea."

He said this so spontaneously that a thought suddenly struck me. " What do you usually pay your doctor in London ? " I asked.

" I always pay my doctor three guineas every visit."

And this is where the blind spot came into operation, for I at once remarked :

" I wish I had known that before."

He offered to double my fee, and I accepted, and with mutual expressions of regard and promises on my part to come again if necessary, I took my departure.

On the landing outside the butler was waiting to show me out. As we went downstairs together I said :

" Who is that old gentleman that I have just been seeing ? "

" That, sir, is Lord So-and So," and he named a name that is a household word in England for the wealth and lineage of its holder.

The following is typical of night calls such as I have often received in the years as village doctor.

Brr ! Brr ! Brr !

It was the district nurse with the usual " Can you come as quickly as possible, please, doctor ? "

With a feeling of resigned resignation I went. It was a most isolated cottage and took a certain amount of finding on a pitch-black night.

One can clearly picture the scene inside. Myself, with my coat off, a mask on my face and an overall tied about my middle. The nurse similarly dressed. Nowadays many babies are born in the efficient, aseptic atmosphere of a nursing home or hospital, but not so on this occasion. The patient is biting back her cries ; the flickering of the firelight is on the ceiling. Suddenly a silence —something has gone wrong. The nurse and I look at each other, and though no word is spoken the patient realises that all is not well. We do everything that our training and our skill suggest. The woman has grown silent now. We can only wait. At last our efforts are rewarded and the child is born. The whimpering cry of a baby breaks the silence of the cottage.

The mother, who has stood on the very brink of death, takes her child in her arms. There is nothing more dramatic that I know than the sudden light that comes into a woman's face when she feels her new-born child in the crook of her arm. I get into my car with the light just breaking in the east, and creep into my bed tired but triumphant. How often have I had experiences similar to that which I have described above.

As a rule patients were most considerate, especially the working class. I only remember being called out needlessly on one occasion, and then it was to reassure a rich man who couldn't get to sleep and who said his reason for calling me out was that he had to be at his office next day at nine o'clock.

About this time I was responsible for making one of the biggest mistakes I have ever made in my life. I was doing a colleague's work at his house and a mother had brought her child to see me. As the mother thought the child's kidneys were affected she had very wisely brought a specimen with her in a bottle. Unfortunately, I could not find any testing reagents, so as the specimen was bright red I took it that blood was present in large quantities and that the child was suffering from inflammation of the kidneys—or acute nephritis. I rang up the hospital and persuaded them to take the child in at once. In the course of the evening I phoned up to know how the patient was. What was my horror to learn that the child was now safely at home. The mother had put the specimen into an uncleaned red ink bottle.

For obvious reasons I can't say much about the medical side of my work. In the cases which I describe here all the principal actors are dead. I must, however, take this opportunity of describing my one and only venture into the rôle of bath-chair attendant. The patient had had a long and trying illness with two nurses looking after her. She had reached the stage of being taken out for short walks by one or other of her nurses. It so happened that the day of my visit coincided with the arrival of a new bath chair, one with specially narrow wheels so that the patient could be taken up and down stairs. I was given the honour of taking the patient downstairs for the first time in the new chair. I may add that the patient was an imperious old lady.

A short flight of steps led down from a landing above to a small square landing on the staircase. Another and longer flight at right-angles to the first led to another small landing with a lavatory door opening off it. Another short flight at right-angles to the long one led to the hall. Thus the stairs formed three sides of a rectangle. I was getting along splendidly and had reached the middle of the long flight leading down to the second landing when suddenly a nurse, who was watching the proceedings from the top landing, spoke to me. I turned my head to reply to her. Alas ! the force of gravity was too much. It was a fatal movement. Like a flash the bath chair and its occupant shot out of my hands and down the rest of the straight part of the stairs with a horrid bump, bump, bump. Luckily the chair remained upright and to my horror shot across the landing and through the lavatory door opposite, which, luckily, was not bolted. She was none the worse for her experiences and was not hurt in any way. Such was the only time I undertook the duties of a male nurse.

This reminds me of another person who was taken ill on the road with heart trouble and was carried into a nearby house. I was sent for urgently and found the patient lying on a camp bed in the hall. The kind owner of the house had put it up to save the patient the effort of mounting the stairs to a bedroom. When I got there the blind spot of which I have spoken made itself manifest once more. Without thinking, I sat down on the edge of the camp bed. Alas! the camp bed was built for one and not for two. There was a sound of splintering wood, and the patient and I arrived together on the floor. Unfortunately, the patient was underneath. The incident seemed to do her a world of good and appeared to restore her sooner than any other treatment.

I did a lot of life insurance work in this practice. One of the questions nearly all companies ask is, "How much does the applicant drink?" (State the actual number in pints, provided the applicant drinks beer.) I put this question to the man I was examining.

"I am practically a teetotaller," he replied.

"Well, I've got to put it down in terms of pints per day. One pint?"

"Oh, more than that."

"Two?"

"Oh, a little more than that."

"Three?"

"A little more than that."

"Four?"

"A little more than that."

"Five?"

"A little more than that."

"Six?"

"That's about it."

And he called himself a teetotaller.

The most dramatic death I ever witnessed took place in this practice. One day I was having my breakfast when an urgent call came to go to a man who was having a heart attack. I left my meal at once and hurried to the house. The patient's wife was in the bedroom when I arrived, giving him restoratives and any homely assistance within her power. Apparently the worst part of the attack was over when I got there. I knew from the type of heart disease from which he suffered that an attack would come on suddenly just as it would depart suddenly. I stayed chatting for a few minutes and then rose to go. I actually had my hand on the door handle and was replying to some remark of his when I noticed something peculiar about him. I crossed to the bed and took his pulse. He was dead. The wife was sitting at the foot of the bed chatting away and laughing, completely unaware that anything had taken place.

It gave one a strange feeling to resume one's interrupted breakfast, realising that in the interval one had been present at one of the most dramatic incidents possible. It made one realise how true are the words " In the midst of life we are in death."

The years passed away, and in the course of time the Disseminated Sclerosis from which I am now suffering made it impossible for me to carry on. At the same time my partner decided to give up work here, and the practice was run from my partner's house in the neighbouring village. The cottage in our garden is still the surgery of the practice, and the village people still sit in the room of the weaver's loom, but I remain in the house where I have been for the last fourteen years, and where I hope I shall be for some considerable time yet.

CHAPTER XIV

KING FOR AN HOUR

DURING the war I was in a civilian practice, but one of my duties was to act as medical officer to a large convalescent home in the neighbourhood.   It had eighty beds and an appropriate staff of V.A.D.s and nurses to look after them.

The hospital was a mansion which had been lent for the duration of the war, and a winding drive led up to the forecourt of the house.   It was a hospital which V.I.P.s were accustomed to visit, and I laid my plans to impersonate one of them.

My first object was to get a good partner—if possible two—and I was lucky to get two excellent confederates.   The female was one of the V.A.D.s from the hospital, and an excellent amateur actress.   The other member of the triumvirate had no connection with the hospital, and therefore was unknown there, so his abilities as an actor were unlikely to be put to the test.

I determined to finish my career as an impersonationist on the highest note.   I would be nothing less than a king.   I surveyed the available kings and decided that the King of Norway offered the best possibilities for me.   King Haakon was tall and thin, like me, and with suitable alteration I could be made to resemble him.

I first of all procured two cabinet-size photographs of the king from a press agency in town, one of his head and shoulders, the other a full-length portrait.   I spent a considerable time studying these photographs.   It will be recalled that during the war the Norwegian King generally appeared in admiral's uniform.

Somehow or other I must become an admiral.   I did, and the whole outfit only cost me a few shillings—five, I think, at the local draper's.

I had a friend who at one period of his career had been a medical officer in the ships of the Canadian Pacific Railway.   His merchant navy officer's uniform was about my size, and I determined to borrow it.   A few feet of gold braid soon converted me into an admiral—a very high admiral—with gold braid from cuff to elbow. The uniform fitted like a glove, and I had three rows of fictitious medal ribbon fastened on in the appropriate place. This was achieved by painting a portion of the gold braid to the colours I required. I think I'm correct in stating that King Haakon only wears one row of ribbons, but I felt that if I were going to be a king I would do it in a blaze of glory. The result was most imposing—most.

The next thing was the car. I noticed at the house of a patient one day a very impressive Rolls Royce with a uniformed chauffeur bending over it. I asked my patient if I could borrow his car plus the chauffeur, and with great good sportsmanship he entered wholeheartedly into my plan.

A Norwegian pennant was manufactured at home to fix on the bonnet of the car when the time came.

The night before our visit the female member of the party paid me an unexpected visit with a view to trying herself out. She visited me as a patient, dressed as she intended to look next day. She is naturally blonde, but, without dyeing her hair, she gave one the impression of being a brunette. She looked *très chic*. I thought she was a patient and had no idea that it was she I was talking to. Her disguise was complete.

And so the great day we had fixed on arrived. About nine o'clock a member of the family phoned up the hospital to say that King Haakon was staying at a house in the neighbourhood and would greatly like to see over the hospital—informally, of course. Would eleven o'clock be convenient? It was, and eleven o'clock was fixed for the time of his visit.

At this point I had better make it quite clear that two members of the hospital staff had to be warned of our real identity. They were the matron and the commandant. It was necessary to notify them in order that the members of the committee and the high Red Cross officials should not be summoned to what they would subsequently find to be a hoax. Moreover, they might find out that the hoaxer was their medical officer, and doubtless they would be far from pleased. They both entered into the spirit of the affair with complete sympathy.

We dressed at the house of the V.A.D. who had come off duty only at ten o'clock. She was to go as a mythical grand duchess Helga—" a friend of my daughter-in-law's," who chanced to be staying at the same house. My other friend was to go as my equerry, for a king must have an equerry in attendance.

We couldn't, however, create a uniform for him, so he had to go as a civilian, and certainly no one remarked on it either then or afterwards.

As I say, we dressed at the house of the V.A.D. and I made up with the portrait of King Haakon in front of me. I must say I did him justice and felt fairly sure that I was all right. However, disaster threatened. It is extraordinary how things get about, but somehow or other the rumour that it was a hoax had circulated, and my fellow-conspirator had been told confidentially that it was just our M.O. up to some of his jokes. Nevertheless, we decided to go through with it.

Just as I was stepping into the car my wife rushed forward.

" That'll never do," she cried. " You'll be spotted by the shape of your back."

It was not that I have an unusual back, but everyone has a carriage of which they themselves are quite unaware. It was not too late. Hurriedly I ran upstairs and looked around for something to alter the contour of my back. All I could find was a pair of pyjamas, and quickly I stuffed the pyjama trousers inside my coat as high up as I could reach. They stayed in that position, quite unsupported, and it was no impossible thought that at the critical moment a pyjama leg would make an unregal appearance. In fact it was the thought of these pyjamas which was uppermost in my mind during the subsequent proceedings.

You can imagine how good the resemblance was when I learned afterwards that a gentleman passing along the road and seeing the car ran into a house excitedly exclaiming, " The King of Norway has just gone past."

It seemed no time before we had arrived at the entrance to the hospital grounds, and we stopped at a suitable spot in the drive for the purpose of fixing the pennant to the bonnet. We thought, I believe correctly, that it was not allowable on a public highway, but it did not matter inside private grounds. The car drove on. My own feelings were quite calm, and I deliberately made conversation so as to keep the minds of the others off the ordeal ahead. At last the moment had come. The car swung slowly round the bend of the forecourt.

The commandant stood at the head of the various hospital officials, the matron at the head of the nurses and V.A.D.s, who were drawn up in two long lines for my inspection. Bless 'em both. I remember the sergeant-major in good shouting voice. I remember the red frock of the commandant. And then I nearly ruined everything by instinctively reaching out my hand to open the door myself. The grand duchess caught my arm in time, but for one hurried moment I thought that everyone had noticed my *faux pas*. The chauffeur opened the door. I stepped down, and the commandant came forward. The officials were presented one by one.

I felt very embarrassed when one lady wept as she thought of all that King Haakon had endured.

We heard afterwards that as the grand duchess passed up the lines of the V.A.D.s one was heard to whisper to another, " I bet she's never done a day's work in her life."

As a matter of fact she had been scrubbing the hospital floors only an hour before. A procession was formed behind me, everyone graded according to his or her position.

I must say that I thoroughly enjoyed being a king and having the sensation of many eyes watching one's every movement. I thoroughly enjoyed heading the procession round each ward.

Two incidents come back to my memory. The first concerned the mythical grand duchess. As a V.A.D. she had, for a long time previously, attempted to persuade a Tommy to give her a little imitation toy dog, a product of occupational therapy, on which she had set her heart. The Tommy as consistently refused to part with it. The grand duchess saw it on the top of his locker. Here was her chance. She admired his handiwork. In fact she admired it so much that the poor man had perforce to say, " May it please your Royal Highness to accept it ? "

She did, and popped it straightway into her handbag.

The other concerned myself. It must be remembered that I, as M.O., had full knowledge of every man's complaint. The devil entered into me. I stopped in front of an undersized youth who was in for convalescence after a common operation that is not mentioned in polite society.

" Where are you hurt ? " I asked.

Falteringly he told me.

" Ah," I replied. " In ze throat ? "

" No, other end, your majesty."

Nobody dared laugh, but I could positively feel the waves of suppressed laughter which emanated from the procession behind me.

Incidentally, with a view to hiding my marked Scots accent, I spoke with a strong guttural accent, and my English was sufficiently " broken " to be mistaken for that of a foreigner. When

I spoke to the grand duchess I used every opportunity to exploit my few German words, and referred, in audible terms, to the similarity between her "Schloss" in Norway and the present building. As a matter of fact, I found out later that King Haakon speaks perfect English, for which I owe him a belated and sincere apology.

I was well versed in the technique of V.I.P. inspections and spoke to an occasional man here and there. Altogether I must have spent about forty-five minutes inspecting the wards, then I requested the commandant to assemble every available member of the hospital in the recreation-room.

When they were all assembled I made a speech from one end of the room. It was all about the "gallant Allies", and just such phrases as I thought the King himself would use. At the close I was cheered to the echo, and then I played my trump card.

I announced that I was about to confer decorations on the matron and commandant. Matron was to get the Order of the Black Walrus, 4th class, and the commandant the Order of the Midnight Sun, 3rd class. Unfortunately, the only medals I had been able to obtain were old school running medals with my own name printed on them. I had hung them on ribbon composed of the Norwegian colours.

At the appropriate moment the equerry entered, carrying the medals on a cushion. I was terrified that someone would ask to see the medals after the ceremony and notice my name on them. With a view to preventing this I had banked on the superstition of the opposite sex. As a result I made the following remark before hanging the ribbon with the attached medal around their respective necks.

This is what I said : " In Norway we have a saying that it brings bad luck to the winner of a prize or medal if he or she lets anyone look at it within the first twenty-four hours. When I give it to you, therefore, please remember that if anyone looks at it, it might bring bad luck to the owner."

I then hung the ribbon around their necks and took the opportunity of kissing them on both cheeks. I'm not sure whether that is one of the perks of a king, or whether it would be looked upon as part of my official duties. Anyway, I kissed in approved continental fashion, and the men enjoyed it immensely. Each of the recipients of the medals tucked them away immediately inside the bib of her apron, and no one saw my name inscribed in large letters on them.

I was then escorted to the car. The troops lined the avenue and, amid tremendous cheering, the car drove slowly away. I sat in the back and saluted in the approved fashion. By this time, with the ordeal behind me, I was able to enjoy it to the full. A small knot of people had gathered at the entrance to the drive, and we drove out into the highway to the accompaniment of hurrahs and doffed hats. I repeat, I enjoyed being a king.

We drove back to the house and changed into our normal clothing before getting into my car and returning to the hospital. The door was opened by a V.A.D., who informed us, in tones of great excitement, that the King of Norway had been there that morning and that the staff had been trying to contact me everywhere in my capacity as M.O.

The men were having their dinner in the dining-hall, and thither we repaired. I thumped on the table and announced that I wanted to make a statement. I told them that I regretted that the whole affair that morning was a hoax ; that I had played the part of King Haakon and these other two with me were respectively the grand duchess and the equerry. Not a man spoke. It was obvious that I was not believed. I repeated the words of the undersized youth. Then a sergeant spoke up. " Somebody who was there repeated that conversation to you."

To this there was no answer. Then up spoke the ex-grand duchess, as she opened her handbag and held aloft the little imitation dog, " Now do you believe us ? "

I hastened away to phone up the local papers, who good-naturedly agreed to make no mention of the episode.

The next day as I came out of my own front door, a long queue of men in hospital blue was waiting for the bus. With one accord the long queue bowed themselves almost to the ground. I was saluted with the good comradeship of the British Tommy.

One thing more. In due course King Haakon himself heard the story and enjoyed the joke as much as anyone. Across the years I accord him my grateful thanks and my salutations as one monarch to another.

CHAPTER XV

NOT THE END BUT THE BEGINNING

IT was one of these August days when the great heat was tempered by a light breeze off the sea. It blew little puff-ball clouds over the sky and across the face of the sun. An altogether perfect day.

I was standing on the first tee of a golf course on the coast of Cornwall. I looked down the long stretch of vivid green which lay before me, and then I practised some swings until my partner should emerge from the Club House to join me. I remember the feeling of well-being and contentment which I had at that moment, the feeling an eight-handicap man has when he is about to play against bogey and win. It was a day when he feels in his bones that he can beat seventy-two, that rare day when he knows that he can make the little white ball go exactly where he wills.

Well, I felt just like that on this particular morning. It was the first time I'd had a chance to hit a golf ball since the war had finished. In fact there hadn't been much chance of a game since nineteen thirty-nine. All the war I had worked very hard. The life of a busy G.P. is always strenuous, but during the war it was much more so. The departure of nearby medical men ; the great increase of the local population, partly due to evacuation and partly due to those whose homes had actually been destroyed, and the increase of work due to the actual war itself—things like convalescent homes and sick people on leave—these all had made it impossible for me to get away to the peace and restfulness of a golf course.

So this summer's day was actually the first time I had stood on a tee for several years. As I looked down the fairway that morning I felt that the world was altogether a very good place to be in. I remember my first shot off the tee. It wasn't even on the fairway. It sailed over to the right and landed in some long grass. A complete slice. I also remember my partner's shot. A short ball. The sort of thing I could have played easily with one hand. But nevertheless it went straight down the fairway, and in due course I lost the hole. The same thing happened at the second and the third, and the fourth and so on to each succeeding hole. I couldn't hit a ball. I saw my partner looking at me in a quizzical sort of way. His face seemed to say, " Eight handicap ? Why doesn't the fellow speak the truth and admit that he's only a beginner ? " I can't remember what the score was. I know that I lost a very large number of balls and that I was thoroughly tired with looking for them when I entered the Club House in a very bad temper.

A visit to the pro was indicated. He took me out to an unfrequented part of the course and I started from the beginning. I swung without a ball and beheaded numberless daisies before eventually being promoted to an actual ball itself. Then I fired off a dozen balls in a row. Every shot was sliced and I lost four of them. I thought it was my grip and tried holding my club differently. Ultimately I bought a new set of clubs and retired to a secluded spot to practice by myself.

I was ashamed to ask anyone to play with me. I noticed that when I asked another fellow to play, he was invariable fixed up for a game. Evidently my reputation as a loser of balls was notorious and my prospective opponents did not relish a morning devoted to exploring every bush and every patch of long grass on the course. I no longer said that my handicap was eight. I claimed to be only a beginner, but even the rabbits of the club got no satisfaction from beating me.

Ultimately I went round by myself and became an authority on lost balls. Anyone on the course could recognise me from afar by the way I steadfastly spent most of the morning hunting for balls. Golf became an expensive hobby and at last the day came when I decided very reluctantly that the remainder of my holiday would be more profitably employed on the beach then on the golf course. But a queer thing happened there, too.

Parts of North Cornwall are noted for surf bathing. Breakers from afar roll on to the gradually sloping beach and if one can ride in on the crest of these waves one might well be carried a quarter of a mile or more before being washed up on the sand with its last expiring gasp. To achieve this result it is necessary to use a surf board, which is an ordinary thin piece of wood somewhat more than a foot in width with one end bent up like a prow of a boat. One would see a long procession of bathers making their way down to the beach or climbing down a short cut by the cliff to reach the smooth semicircle of sand down below.

It was my custom to take this short cut. It was always an awkward climb when carrying one's surfboard. It was, however, quite a practical proposition for an active person, and I was a very active person. Several times, more especially when descending to the beach, I stumbled at narrow parts of the little path and once I nearly fell at a hairpin bend. Had it not been for the quickness of my daughter in grabbing hold of me, I would have been hurled on the rocks below. Gradually, it came to be an accepted thing that one or other of the family was always at hand when I went up the cliff. It was only a small step from this to the one of them carrying my surfboard along with their own.

" It's really no weight at all, Pop. I'll just carry it till we reach the level ground at the top."

However, thanks to the family, I had no serious spills—and whatever they thought, they kept to themselves. Probably it occurred to them that Pop was getting a little elderly and infirm, though after all I was only in the late forties.

After our holiday in Cornwall I went home and—nothing happened. Nothing—well, hardly anything. I asked a lady to play me at golf. I thought I was safe with the female of the species. But, alas, the same thing happened as in Cornwall. We spent most of the afternoon exploring the long grass in the rough. I was ultimately beaten ten and eight. I took her in to tea *sans* pride, *sans* balls and *sans* temper. I have never played golf since.

As I say, I returned home and nothing happened. I was feeling fine. I won't say I sang in the bath, but I was as cheerful as usual and my tactful family heroically forebore to mention the word " golf." During all this time I think I was like the proverbial ostrich. I knew that there was something seriously wrong with me, but deliberately refused to think about it. Curiously enough I thought it was some other type of organic disease and the diagnosis of Disseminated Sclerosis did not enter my mind. Only once do I remember setting myself to face the future. It was during the night and I got up and went across to the surgery to re-read the symptoms of the different diseases of the nervous system. I seemed to fit into none of them, so I went back to bed convinced that I was suffering from a new disease.

Things became steadily worse. I was unduly fatigued after strenuous exercise. We went up to the Highlands for our summer holidays that year and I climbed one of the very high peaks. I found myself unusually tired at the end of it. At the close of our holiday we came down the east coast of Scotland and I visited many of the haunts of my boyhood. It was only marred by one thing. My driving had all of a sudden deteriorated badly and several times the car hit the kerb at the side of the road.

The winter passed away. Things were a little easier now that the war was over and help was more available. I took a partner, but the winter is always hard going. The first three months of the year are the worst. If you've got 'flu, well, that's just too bad. You must keep going as long as you can hobble in and out of your car. When the days began to lengthen and March had blown itself out, I began to get my head above water and to think about a holiday. I needed one.

For ninety days since Hogmanay I had gone into the waiting-room at nine o'clock each morning. Each morning I had seen a similar row of faces buried in last year's *Punches*. Each morning I had seen a row of depressed-looking people draped around the wall. I had dressed the leg ulcers of the elderly ; given advice about taking out little Willie's tonsils, and taken the blood pressure of the expectant. Yes, I needed a holiday. Easter approached. Where to go ? That was the question. The previous summer one of the family had gone to a Church of England centre, Lee Abbey near Lynton on the Devon coast. It seemed to offer all the facilities of religious stimulation along with the essentials of a good holiday. My daughter was very keen for us to go. I can't say I was keen on the religious stimulation, but at the same time I was prepared to put up with a certain amount provided the holiday part was all right. I booked places for the family and one April morning we set off for Devon in the car.

Now, somehow a journey like that ought to end with the sun shining, the birds twittering, and the peace of a great content in our hearts. It wasn't like that at all, however. The rain was coming down in torrents. It was tea-time when we arrived. Luckily they hadn't finished. We sat at long tables. Apparently there were no fixed places, but our family stuck together.

Someone tinkled a glass, and a man of about forty in a pair of corduroy slacks got to his feet. In a jocular tone he gave out some notices. It was interspersed with a certain amount of back-chat with a person who was presumably the cook. After tea, the entire human contents of the room departed and we finished our meal alone. The one of the family who had been here before was conductress-in-chief, and after tea led us into a large room where a group of people were singing around the piano.

I noticed one man in particular, not only because he had a very fine voice, but because his hair was cut shorter than anyone I had ever known. I got to know him over the washing-up sink and found that he had been a prisoner of war in Germany. He was now repatriated and was in charge of a prisoner of war camp for Germans over here, on the principle, I suppose, of " set a thief to catch a thief ".

As I say, I found myself sitting in a large room taking stock of my fellow internees. Time wore on and the group around the piano swung over to hymns, with the ex-P.O.W. obviously enjoying himself and letting his voice have full scope. I, too, was enjoying it, until someone thrust a hymn-book into my hand and invited me to join them. I didn't think I could very well refuse, or rather an excuse didn't spring to my mind soon enough. I joined the group and was slightly chagrined to find that nobody seemed to take any notice of me. At first it seemed like taking off one's clothes in public. But after a while I forgot my self-consciousness and thoroughly enjoyed the hymns. I like a sing-song occasionally and the hymns brought back old memories with just that touch of melancholy without which no Scotsman is really happy.

After supper there was an epilogue. Apparently one holidayed all day and was religiously stimulated at night. There wasn't any " buttonholing " or anything of the " are you saved, brother? " type of thing. There was just a hymn, a short prayer and an address of about twenty minutes. That was the general set-up of the establishment. I had come for a holiday. I got one.

I was struck with one aspect of the place—its tremendously friendly atmosphere. I had often been for holidays to hotels where people sat in the lounge and buried themselves behind the daily papers, or families whispered in corners as though they were attending the funeral obsequies of a relative. Well, in this place there was none of that.

One of the first people who spoke to me was an attractive elderly lady. I visualised her as an elderly spinster with lots of money and an unlimited capacity for playing bridge. I was wrong in both respects as she turned out to be as poor as the proverbial church mouse and the only grand slam that she knew was when she dropped her hymn-book on the floor. And I thought I was rather a good judge of people !

Then there was a young chap with a very expectant wife. To begin with, I thought it was he who was going to have the baby instead of his wife. He clucked over her like a broody hen, but otherwise he was a very normal young man. I cast my mind back to that dim and distant past when we were expecting our first baby. It seemed as though he was just behaving as I had done. But there they were, scores and scores of them, all seeming to enjoy themselves. I was to learn later that there were exceptions.

As I have said, the epilogues were held in a large lounge after supper. At first I thought it rather a nuisance having to attend them. But there was no compulsion whatever. I could have sat somewhere else during that half-hour and none would have remarked on it or even have thought that I was a bit of a slacker. No, I must admit that I attended these first few epilogues out of a sense of fairness and of a feeling that somehow if I didn't I ought not to be there.

Then I began to be interested and to wonder what the fellow—and there were three different speakers—was going to talk about that night. Of course, it wasn't all new to me by any manner of means. I had been brought up in a Christian home. My father was a keen Evangelical and I, in turn, had tried to carry on the Christian tradition. Probably I sound rather like the Pharisee in the Bible, but I certainly went to church more or less regularly, and I prided myself on my generosity, which was exemplified by putting half a crown in the offertory on Sunday. I knew I was kind. I treated patients as human beings.

No, I wasn't an agnostic or anything like that. I believed in the fundamental facts of the Christian faith. Let me choose a simile from my own experience. When a person is studying medicine he attends a series of lectures and learns about—say pneumonia. Later on he attends the bedside of someone suffering from that particular disease. That is called " clinical " medicine. The first is called " theoretical " medicine. There is all the difference in the world between the two. It is the same with religion. I had —so to speak—completed my course on the theory of religion. I gathered from the speakers that Lee Abbey specialised on the clinical side.

To return to the epilogues. One night the Chaplain spoke about prayer. He said that personally he subdivided prayer into several divisions which he designated by the letters P.S.A.L.M. P. standing for Praise ; S. for Surrender ; A. for Asking ; L. for Listening and M. for Meditation. Apparently the whole operation took upwards of an hour to do and the early morning was the time to do it. Mentally I visualised myself taking an hour to say my prayers and decided that such a procedure was not for me. I was to learn that the morning prayers may take considerably less than an hour however.

I went to bed that night turning the matter over in my mind and the letters P.S.A.L.M. kept recurring. I couldn't sleep that night. I tossed this way and that. I counted sheep. There was only the very deep silence of the countryside and not even a chiming clock to tell me how the hours were passing. Mentally, I made a survey of what it would cost if I were to become a Christian in the clinical meaning of the word. It was going to cost a great deal—a very great deal. The hours sped away and slowly the dawn of an April morning lit up the room. I am naturally sceptical about people who say they haven't slept a wink. Looking back, I am sceptical of myself that night, but at least it seemed like that to me. I decided to get up when the room was really filled with daylight and go down to the chapel and carry out the suggestion of P.S.A.L.M.

There was no one in the chapel at that hour of the morning, so I knelt down and prayed. I started with P. for Praise. I found I could thank God with complete sincerity for all He had done for me. I had no difficulty whatever with P. Mentally I passed on to S. S. stood for Surrender. I was no fool. I knew what surrender meant all right. I had counted the cost and added up the total during the night, and the total came to a mighty lot and I had come to an impasse on my very first attempt. Either I must stop praying and not pray any more, or surrender. I was driven into a corner. I wasn't such an ass as to think that I would become a sort of saintly individual by merely choosing God to run my life instead of myself. I rather looked on conversion as a sort of bend in a person's life, an all-out drive in the direction of God, an absolute willingness to let God take complete charge of me. It meant keeping nothing back —time, money, relationships—all these and a lot more, everything in fact.

I hesitated a long time. I wasn't for any emotional resolution even at half-past six in the morning. Have you ever taken a dive off the highest step of a diving board ? It is your first time. You stand there hesitating. The water seems very far away and the steps bringing one back to normality seem so very secure. And then one says to oneself, " *Nil desperandum*," and one jumps into space. Well, it was just like that. Just like diving off the high step into the deep end of the baths. I said to myself, or rather to God,

" Oh Lord, I surrender, and if there is anything which I have not surrendered, please show it to me." That was all. Nothing dramatic. Nothing spectacular and yet like all the really great victories and really great defeats it was fought in absolute silence.

Shortly after that, a clergyman came into the chapel and started moving about preparing for Holy Communion. Somehow I didn't feel like staying. My head was too much in a whirl. One reads of a feeling of peace which comes over one at such a time. My only feeling was one of complete confusion. And so I found myself outside on the path leading to the sea at seven o'clock on an April morning with the birds all singing and the rabbits scuttling to their holes as I approached. At this point I must digress. . . .

It is nineteen eighteen. The last year of the war. I was then eighteen. (The curious can find out how old I am by doing a little mental arithmetic.) I don't propose to go into particulars, but I underwent an experience during which I was tremendously afraid. I don't think I showed it, at least I hope not. For many months I was in hospital and I was ultimately discharged as cured. Yes, I was cured, but only outwardly. The experience left a scar on my mind which was lasting and which seemed to be permanent. It showed itself in a curious way.

I had an unreasoning unnatural panic when I was farther away from other folk than about four hundred yards. Yes, I know it sounds mad. It *was* mad. Whenever I tried it, the same thing invariably happened. My palms would immediately get clammy, my heart begin thumping and in the end I would start running, but in one direction which never varied. I always made for the nearest human being, preferably an adult, but a child or even an imbecile was not to be despised. I was suffering from a thing called agaro-phobia. Luckily, this unreasoning affliction did not affect me when in a car. I always looked on a car as a salvation, but there was no rhyme or reason in my actions ; I suppose I looked on a car as something that could be trusted to carry me to my fellows and to safety.

Naturally I worried about it. Who wouldn't ? Being a doctor, the best psychologists in England were mine for the choosing, and I chose with care and with discrimination. All the psychologists whom I consulted said more or less the same thing.

" Relax. Don't be so taut. Uncover the cause and when you have uncovered that you ought to be better."

I knew the cause all right but I was no better. For twenty-nine years I had this curse dogging my footsteps. Most of the years I was a medical student. All the years I was a doctor. In the end I came to accept it as part of myself. I just didn't put myself in a position where such a situation would be likely to arise.

I found many patients with the same trouble. They must have wondered at my being able to describe their symptoms so exactly. And if any doctor should read these words, don't repeat the word " psychosis " to yourself and ring up the nearest psychologist on your patient's behalf. Do remember that these people suffer just as much as a person with an acute appendicitis. Be kind to them by explaining that such a thing is a habit of the mind and not merely a figment of the imagination. Don't just prescribe bromide and give them a pat on the back.

Well, to return to myself. Of course I was ashamed of such a thing. It was something one couldn't explain to people and, if one did, ninety-nine people out of a hundred would put it down to incipient insanity. I became adept at the subterfuge which prevented me from being left alone in such a position. I don't think anybody knew—except my wife. . . .

And so I found myself on my way to the sea at seven o'clock on an April morning. I must have gone some way before I realised what I was doing. I nearly turned back, but I said to myself—or was it the voice of God speaking to me in my own mind? Go on. I went on. It wasn't very far to the edge of the cliff, just a before-breakfast stroll, but all the same it was further than my agarophobia would take me. I had got about half-way there when my ghost laid his clammy fingers on me. My heart felt as though its thudding would burst through my chest ; my breathing became a rapid series of gasps ; my mouth became dry. Sheer panic. I stopped in my tracks. Out of the depths of my soul I prayed, as I had prayed so often before, " God take this thing away from me ". I can best describe what happened next by saying it was as though I had taken off a heavy overcoat on a summer's day. In a few moments my heart stopped thumping—my breathing became natural—my mouth became moist. I was a free man. I knew in an instant that the spectre had vanished. I remember singing at the top of my voice as I completed my journey to the sea. On my way back I met the warden. He must have thought I was off my head. I was still singing. To reassure him I told him the whole story.

Next morning before anyone was up I went away to the loneliest place I could find to see if it was true. The panic did not come back, it has never come back. Psychological laws. Maybe. But who makes the psychological laws work? I am content to thank God for answering my prayer on that April morning—and to leave it at that. One thing more before I come to the close of that eventful day. Before the epilogue began, I told my tale to the assembled guests in the lounge. God works in a mysterious way. Some two years later I was invited to tell my story once again as part of a broadcast service from Lee Abbey. Since then I have repeatedly spoken over the wireless, though naturally, as my speech has since been affected by the disease which I developed, someone else reads the scripts for me. As I say, God moves in a mysterious way. That was the direct result of having a modicum of moral courage to speak that night and as a result I have received thousands of letters from people in distress.

And so I went home with my centre of gravity changed. I resumed my normal life. I don't think the internal revolution I had gone through was very evident to my patients. Much the same row of people was there in the waiting-room when I opened its door at nine o'clock every morning. Yet there was a difference, and the difference was in me. Previously I had been a confirmed worrier, not over my patients, but over my personal security. My pride was a little piqued if my monthly totals of work and of income were not as good as last year. I thought the world was coming to an end if my income dropped slightly. Now, it was very different. " Thou shalt not want " was as true for me now as it was thousands of years ago for others. I didn't need to worry any more and because I didn't worry, I was a happier man.

It is strange that even a medical man can fool himself. Slowly, insidiously, I began to develop things that seemingly had no relation to each other. I began to be unsteady on my feet. I have never been a teetotaller but now I was almost compelled to be one. If people were to notice a slight unsteadiness in my gait, they would at once say, " Ah, he has been drinking," which sounds dreadful when said about a respectable citizen, and just to prove I had not I breathed hard in the faces of everyone I met on my evening stroll.

I don't remember when I first noticed this unsteadiness. It came on so gradually that I could not name a month when I noticed it first. Certainly by June I was aware of it. It was my custom to take a walk for a mile or two at the close of the day and I began to pretend that I was tying my bootlace when it was necessary for me to pass anyone whom I knew. It was worse when I was tired.

The second thing was to do with my voice. Queer things were happening to it. I found I was always a little hoarse. Sometimes more than a little. The other thing was that my words were pronounced indistinctly. Sometimes they were like the words of a man who had drunk not wisely but too well.

After the hoarseness had gone on for some months, I came to the conclusion that I must be developing a growth in my throat. With that nagging fear in my mind, I consulted an ear, nose and throat specialist. He told me there was a slight time lag in one of my vocal chords for no apparent reason. But they were otherwise healthy and definitely no growth was present. I went home walking on air.

Things came to a head towards the end of October. It happened in this way. One morning I was seeing patients when the telephone rang. It was a call to go to a patient. I jotted it down in my notebook which was lying open on the desk in front of me. After the consulting hour was over I proceeded to make up my visiting list for the day. When I came to the call which had just come in I found that by no possible deciphering could I understand it. I had always been a bad writer, but during the past few months my handwriting had deteriorated considerably, so that by this time my writing resembled the marks which a child makes with a pencil before it learns to write. I was unable to read either the name or address of the patient to whose house I had been called. Unfortunately, neither could any of the people to whom I showed it. To make matters worse, I was unable to remember who had phoned me. The net result was that that patient has never been visited to this day. They must have wondered why no doctor called after hearing me say with such certainty that I would definitely be along quite soon. To my surprise they did not phone up again, either that day or the next. They must have got another doctor.

That incident decided me. There and then I phoned a doctor and asked him to see me professionally. The incidents of that consultation remain vividly in my mind. He thumped me and pinched me and pummelled me to such an extent that I was convinced it was the most comprehensive examination that a man could have. In the end I asked him what he thought was wrong with me. He hummed and he hawed, and then he said he would like the opinion of a colleague who specialised in my particular type of trouble. Like a wise man he did not commit himself. I knew the diagnosis was going to be none too easy and that he wanted to make reasonably sure.

In due course an appointment with the colleague was fixed. I was again pummelled and prodded and pinched and was ultimately told to get my things on while the two other doctors retired to another room to discuss my case. How often had I done the same thing with other medical men whom I had called in for consultation. The whole chain of events had a familiar ring about them. I can't say I was worried. I was just interested. They seemed to be away a long time. Ultimately they returned.

When a doctor wants to tell a patient something unpleasant he often wraps it up, and it can be wrapped up so well that the patient can swallow almost anything, however unpleasant. In this particular case they didn't wrap it up very much. I gathered that they thought there was a possibility that I might have a tumour on my brain. It was arranged that I was to go into hospital to have various tests, including an injection of air into my spine so that the air would rise to the ventricles, or cavities, in my brain, and an X-ray could be taken which would show the presence or absence of a tumour. I was to go into hospital the following Wednesday.

The day before I was due to enter hospital I did my normal day's work. It came to the evening surgery. Little did I think that was to be the last surgery I would ever take. I remember an elderly man sitting in the chair in front of me telling me about a pain in his chest which came on when he cycled uphill. He was suffering from advanced heart disease. He didn't know it, but he was standing on the very edge of a volcano. I advised him what to do. I heard afterwards that he died suddenly and unexpectedly. It was the end I had expected.

After the patients were all gone I took down a book and proceeded to read up all I could find about tumours of the brain. It was rather an old edition which I had, but I made a mental note that eight per cent. made a recovery of sorts. Out of every hundred that were operated on, therefore, eight survived. I wondered if I would be one of the eight or whether I would be numbered among the other ninety-two. I remember kneeling down and asking God to give me courage to face whatever the future might hold. I did not say anything to anybody about what I had learned.

Next day I went into hospital. It is a strange feeling when one is in one's apparently normal health. I walked along the corridor between the rows of cubicle beds to my room at the end which was going to be my home for the next few weeks. The sister advised me to go to bed. I did so, but felt rather a fraud as I climbed in between the sheets.

The days passed and various doctors came to carry out tests, none of which required any fortitude on my part. Then a queer thing happened. The method of diagnosing cerebral tumours had not been discovered when I was a student, but there had naturally been patients in the hospital from time to time with the same condition, at least the sisters knew all about it. Three nights before the investigation was to be carried out the night sister in the course of her round paid me a visit. We naturally discussed the investigation which was to take place. I had never seen it carried out, but she was familiar with it and naturally assumed that I was also.

" I think you are a very brave man," she said, and then the talk turned to other things.

After she had gone I scratched my head and wondered what I was being brave about. I decided to ask the day sister about it.

" Yes," she said, " it requires considerable courage, but you will be all right, I feel sure."

I was not reassured. In due course the house physician came round, and I asked him to tell me all about it.

" Well," he said, " it's a bit grim. Most people become unconscious during the procedure, so you will probably not feel it very much."

I was less assured than ever. In fact, as the day and the hour approached, I had a sinking feeling in my stomach which nothing would allay. Ultimately the hour arrived. Five p.m. It wasn't the hour one would have chosen oneself as it meant having the whole day to think about it. Deep down within me I had a very strong conviction that nothing could happen to me beyond what I could bear. God would give me the strength to endure.

At five o'clock I went down to the X-ray room on the trolley. It had previously been explained to me that any form of anæsthetic was impracticable and that even morphia made the condition worse. However, they gave me a sedative of sorts. I sat in a chair and the doctor proceeded to inject air into my spine. I think I was more curious than otherwise. At least the pain didn't come on suddenly like a dentist drilling the tender part of one's tooth.

There was another thing, too. I gathered that usually the air is injected into one's neck. It was decided to do the deed lower down my spine. Somehow one has more control of oneself when the injection is lower. The neck is such a wobbly and uncertain place to have anything done. I did not like having my neck interfered with. It reminded me a little too much of King Charles and his execution. This is not the Chamber of Horrors, so I don't propose to describe in detail how the pain grew to a crescendo and how ultimately my head was shaken from side to side by an assistant in order that the air should rise satisfactorily and the photographs could be taken. Sufficient to say that I did not " pass out " and I have the most vivid recollection of every detail.

At last the time came when the plates were ready to be developed and the doctors in charge retired to inspect them. It was a lasting lesson to me not to let a patient hear what one was saying. In a perfectly clear voice I heard a young doctor, who chanced to be present say " There it is, just there." And so I returned to my bed, but it was almost a fortnight before I had recovered sufficiently to be able to resume my normal activities.

One day, shortly after I had recovered, I was invited to go to the hospital with my wife and hear the considered verdict of the doctor who had examined me on the second occasion. Everything was made very nice. We had tea in the sister's room. It was altogether too friendly. I wondered what was coming. I was soon put out of my misery. I was told that the X-ray had shown a suspicion of a tumour, but that further investigation must be carried out at another hospital. These investigations would involve an operation on my brain which would prove conclusively the presence or absence of the growth.

A bed had been arranged for me in the hospital which specialised in such troubles. So one fine day my wife and I set out for London in a hired car. The hospital was divided into two parts like the St. Andrew's Golf Club—Royal and Ancient. I was in the " Royal " or modern part. It wasn't like any hospital I had been in before. There were four beds to a ward and all the " up " patients sat in a little sitting-room by themselves. It was all very efficient and up-to-date, but I distinctly had the feeling that I liked the old-fashioned hospital best.

The day before my operation a strange thing happened. It had been my custom for many years to play chess on a Saturday night with the local Roman Catholic priest. I am not a Roman

Catholic myself, nor am ever likely to be one, and by tacit consent we avoided the subject of religion. He was an old man and an ill one, and had recently retired from his duties and gone to live at a convent in Surrey. What was my surprise, therefore, to see him come through the doorway. He had treated me as he would one of his own flock and had come up all that way to see me.

We chatted of this and that and at last the hour came for him to take his departure. I got out of bed, slipped on a dressing-gown and accompanied him as far as the lift.

"What would you do, Father, if I were a Catholic?"

"I would give you my blessing, my son."

"Well, just imagine I am a Catholic and give me your blessing."

And there and then I knelt down at the entrance to the lift and he blessed me. I never saw him alive again.

At that hospital they had male nurses on the staff. I may be conservative, but I much prefer female nurses. There is something cold, bald and a little unnerving in seeing a man in a white jacket turn round when you call out for a nurse.

One thing I had quite forgotten was that my head would be shaved prior to the operation. I was summoned into a side room, and one of the male nurses began to make me like a human billiard ball. I like my hair cut short, but it was with consternation that I surveyed my shorn tresses. It was even more depressing when I saw my naked head. It looked horribly bald and unclothed. I hastily covered it up, and was only too pleased when it was concealed by the turban-like layers of sterile dressing.

I was always a bad sleeper, and, like the soldiers at the burial of Sir John Moore, "I bitterly thought of the morrow," and did not sleep much in consequence.

I climbed on to a trolley about ten o'clock and was pushed out into the corridor. Then the cavalcade came to a halt. The nurses departed and I was left to my own devices for half an hour. The operating theatre was on the floor above and my trolley had to be taken up in the lift. The doors of the lift were white, and it seemed an eternity before I heard the rattle of it descending. They opened and revealed an unconscious figure lying on a stretcher.

I did not have any feelings of panic or apprehension. I sang the twenty-third psalm over and over to myself to that haunting tune of Crimond, which I had been brought up to know in Scotland. "The Lord is my Shepherd". I repeated it, and I was not in the least afraid—only curious and interested. I watched the doors until the trolley with its human burden was trundled out and I myself pushed in to take its place. The lift quickly rose to the upper floor. The doors swung open and in a very short space of time I was in the operating theatre itself. The whole performance reminded me of a paragraph in the newspaper which stated that " it was only a step from the condemned cell to the execution chamber and the accused mounted the gallows with a firm step ".

As a matter of fact I was still singing to myself " The Lord is my Shepherd ". I do not want to convey the idea that the Christian faith is only a soporific against fear, but I am sure that God stands by our human frailty in its need. He will keep His side of the bargain as we, feebly, falteringly try to keep ours, and so I climbed on to the operating table. Luckily, I was used to the technique and to the lay-out of a theatre. What a lay person must have thought about the five or six white garbed and hooded figures, I shudder to think.

It was explained that it was impracticable to give me a general anæsthetic. I would have to be content with a local. I wanted to pay a tribute to that local. It was certainly effective. I never felt a thing during the operation except maybe when the coverings of the brain were being cut, but then they are extremely sensitive.

My eyes were covered with a sheet. An instrument for recording my blood pressure was put on my leg. A tinkle of instruments and the operation had begun. I asked the surgeon what my sensations were likely to be at each successive step. Never as long as I live will I lose the memory of that circular saw which cut the actual bone. It must be remembered that bone is one of Nature's sound conductors and the noise was simply appalling. It was as though all the tramcars in creation were magnified a thousandfold and were clattering past within an inch of my ear.

Luckily the brain was painless, absolutely painless. But I knew that if the surgeon did not go dead straight, well, that was just too bad. I hummed Crimond silently to myself. " The Lord is my Shepherd, I shall not want ".

By the time I climbed into my bed again I knew that I had no cerebral tumour. A few days later I was told definitely that I was suffering from Disseminated Sclerosis.

During the past years I had had a considerable number of patients who suffered from this disease. In many respects it is like the tide on the seashore ; its progress is hardly perceptible, sometimes, indeed, it seems to retreat and the individual to have a remission of his symptoms, but generally it is steadily progressive —a form of gradually progressive paralysis. Neither the cause— nor, even more unfortunately, the cure—is at present known. It may last twenty years ; on the other hand, it may run its course in two or three. An average of its duration would be eight to ten years and almost any part may be affected. This, then, was the future I had to contemplate as I lay and recovered from the operation.

Shortly after coming out of hospital I sold my share of the practice, and as my partner retired at the same time the medical work in this village passed into other hands.

CHAPTER XVI

THE BEST YEARS OF MY LIFE

IT is over four years since I came out of hospital, four years of a gradual shrinking of the perimeter, four years which have led me to this chair by the fireside. Often in the past I have seen someone sitting there like this and I have said to myself, "Poor fellow, what on earth does life hold for him?"

Little did I ever think I would be in that position myself some day. I get many a visitor whose lips don't say these actual words, but whose eyes say them nevertheless, and yet—strange to say—these last four years have been the happiest of my life. Here are some snapshots taken from them.

In the early days I was only slightly handicapped and spent an increasing amount of time at Lee Abbey. I had a most amusing experience there. I arrived alone, my wife being unable to accompany me, and was given a bed in an all-male dormitory of five beds. My bed was between that of a parson and a very vocal Socialist. Unfortunately, I forgot to warn the other occupants of the room that I was liable to have nightmares. About two o'clock in the morning I was wrapped in deep slumber. In my dreams I was playing rugger for Scotland. I can't remember if I scored a try or whether I was only leading a forward charge—anyway, I went through the opposing forwards as a knife goes through butter. Unfortunately, in doing so I let out a terrific yell which must have echoed and re-echoed all over the building. When I opened my eyes to see what the commotion was about, the Socialist was sitting up in bed looking as though the end of the world had come and the parson was making soothing noises with his tongue. I assured them that all was well and gradually they settled down to sleep again. An hour later a deep silence reigned in the dormitory. My dreams continued with the rugger match. Once again I went through the opposing forward line ; once again a bloodcurdling yell rang out through the building. It had a sequel in the morning. The secretary offered me a room to myself. I took it.

These nightmares of mine generally took the same form. I would wake myself up, generally with a peal of laughter. If the laughter was sufficiently loud to awake my wife, she usually asked me what the joke was, as one does at such a time. I would murmur something unintelligible and almost immediately go off to sleep again. I simply couldn't remember what it was that had made me laugh. The memory of the dream had departed from me entirely. On one occasion, however, I was able to remember what I was laughing at. It explained a lot of things to me. Why, for instance, I had these grotesque dreams. It explains how something lies buried on one's sub-conscious mind. Here is the dream and the cause of it.

I dreamt I was seated in a theatre. I have no recollection what the play was about. In fact, the play did not come into the dream at all. My attention was rivetted on a man in the gallery. He was a very fat man with a beaming face and he was seated on the top step of the gangway, which, as everyone knows, is very steep. The fat man was clapping effusively. He continued clapping—much as they do at the Orchestral Concerts. The impetus of his clapping propelled him down the gangway and he went bump, bump, bump, down to the foot. From where I sat I could see a very large nail sticking up from the lowest step. The fat man continued to bump down the steps and ultimately bumped right on to the nail, which was the father of all nails, and to my astonishment the man continued clapping. I was so amazed that I left my seat in the stalls and climbed to the top of the gangway in the gallery, to reach which I had to go outside the building and up a spiral staircase. I walked down the gangway and tapped the fat man on the shoulder.

" Excuse me," I said, " but you're sitting on a large nail."

He beamed round at me and continued clapping.

" Oh, it's all right," he replied. " I have a cork behind."

It was at this point that I burst out laughing in my sleep and I woke not only myself but my wife.

The point was that I know why in my dream the man made the ridiculous remark that he did. A day or two previously I had been walking along the corridor of a hospital with a doctor whom I had known intimately for many years. Suddenly he bent down and, picking up a drawing-pin, pulled up his trouser leg and thrust it through his sock.

" Just the thing I've been looking for," he exclaimed.

" Well," said I, " I hadn't the slightest idea that you had a cork leg."

" Oh yes, I've had a cork leg for years. As a matter of fact I lost my leg in the first World War."

I think it was during that visit that I made one of the biggest *faux pas* I have ever made in my life. It is the custom at Lee Abbey to have prayers after breakfast. Prayers which are generally taken by one of the guests on the invitation of those in charge. On this particular occasion I was asked to take them. It is really quite simple. One is generally allotted a subject about which one reads an appropriate part of scripture. Then one says a little bit about the subject and finishes with a short prayer. They were doing " the fruits of the spirit," so I was asked to speak about love which is the first " fruit of the spirit". Unfortunately I am no good at speaking in public, nor ever could without getting in a flap over it, so I prepared my subject very carefully. I determined to read the thirteenth chapter of the first Epistle to the Corinthians, which is all about love. The part I had to speak myself I wrote out and carefully committed to memory. The prayer I did not prepare as—having been brought up a good Presbyterian—I thought it ought to " come from the heart ". The night before the ordeal was to take place I could not sleep and rose at three in the morning and made my way down to the seashore and repeated my little piece to the wild waves. Breakfast came and then prayers. I read the passage from the New Testament that I had had in mind and then—unfortunately —every word I had memorised went out of my head. What I actually *did* say must be the shortest address on record. " After reading those words of St. Paul it would be presumption on my part to add anything further ". And so we came to the prayer— which I had not prepared. I prayed for this and that, and then I dropped the most dreadful brick on record. I don't know what made me say it. I still don't know. I said. " Lord, make us good, but not too good ". There was a half-suppressed titter over the room. Hurriedly I said " Amen," and drew the proceedings to a close. I have never been asked to take prayers at Lee Abbey again and now my voice is affected and I probably won't be asked in the future.

This experience was hardly as bad as that of a friend of mine who was asked to speak at a Mothers' Union meeting on her first mission. The Chairwoman was almost stone deaf and all conversation with her had to be conducted through a speaking-tube. My friend was asked if she would give a short extempore prayer before the address —to which she readily agreed. When it came to the prayer all those present bowed their heads in a reverent attitude. In due course my friend finished her prayer and the audience assumed their normal upright position, all—that is to say—except the Chairwoman who continued to sit with bent head and reverent mien. The speaker wished to indicate that she had finished and gave a cough to that effect. There was a general shifting of chairs and shuffling of shopping baskets. Still the Chairwoman remained with bowed head and in a reverent attitude. The speaker coughed again, but without avail. In despair she turned to her audience and appealed to them, " What do I do now ? "

Apparently the audience were used to the dilemma, for someone got up from the front row and crossed to where the Chairwoman was sitting. Grasping the business end of the speaking-tube she shouted down it " She's finished ". The lady in charge sat up and those present apparently took it as a perfectly normal procedure for no one even smiled.

The years passed away. Four of them have gone. What am I like now ? I can best answer that question by quoting from a broadcast which I was asked to do recently about Christianity and one's illness. First of all I apologised for talking so much about oneself and then I went on, " Each year the illness has advanced, but its progress is very gradual. As a matter of fact, one has to compare what one was like several months ago, or even a year ago, to be able to see any great difference. I must tell you what I am like at the moment so that you can have some idea of the person who is speaking to you. I look perfectly well when sitting still (which is often) and keeping my mouth shut (which is seldom). But if I get up you would soon see that my sense of balance is seriously affected so that I can't get about unless I hang on to somebody's arm. Likewise my ability to do fine movements, such as writing, is affected. My sense of heat and cold is also affected, so that I might get into a hot bath and scald myself without knowing if I were not careful. My words sometimes get very indistinct, though this varies from day to day. I can't do much without getting excessively tired and, lastly, I have a form of blackout which is very uncommon in this type of illness, which has to do with my blood pressure ; but which unfortunately comes on fairly frequently and causes much more worry to my family than it does to myself.

On the other hand, I am not mental. At least I don't think I am. Doubtless my family, with that keen perception which youth claims to have, would have been sure to tell me had they noticed any sign of it. Likewise, I am not terribly depressed about it all.

I mean by that that I don't sit in a corner with an artificial smile hiding a secret sorrow and being very brave.

* * * *

How does being a Christian affect it? When I had this illness first I panicked badly. I, so to speak, battered at the gates of Heaven demanding to be made well. I just couldn't believe it. Any kind of healing—medical healing or spritual healing—I didn't care so long as I was cured. Then the first panic began to subside. I no longer lay awake at night sweating with apprehension. Gradually it dawned on me that it wasn't such an unmitigated disaster. After all, my life was in God's hands and it wasn't just a jigsaw puzzle of chance.

* * * *

There is another thing, too. I have got a different idea of God from what I had before. In my childhood I had a recurring dream which in time came to colour my waking thoughts also. I used to dream it was the day of the last judgment and I was the last to be judged. I stood there alone in the middle of a sort of enormous pavement. God, in the form of an elderly and somewhat severe-looking gentleman, was running a rather podgy forefinger down the list of my somewhat petty little sins. Not many really ripe ones —not many purple patches—rather a long list of small pettinesses. Of course it was exit to the goats.

Or let me put it another way. Everyone who is born north of the Tweed has heard this story and not a few who come from the south of it also. The story is that a Scotsman—not a particularly wicked man—but one who had led rather a selfish life, died, and in due course found himself at the Last Judgment. He was condemned to everlasting punishment among the goats. In his torment he cried out: "Oh, Lord, let me oot. I didna ken I was daen' wrang."

And the Lord in his infinite wisdom replied, "Weel, ye ken noo."

Now that's not just a funny story. It presupposes a very stern God, a God who secretly gloats over the misdeeds of his victims; one who, as in my childhood dream, was rather to be feared than loved. It took me nearly fifty years to lose that idea of God.

I found a friend in Him. Someone who really understands me

at last. A captain worth serving. Someone who will be with me to the very end. There's no need to worry about the future for, as it says in the twenty-third Psalm, " Goodness and mercy shall follow me all the days of my life ". The Bible isn't just a " good book " of beautiful thoughts and stories. It contains the promises of God. The greatest promise that the whole Bible contains for me are these words, " I will never leave you nor forsake you ", and knowing that to be a fact it makes my paralysis seem a little thing and the future to be radiant and bright instead of being fearsome and dark.

I have a strong feeling that this book is not finished yet ; that I shall write another chapter some day ; and that I shall call it " The way back ". So far I have nothing but the heading for the chapter. I am waiting for the contents.